The Absent Man

The

Absent Man

*The Narrative Craft
of Charles W. Chesnutt*

Charles Duncan

OHIO UNIVERSITY PRESS

Athens

Ohio University Press, Athens, Ohio 45701
© 1998 by Charles Duncan
Printed in the United States of America
All rights reserved

Ohio University Press books are printed on acid-free paper ∞ ™

05 04 03 02 01 00 99 98   5 4 3 2 1

Library of Congress Cataloging-in-Publication Data
Jacket photograph of Charles W. Chesnutt
by Edward J. Solotko, courtesy of Cleveland Public Library
Photograph Collection / *Cleveland Plain Dealer*
Duncan, Charles, 1962–
    The absent man : the narrative craft of Charles W. Chesnutt /
Charles Duncan.
        p.   cm.
    Includes bibliographical references and index.
    ISBN 0-8214-1239-6 (acid-free paper)
    1. Chesnutt, Charles Waddell, 1858–1932—Technique. 2. Afro-
Americans in literature.   3. Afro-American aesthetics.
4. Narration (Rhetoric)   I. Title.
PS1292.C6Z69 1998
813'.4—dc21   98-22063

To Rebecca and Graham

Out of the dimness opposite equals advance,
always substance and increase, . . .
Always a knit of identity, always distinction,
always a breed of life.

To elaborate is no avail, learned and
unlearned feel that it is so.

—WALT WHITMAN

Contents

Preface   xi
Acknowledgments   xv
Chronology: Charles W. Chesnutt (1858–1932)   xvii

1. Introduction   1

2. The White and the Black . . .
   and the Limits of Authorship   27

3. "Through My Leafy Veil":
   Chesnutt's Narrative Witnesses   47

4. Negotiating Belief and Voicing Difference   77

5. Speaking For (and Against) Each Other:
   The Inside Narratives   107

6. Shortening His Weapons:
   The More Detached Voice of Realism   137

7. Conclusion: The Blackballing of
   Charles W. Chesnutt   166

Notes   177
Bibliography   197
Index   207

Preface

Between the appearance of "Uncle Peter's House" (1885) in the *Cleveland News and Herald*—his first significant, national publication—and his death in 1932, the African-American writer Charles Waddell Chesnutt published more than fifty stories in newspapers and magazines, including several in the *Atlantic Monthly*, upwards of twenty essays in periodicals such as the *Boston Evening Transcript* and W. E. B. Du Bois's *The Crisis*, a biography of Frederick Douglass (1899), and even a handful of poems. His literary reputation rests primarily, however, on two collections of short fiction, *The Conjure Woman* (1899), and *The Wife of His Youth and Other Stories of the Color Line* (1899), and three novels, *The House Behind the Cedars* (1900), *The Marrow of Tradition* (1901), and *The Colonel's Dream* (1905). Based on the artistic control and deft characterizations typical of the stories found in the two collections, they have generally been considered, by readers of his day and of ours, as superior to the more openly polemical novels, and it is impossible not to agree. Despite that critical consensus and the fact that his literary reputation has improved dramatically over the past thirty years, no study of Chesnutt has yet been devoted exclusively to his short fiction. This book is intended to address in part that shortcoming. In determining the scope for this study, I have elected to consider not only the sixteen works collected in *The Conjure Woman* and *The Wife of His Youth* but indeed all of the short fictions Chesnutt wrote, some few of which remained unpublished in his life.

Any consideration of Charles W. Chesnutt must, as a matter of course, address the central role played by race in his writings. While acknowledging the importance of that subject and its implications, this study also focuses on the crucial relationship between Chesnutt's thematic designs and his sophisticated narrative presentations. As the first major African-American fiction writer, Chesnutt compelled his largely white reading audience to reimagine its collective sense of black Americans. For while the authors of slave narratives had had a rhetorical imperative to present themselves as truthtellers, Chesnutt emphatically called attention to his work as fiction.

In organizing this study, I have thus sought to emphasize the ways Chesnutt manipulated narrative strategies that both describe and enact his fictions of identity. Rather than grouping the stories by chronology or theme, then, I have considered them according to shared narrative framework. Fictions narrated by the protagonist, for example, are treated in chapter 2, while all of the stories featuring two first-person narrators (usually John and Julius) have been grouped together for discussion in chapter 4. The order of the chapters reflects Chesnutt's gravitation toward increasingly impersonal modes of narration. Hence, those stories told by a first-person protagonist—the most personal form of narration—are examined first (in chapter 2), while his stories with a first-person narrator who functions primarily as a witness to the action provide the subject matter of chapter 3. Similarly, the dual first-person narratives examined in chapter 4 differ materially from those stories narrated collaboratively by both first-person and third-person narrators, as discussed in chapter 5. And Chesnutt's detached and ironic third-person narratives—the least personal mode—are analyzed together in chapter 6. The chapters have in common an internal organization as well. The first part of each chapter examines, in general fashion, the stories that share a given narrative framework; the second part of the chapter then considers one work that best represents (and, generally, is the most polished example of) that framework. There is one exception to this rule. I examine "Baxter's Procrustes" in the conclusion rather than in chapter 3 because that story so fittingly recapitulates Chesnutt's ironic acknowledgment of his position within the white literary tradition and anticipates the twentieth-century construction of his reputation.

Acknowledgments

My interest in the writings of Charles Chesnutt originated with my work as a research assistant gathering primary materials on Chesnutt's periodical publications for Joseph R. McElrath, Jr. Since that time Professor McElrath has generously guided my study of Chesnutt, and I am grateful. Ralph Berry, Anne Rowe, Craig Stroupe, and Dennis Moore also offered much-appreciated support by graciously commenting on, and talking with me about, early versions of this book.

I wish also to thank the Florida State University, which, by granting me a Fellowship, made this book possible. I likewise want to acknowledge the helpful professional guidance provided by the people at Ohio University Press, especially David Sanders, Nancy Basmajian, and Gillian Berchowitz.

I am also deeply indebted to William Hardin, Jennifer DiLalla, and Jeren Goldstein, who provided thoughtful commentary on the manuscript at various stages of development; I cannot thank them enough. My wife, Rebecca, gave me invaluable help and support throughout the entire process. I could not have finished the book without her.

Chronology

Charles W. Chesnutt (1858–1932)

1858   Born 20 June in Cleveland.

1866   Chesnutt family moves to Fayetteville, North Carolina.

1872   Publishes first story (in a local newspaper).

1873   Drops out of school and begins teaching in order to supplement family income.

1874   Earns teaching certificate.

1878   Marries Susan Perry, a fellow teacher.

1880   Becomes principal of the new normal school in Fayetteville.

1881   Daughter Helen, who would later write a biography of her father (1952), born.

1883   Resigns from position at normal school. Travels alone to New York, where he works for six months as financial news reporter for the *New York Mail and Express*. Moves to Cleveland in the winter and works as bookkeeper and legal stenographer with Nickel Plate Railroad Company.

1884   Moves family to Cleveland.

1885   Begins studying law. Has first national publication of short story, "Uncle Peter's House," in the *Cleveland News and Herald*.

1887   Passes Ohio bar examination with highest score in group, and begins practicing law with the white law firm, Henderson, Kline and Tolles. Publishes "The Goophered Grapevine," first significant conjure story, in *Atlantic Monthly*.

1888   Opens own office as court reporter. Publishes "Po' Sandy," second significant conjure tale, in *Atlantic Monthly.*

1889   Declines offer from George Washington Cable to become his secretary. Publishes both "The Sheriff's Children"—first major non-dialect story—and "What Is a White Man?"—a provocative essay on the vagaries of legally determining race—in the *New York Independent.*

1890   Richard Watson Gilder, editor of *Century*, rejects Chesnutt's "Rena Walden," a story *Atlantic Monthly* likewise declines to publish. The much-revised and expanded story is eventually published as *The House Behind the Cedars* in 1900.

1891   Houghton, Mifflin declines to publish volume of short stories containing "Rena Walden," "The Sheriff's Children," "A Victim of Circumstance," and conjure tales.

1893   Declines Albion Tourgée's offer of associate editorship for new journal, the *National Citizen.*

1897   Houghton, Mifflin rejects "Mandy Oxendine," a novel that explores the possibilities of a young woman "passing" in North Carolina; it is subsequently published in 1997, sixty-five years after Chesnutt's death.

1898   Publishes "The Wife of His Youth" in *Atlantic Monthly.* Learns from Walter Hines Page of Houghton, Mifflin's decision to publish collection of Chesnutt's conjure tales. Houghton, Mifflin declines to publish "A Business Career," a novel.

1899   Houghton, Mifflin publishes *The Conjure Woman* and *The Wife of His Youth and Other Stories of the Color Line.* Small, Maynard publishes *Frederick Douglass* (a biography). Retires from business to concentrate on writing as profession.

1900   Houghton, Mifflin publishes *The House Behind the Cedars,* a much-revised version of "Rena Walden." Chesnutt publishes several controversial essays on race, including "Future American" series for the *Boston Evening Transcript.* Houghton, Mifflin, *Century,* and, later, Doubleday, Page decline to publish "The Rainbow Chasers," a novel.

1901   Houghton, Mifflin publishes *The Marrow of Tradition* (novel).

Chesnutt publishes "The White and the Black" (essay) in the *Boston Evening Transcript.*

1902   The Rowfant Club, an exclusive social club (known for book collecting) that would serve as the model for the Bodleian Club in "Baxter's Procrustes," rejects Chesnutt's application for membership, presumably because of his race. Returns full time to business.

1903   Publishes "The Disfranchisement of the Negro" (essay) in *The Negro Problem: A Series of Articles by Representative American Negroes of To-day,* with contributions by, among others, Booker T. Washington.

1904   Publishes "Baxter's Procrustes" in *Atlantic Monthly.*

1905   Doubleday, Page publishes *The Colonel's Dream.* Attends Mark Twain's seventieth birthday party. Essentially retires from writing as a profession. Publishes "Peonage, Or the New Slavery" (essay) in *Voice of the Negro.*

1906   Writes "Mrs. Darcy's Daughter" (a four-act play).

1910   Accepts membership in the Rowfant Club.

1912   Becomes member of Cleveland Chamber of Commerce. Publishes "The Doll" (story) in *The Crisis.*

1915   Publishes "Women's Rights" (essay) and "Mr. Taylor's Funeral" (story) in *The Crisis.*

1919   Small, Maynard declines to publish collection of dialect stories titled "Aunt Hagar's Children."

1921   Writes "Paul Marchand, F.M.C.," a novel that Houghton, Mifflin, Harcourt Brace, and Alfred Knopf all decline to publish.

1923   Oscar Micheaux produces movie version of *The House Behind the Cedars.*

1924   Publishes the first installment of "The Marked Tree," the last of the conjure tales, in *The Crisis* in December; the completion of the story followed in January.

1926   Publishes "The Negro in Art: How Shall He Be Portrayed?" in *The Crisis*

1928   Receives Spingarn Medal from National Association for the Advancement of Colored People for his distinguished service to Afro-Americans.

1930   Publishes "The Negro in Cleveland" (essay) in the *Clevelander* and "Concerning Father," the last story published in his life, in *The Crisis*. Submits "The Quarry," a novel, to Houghton, Mifflin and later to Alfred Knopf; both decline to publish.

1931   Publishes "Post-Bellum—Pre-Harlem," an essay that provides Chesnutt's assessment of his own career; it appears in both *Colophon* and *The Crisis*.

1932   Dies at home.

1954   *List of Manuscripts, Published Works and Related Items in the Charles Waddell Chesnutt Collection of the Erastus Milo Cravath Memorial Library, Fisk University* appears.

1966   The Rowfant Club reprints "Baxter's Procrustes" as a rare book *(Baxter's Procrustes)*.

1972   *Guide to the Microfilm Edition of the Charles Waddell Chesnutt Papers in the Library of the Western Reserve Historical Society* appears.

1973   *Charles W. Chesnutt Collection* (Fisk University) appears.

1974   *The Short Fiction of Charles W. Chesnutt*, edited by Sylvia Lyons Render (containing most of Chesnutt's previously uncollected short fiction), is published.

1993   *The Journals of Charles W. Chesnutt*, edited by Richard H. Brodhead, is published.

1997   *"To Be an Author": Letters of Charles W. Chesnutt, 1889–1905*, edited by Joseph R. McElrath, Jr., and Robert C. Leitz, III, is published. *Mandy Oxendine: A Novel*, declined by Houghton, Mifflin in 1897, is published.

The Absent Man

I / Introduction

Nearly a hundred years after he published his last book-length work, Charles Waddell Chesnutt (1858–1932) remains an enigmatic figure. The first African-American fiction writer to earn a national reputation,[1] Chesnutt appeared until recently as little more than a footnote in modern accounts of black literature.[2] While Gayl Jones, for example, asserts in *Liberating Voices* the crucial role played by oral forms in the development of a distinctly African-American literary tradition, she minimizes Chesnutt's role in that development. She suggests that not until the Harlem Renaissance did black writers make what she calls "serious" use of their "literary double-consciousness." It was only then, Jones writes, that

> African American writers whose tradition serves as a parallel to that of Twain, Lardner, Hemingway, and Salinger began to make a serious literary use of that other "unique language of American literary art." Among the fiction writers in this tradition were Zora Neale Hurston, Jean Toomer, Rudolph Fisher, John Matheus, Eric Walrond, [and] Bruce Nugent. . . . The range of sensibility broadened beyond the traditional literary dialect of Paul Laurence Dunbar, Charles Waddell Chesnutt, and William Wells Brown. This shift in attitude made possible a new seriousness and range in subject matter, experiences, and concerns, as well as deeper, more complex characterizations. (9)[3]

Not only would this relegation to the literary realm of un-broadened sensibilities have been personally galling to Chesnutt,[4] but it also summarizes his curiously ambiguous place in our current conception of both American and African-American letters. For, despite being classed by William Dean Howells in "the good school" of fiction—along with contemporaries Henry James, Mary Wilkins Freeman, and Ivan Turgenev[5]—Chesnutt seems to be something of a cipher for modern readers. Or, in terms Chesnutt used in his fiction, he became and continues to be an "absent man."

Such a cryptic characterization might initially seem an incongruous one for Chesnutt, who was very much a man of his times, especially the period between the end of the Civil War and the turn of the century. While designating someone a "man of his times" often carries with it a faintly apologetic connotation—usually implying that the subject indulged in behaviors no longer officially or popularly sanctioned—I use the expression here not to excuse or justify, but to emphasize the degree to which Chesnutt strikingly exemplified the social, cultural, and intellectual climate of his day. Living through the Civil War, Reconstruction, the turn of the century, World War I, and the Harlem Renaissance, Chesnutt witnessed and wrote about the dramatic changes the United States underwent between the mid-nineteenth century and the early 1930s, and he did so having lived substantial parts of his life in both the New South and the industrial North. Born in Cleveland (and so a northerner by birth),[6] he moved with his family in 1866 to Fayetteville, North Carolina, which provided the backdrop for his childhood and early adult years, as well as the setting for his *Conjure Woman* tales; he thus grew up as a man of mixed race in the South during Reconstruction.[7] Regularly expressing discontent in his journals about the social restrictions for an African American in the South, he moved as a young man back to the North, eventually resettling with his family in Cleveland, where he lived until his death in 1932.

As an African-American businessman and writer, he not only

personified the rising black professional class, but also documented the profound (and ongoing) importance of race to the turbulent process of national metamorphosis. Although he had hoped to gain fame and fortune exclusively from a writing career,[8] his own financial ambitions and the consistently disappointing remuneration he realized from his writings kept him from devoting himself solely to literary pursuits. From the mid-1880s until 1905, with a brief exception between late 1899 and some time in 1902 during which he wrote full-time,[9] he subordinated writing to his highly successful court reporting and stenography business.[10] Despite the years of dividing his energies between literature and commerce, he nevertheless produced an impressive list of publications, including three novels, several provocative essays on race, a biography of Frederick Douglass, and the two 1899 collections of short stories for which he is best known, *The Conjure Woman* and *The Wife of His Youth and Other Stories of the Color Line*. By the end of 1905, essentially all of Chesnutt's significant literary productivity was behind him:[11] he published only a handful of stories— "The Prophet Peter" (1906), "The Doll" (1912), "Mr. Taylor's Funeral" (1915), "The Marked Tree" (1924–25), and "Concerning Father" (1930)[12]—and essays, among them "Women's Rights" (1915) and "The Negro in Cleveland" (1930), thereafter.

But between 1887 and 1905, he had been a player in the belletristic universe. The writings he produced during that period epitomized, with a difference, the evolving American literary scene at the turn of the century, his best fictions seamlessly combining elements of the romantic and the realistic to form what William L. Andrews calls a "peculiar blend of realism and fantasy" ("Introduction" xi). The stories of magic (or "goopher") collected in *The Conjure Woman*, for example, may well depict elements of the supernatural in a Hawthornesque manner, but they also precisely render—in an understated style very like that of such prominent realists as Howells and James—the social and racial conditions of pre– and post–Civil War America, especially Cleveland and the sandhill region of North Carolina. Based on this tendency to bring to life specific venues in such particularized detail, Chesnutt's works seem to belong to the local color tradition as exemplified by Mary Wilkins Freeman, Sarah Orne Jewett, Bret Harte, Kate Chopin, and Mark Twain. And in his portrayals of the South in transition from slavery through Reconstruction, and especially the effects of race on those transitions, Chesnutt seems also to echo such figures as Thomas Nelson Page, Albion Tourgée, George Washington Cable, Joel Chandler Harris, and Ruth McEnery Stuart.[13] Ultimately, though, his often subversive use of the materials typical of those traditions, his near-preoccupation with race matters, and his subtle narrative presentations all combine to distinguish his writings from those of his contemporaries.

Despite the impressive range of his experiences and historical interests, virtually all of Chesnutt's writings act as a literary recapitulation of Reconstruction. His works, that is, repeatedly play out in microcosm—usually by concentrating on individual families attempting to make or, more often, to remake themselves in the face of late-nineteenth-century social upheaval— the national drama of repatriation and tentative reconciliation that began after the Civil War (and, in many ways, continues even now).[14] In each of the novels, *The House Behind the Cedars, The Marrow of Tradition,* and *The Colonel's Dream,* and in most of the short fiction, Chesnutt attempts to reimagine the American family (and thus America) in a broader context, a family able to resist or, perhaps, even to transcend the racial and social pressures of American history. But because Chesnutt is finally no weak-kneed sentimentalist, he can never quite bring himself to write a story or novel that enacts that transcendence. He seems finally to conclude that the very cure for racial ills—an understanding of, or a coming to terms with, the past—constitutes a sort of poison pill. For, in many of his fictions, the past functions both to sustain and to overwhelm his characters as they seek to establish a place for themselves and their families in the American social universe.

In thus habitually locating families in transition at the center of his fictional worlds, Chesnutt investigates the broad social and cultural implications of race on Reconstruction and post-Reconstruction America. The stories collected in *The Conjure Woman,* for example, focus on the obstacles that impede meaningful communication and understanding between a (presumably representative) northern white businessman who has recently relocated to the South after the Civil War and his coachman, an ex-slave raconteur whose stories in part depict the residual consequences of slavery on black families. In *The Wife of His Youth,* also published in 1899, Chesnutt again explores the logistical complications of a reconstituted America, this time by contemplating the fates of those with mixed blood as they try to make a place for themselves and their families in the tumultuous late-nineteenth-century milieu. And in much of the short fiction uncollected during his life (as well as in the novels), Chesnutt likewise uses the family as a lens through which to interrogate the very notion of American "reconstruction." But because Chesnutt, especially in the short fiction, skillfully disguises those trenchant interrogations—thereby leaving his intentions difficult to "read"—he continues to be an enigmatic figure.

Such a fate might well appeal to an author whose affinity for manipulating complex narrative strategies often resulted in texts so subtly layered as to confound readers' expectations. Short stories such as "Baxter's Procrustes" and "Her Virginia Mammy," for example, embed so many plausible "meanings" that Chesnutt's position in relation to the issues he raises in these works remains cryptic. The former story, built around a text composed of "all margin" (*Collected Stories* [hereafter *CS*] 277), is often cited as Chesnutt's best: Andrews, for example, notes the "excellence" of its "multi-layered satire" (*Literary Career* 220).[15] Even more telling, though, is Andrews's assertion that "one still imagines the author and his intention standing just a little apart from the reader, the enigmatic smile of Baxter reinforcing the author's reticence toward the reader" (220).[16]

This authorial "reticence" derives partly, of course, from Chesnutt's nature. But his cryptic relationship with readers of his own generation and ours has other causes as well.

The literary tradition Chesnutt inherited from earlier black writers and his innovations with the forms of fiction have both contributed to his enigmatic position within the American canon. He gleaned much of the material for his fiction from sources used previously by the writers of slave narratives, partly basing his *Conjure Woman* (1899) tales, for example, on familiar folktales he had heard as a child.[17] But while mid-nineteenth-century black writers such as Frederick Douglass and Harriet Jacobs needed to establish themselves primarily as truthtellers, Chesnutt had to negotiate a far different cultural landscape. As the first major black fiction writer, he manifestly violated the terms of literary engagement established by Douglass, Jacobs, and other writers of slave narratives. At the beginning of "The Goophered Grapevine," for instance, his narrator describes to readers "a quaint old town, which I shall call Patesville, because, for one reason, that is not its name" (*CW* 3).[18] Here and throughout his fiction, Chesnutt aggressively calls attention to the artificiality of his productions, thereby locating himself outside of the black literary tradition of truthtelling developed through more than a century of slave narratives. Thus, Chesnutt forced his reading audience to recalibrate its collective relationship with the works of black writers.

Many of the difficulties of that recalibration derived (and continue to derive) from Chesnutt's frequent use of characters and narrators who, for a variety of reasons, "mask" their identities,[19] a theme or motif that appears repeatedly in the African-American literary tradition. Douglass relates, for example, an anecdote in which a slave who answered honestly when questioned about his living conditions is sold down the river as punishment: this type of situation, writes Douglass, "has had the effect to establish among the slaves the maxim, that a still tongue makes a wise head. They suppress the truth rather than take the consequences of telling it" (62).[20] But while Douglass *explains* the practical necessity for slaves to dissemble—thus letting his white readers in on the practice—Chesnutt's characters and narrators *enact* that linguistic deception, thereby leaving readers in the precarious and uncomfortable position of wondering if they have been taken in.

Partly as a result of creating a host of inscrutable characters, including trickster figures such as Julius of *The Conjure Woman* and Baxter of "Baxter's Procrustes" (1904), Chesnutt inscribed for himself a similarly ambiguous position as author. Discussing "A Matter of Principle," J. Saunders Redding attests to precisely that ambiguity when he asks questions which in many ways typify critical response to Chesnutt's work:

> But what is Chesnutt's conviction as an artist? Does he sympathize with the existence of a color caste within the race? Is he holding his characters up to ridicule? Of what is he trying to convince us? In this and other stories one seems always at the point of making a discovery about the author, but the discovery never matures. (71)[21]

Intentionally or not, Chesnutt the author seems to don the mask with which he so craftily disguises his creations. In stories as varied as *The Conjure Woman* tales, "The Shadow of My Past," "The Passing of Grandison," "Baxter's Procrustes," and "Mr. Taylor's Funeral," Chesnutt thus establishes his own peculiarly inscribed absence. And as happens with his protagonists in these stories and others, Chesnutt's authorial self-masking both empowers and binds him. Like many of his characters, Chesnutt—the "absent man"—authors an identity for himself that remains, finally, inscrutable to his readers.

But in the highly self-conscious crafting of that inscrutability, Chesnutt engages in a kind of literary gamesmanship that, though to some extent reminiscent of Poe, has unique perils and consequences for an African-American writer interested both in overturning race prejudice and in establishing a black literary tradition in fiction. Those intentions often seem actively to oppose one another in his writings, an opposition apparent, for example, in *The Marrow of Tradition*, which Eric J. Sundquist calls "Chesnutt's most searching reflection on the divided sensibilities of his own literary career. Both [the novel and Chesnutt's career] concluded in states of tension and irresolution" (453–54). It is that very "irresolution" of his own sensibilities (or intentions or "anxieties") which ultimately makes Chesnutt such an enigmatic figure. While he grappled in his fiction with questions of personal and social identity, of the relationship between textual constructs and the culture that both begot and resulted from them, readers have tended to agree with Richard Watson Gilder, the editor of *Century*, who in an 1890 letter to George Washington Cable described Chesnutt's work as "amorphous—not so much in construction as in *Sentiment*" (qtd. in McElrath and Leitz 67). For Gilder, for turn-of-the-century and modern readers, and for Chesnutt himself, there is ultimately something unresolved and unresolvable about Chesnutt's artistic identity.

Questions of identity have long dominated discussions of African-American literature. When asked during a 1955 interview whether the quest for identity was "primarily an American theme," Ralph Ellison offered a definitive response: "It is *the* American theme. The nature of our society is such that we are prevented from knowing who we are" (177–78).[22] That the investigation of the self forms an essential component of American literature is nowhere more apparent than in African-American writings. Black American literature, especially during the late nineteenth and early twentieth centuries, reflects the struggles of black Americans to construct and articulate an identity for themselves in a social milieu that, while putatively liberating, often imposed on them new forms of confinement.

Although a few black writers—most notably Phillis Wheatley and Olaudah Equiano—published during the eighteenth century, African-American literature originated for the most part with slave narratives that articulated, from an eyewitness and very personal perspective, what it was to be black in the antebellum South. Before the Civil War, writers such as Douglass,

Jacobs, Henry Bibb, Solomon Northrup, and William Wells Brown created what Donald A. Petesch calls "a literature of reportage" (4). Because many whites, especially those in the North, formed their conceptions of black identity almost exclusively through what they read,[23] these writers faced the challenge of inscribing an identity for an entire race. That is, much early African-American literature sought to convey the humanity of blacks to an uninformed but presumably reasonable white audience. "In its early public role," Petesch suggests, black literature attempted "to report on the conditions of black life to a hypothetically decent, Christian, democratic audience in the expectation that once that audience was made aware of the gap between democratic, Christian ideals and daily, mundane practice, change would occur" (8). Change, of course, did occur, and in dramatic fashion: the Civil War obliterated the system—although not all of the underlying causes for, nor the residual consequences of, that system—that had assigned many African Americans their identity. Emancipation meant not only literal freedom for those who had been enslaved; it likewise liberated black writers, for whom the end of the slave system promised freedom of another sort: they no longer had to confine their work to the rhetorical goals established by the slave narrative.[24]

But this literary freedom had its costs. While the writers of slave narratives focused on convincing white audiences of the humanity of blacks, post–Civil War black writers faced an equally daunting, but in many ways more delicate, challenge. First, they struggled to assert, and defend, a place for African Americans within the rapidly evolving sociopolitical landscape of late-nineteenth-century America. As the country fashioned laws and bureaus to remake itself during the years immediately following the War, African Americans had the nearly literal task of reinventing themselves, often in opposition to ingrained prejudices that had flourished during slavery. Where before blacks had been considered subhuman or, as the Constitution mandated, three-fifths of a person, the fall of the Confederacy conferred upon them full legal personhood. Shortly after the

Civil War ended, a cultural backlash began, including both leg-
islative and judicial assaults on the rights of African Americans,
assaults which culminated in the 1896 *Plessy v. Ferguson*
Supreme Court decision validating the "separate but equal"
notion of civil rights.

These largely unhappy events nevertheless made for a rich
vein of material for black writers like Chesnutt, Paul Laurence
Dunbar, James Weldon Johnson, Frances E. W. Harper, and Sutton Griggs. In response to the social and cultural changes
wrought by the Civil War, Reconstruction, and the subsequent
racially motivated backlash, these writers described the constantly shifting roles of black Americans as the turn of the century approached. African-American literature continued during
this period in its role as a lever for social change, but it no
longer had the abolition of the slave system as a unifying goal.
Thus, black writers of the late nineteenth century regularly dis-
agreed as to the best social course for African Americans to
take, an ongoing disagreement personified in Chesnutt's day by
Booker T. Washington and W. E. B. Du Bois.[25] On a more literary level, they also began the equally intricate task of depicting
black individuals making their way in a world profoundly complicated by "freedom."

In addition to inscribing a social and economic position for
African Americans in a time of cultural instability, black writers
of this period faced a second obstacle. While slave narratives
might be compared to the nation-building literature of the
Colonial period, the works of post–Civil War black writers mir-
rored in many ways the literature produced by such American
writers as Charles Brockden Brown, Washington Irving, and
James Fenimore Cooper. That is, after Bradford, Winthrop,
Franklin, Crèvecoeur, and others had produced a literature of
identity constituted by texts devoted primarily to autobiography, biography, and history, the next generation of writers—
Brown, Irving, and Cooper—helped to inaugurate an American
literary tradition that elevated fiction to the status of those earlier genres. Similarly, black writers such as Chesnutt, Dunbar,

and Frances E. W. Harper followed the literally autobiographical tradition of slave narratives with more figurative renderings
of black identity. Ultimately, then, Chesnutt and others faced
the imposing challenge of delineating a poetics of black fiction.
For while a handful of African-American novels appeared as
early as the 1850s, including Douglass's *The Heroic Slave* (1853),
William Wells Brown's *Clotel, or the President's Daughter* (1853),
and Harriet E. Wilson's *Our Nig* (1859), they generated much
less national interest (and acclaim) than slave narratives.[26] In
short, *fin de siècle* black writers continued to inscribe a broad
social identity for an entire race, a process begun by the more
biographically focused writers of slave narratives. But this later
generation—Chesnutt, Dunbar, Harper, Griggs, and others—
also developed, in significant ways, an African-American tradition of fiction writing. And because of his interest in capturing
multiple perspectives in his fiction, Chesnutt in particular re-
envisioned the role of literature as a means to investigate questions of personal and cultural identity for African Americans.

No writer of the period of any race, in fact, explored the
subject of identity, whether literary or social, more comprehen-
sively than did Chesnutt. As a light-skinned, gray-eyed black
man whose grandfather was white, Chesnutt understandably
lacked a fixed or definite position from which to view racial
interaction,[27] and this ambiguity about his own racial makeup
clearly affected his writings, as several readers have noted. Sylvia
Lyons Render, for example, has suggested that the author's heritage formed a crucial element of his work, and she cites the
"double vision of one whose racial antecedents placed him on
the color line rather than on either side of it" (*Short Fiction*
[hereafter *SF*] 3). But such an assertion, although certainly
valid to a point, ultimately oversimplifies the matter. For Chesnutt's short fiction does much more than place binary oppositions in conflict. Rather, his fiction explores the shadings of the
people he writes about; or, more metaphorically, it plays among
the shadows that in large measure constitute human identity.

It is not so much Chesnutt's vision, double or otherwise,

that distinguishes him from his contemporaries, both black and white, but, more fundamentally, his manipulation of sophisticated narrative techniques and strategies to render the turn-of-the-century American social and political landscape from multiple perspectives. Through his experimentation with a range of voices—often within the same text—Chesnutt deploys a host of characters to articulate the American experience from vastly different subject positions. In this way, he also provocatively complicates questions of identity. Peter Carafiol, writing about those who produce what he calls "narratives that take ethnos for a subject in the American context," astutely notes their "problematic and even ideologically uncomfortable understandings of the interplay of self and culture, of individual and ethnos" (44). Although Carafiol's essay focuses on works by Alger, Washington, and Wright, his commentary applies equally well to Chesnutt, whose gift/curse is, I argue, precisely his tendency to make readers of all stripes "ideologically uncomfortable." For, as his fiction explores matters of cultural delicacy—both in his time and ours—Chesnutt forces readers to confront and account for the shifting perceptions (and varied angles of vision) of his many characters and narrators. He returns throughout his career to a literary paradigm that foregrounds the interaction of multiple voices within the text as they "construct" personal and social identities through storytelling within, and quite often against, the cultural framework of turn-of-the-century America. Such a paradigm can disorient even the most stalwart of readers, particularly in light of the often controversial nature of Chesnutt's subject matter, which includes miscegenation, "passing," and natural law.

This skillful handling and arrangement of several voices in addition to his own is clear in his novels, each of which examines issues of racial interaction from varied points of view. In *The Marrow of Tradition* (1901), for example, the narration draws from a broad array of perspectives on the races intermingling; readers are informed by voices reflecting a range of blacks—including an educated assimilationist, a radical separatist, and what we've come to know as a stereotypical "Uncle Tom"—and whites, among them an ineffectual liberal, a Klansman, and an idealized patriarch the narrator describes as "the apex of an ideal aristocratic development" (96). In *The Colonel's Dream* (1905), the narrator depicts most of the action from the perspective of a successful white businessman, who fails in repeated attempts to transform his southern hometown into an example of multicultural capitalism. And in *The House Behind the Cedars* (1900), Chesnutt liberally uses free indirect discourse to attach the point of view to a brother and sister of mixed blood as they make their way in a world ill-prepared to deal with them. Compared with Chesnutt's short fiction, the novels generate much less critical appreciation, due in part to their stridency of tone and the melodramatically propagandistic plots that characterize them. Joseph R. McElrath, Jr., and Robert C. Leitz III suggest that the novels dwell so insistently on issues of social reform that turn-of-the-century readers ultimately grew weary of "paying to be scolded" (23).

Despite their weaknesses, the novels provide compelling insights into Chesnutt's storytelling intentions and strategies; in his first novel, *The House Behind the Cedars*, he most nearly reproduces the complex narrative strategies typical of his short fiction. As often happens in Chesnutt's works, the plot derives from, but ultimately revises, an established genre, in this case that of the tragic mulatto fiction. A mulatto, John Walden (later John Warwick), "passes" for white and becomes a successful lawyer in South Carolina; when he arranges for his sister Rena to join him in white society, her involvement in a romantic relationship with the white George Tryon triggers a series of events culminating in the revelation of their racial background and, finally, Rena's death.[28] In many ways, of course, this plot aligns with, and, according to Eric J. Sundquist, is finally "limited by the conventions of white beauty that define the genre of tragic mulatto fiction" (399). Certainly, Rena's renunciation of passing, reminiscent of Frances E. W. Harper's *Iola Leroy* and Sutton Griggs's *The Hindered Hand,* and her melodramatically rendered

death—"Mary B. threw open a window to make way for the passing spirit, and the red and golden glory of the setting sun, tri-
umphantly ending his daily course, flooded the narrow room
with light" (*House* 294)—conform to typical conceptions of
mulattoes (and their attitudes about passing) in fiction at the
close of the nineteenth century.[29] Sundquist argues, for example, that *The House Behind the Cedars* "capitulates to conventions
of racialized, gothic sexuality," and that finally "the novel,
although it tentatively invokes the hidden promise of mixed-
race 'new people,' thus fails to forecast a new generation of
'future Americans'" (399). William L. Andrews likewise cites
"Chesnutt's choice of the stock tragic ending to his novel of
mulatto experience" in concluding that the novel ends "so com-
fortably for white social prejudices and so melodramatically for
popular literary sentiments" (*Literary Career* 173).

But *The House Behind the Cedars* differs in crucial fashion
from the tradition of the tragic mulatto genre, and in so doing
inlays a pointedly subversive message. In fact, despite Raymond
Hedin's contention that the novel works as a cautionary tale
examining the unhappy consequences for "blacks who step into
the dominant culture's sense of story" (197), I suggest that it
actually co-opts that very "sense of story." For while Rena's tra-
vails and death do follow the conventions of the tragic mulatto
plot, Chesnutt's use of John Walden in this novelistic account of
"passing" anticipates the radical evocations on the same theme
by James Weldon Johnson in *The Autobiography of an Ex-Colored
Man*. In John Walden, Chesnutt introduces a figure who, unlike
his sister Rena, refuses to accept the usual literary fate of the so-
called "tragic mulatto."

That refusal constitutes a trenchantly subversive, if well-
disguised, commentary not only on the genre of fiction from
which Chesnutt borrowed plot elements for *The House Behind the
Cedars,* but also on the expectations of his primarily white readership. If Rena's melodramatic end confirms those expectations, her brother's performance within the structure of Chesnutt's design offers a dramatic counterpoint. Although the

novel opens with an account of John Walden returning to his home of Patesville after years of passing for white in South Carolina—thus seeming to establish John, not Rena, as its protagonist—he utterly disappears two-thirds of the way through the work; neither the narrator nor any character ever so much as mentions John Walden following his departure from Patesville, which occurs more than a hundred pages from the end of the novel. Note the manner of John's leavetaking of his sister (and indeed the reader):

> "Listen, Rena," he said, with a sudden impulse, "we'll go to the North or West—I'll go with you—far away from the South and the Southern people, and start life over again. It will be easier for you, it will not be hard for me—I am young, and have means. There are no strong ties to bind me to the South. I would have a larger outlook elsewhere." (183)

While Rena chooses not to go with her brother, thereby rejecting the option of passing, John here announces both his intention to re-create himself as a white man (again) and his plans to do so "elsewhere." The very indeterminacy of his plan suggests that even his sister apparently does not know his destination. Four pages later, in what becomes the final mention of him, John's mother responds to Frank Fowler's questioning with the simple statement, "'my son's gone'" (187).

Hence, John's disappearance becomes an act of double passing, both textual and social. He fades out of the scope of the novel's plot while, more subversively, he disappears into (*not* out of) the culture at large: like Johnson's ex-colored man and Ellison's Invisible Man, John Walden (cloaked in whatever new identity he contrives for himself "elsewhere") has, by two-thirds of the way through *The House Behind the Cedars,* gone thoroughly underground. And, like Huck Finn, he chooses to "light out for the Territory ahead of the rest," but in this case the "Territory" might be anywhere he can live as a white man. If Rena's death serves to appease the sensibilities of late-nineteenth-century readers uneasy about the morality of passing, the novel's final silence concerning John's whereabouts sends a profoundly inflammatory message to that very audience.

And yet John's role in the novel, and indeed his flagrant intention to establish himself as white "elsewhere," has generated very little commentary. While Chesnutt's contemporaries generally praised the novel for its earnest treatment of delicate social and cultural matters,[30] modern readers have tended to focus on the debt the novel owes to the tragic mulatto tradition. Sundquist contends, for example, that "the power of its melodrama to produce a serious challenge to racialist cultural assumptions is constrained by Chesnutt's own fundamental ambivalence" about the subject of passing (399). "Although the epistemological plane is engaged," writes Sundquist, "in the novel's frequent recourse to the radically ambiguous language of the law and especially to coincidental epistolary revelations as a means to advance the downward spiral of Rena's fall, there are, finally, no secrets" (400). I argue that there are indeed secrets in *The House Behind the Cedars,* the most telling of which is Chesnutt's apparent deployment of John Walden as what Ellison would later term the "spy in the enemy's country." Thus, John ultimately escapes the apparent racial destiny homophonically encoded in his original surname (Walden = "walled in"): through the narratologically embedded misdirection of plot in *The House Behind the Cedars,* John's fade to white is de-emphasized while Rena's story plays itself out in more melodramatic and, for white turn-of-the-century audiences perhaps, more comfortable fashion.

Although *The House Behind the Cedars* and his other novels reveal a command of disparate voices and narratological sophistication, the true measure of Chesnutt's ability to articulate multiple perspectives is most apparent in the remarkable variety of what transpires in his short fiction. In these works, Chesnutt developed his ear for dialogue and perfected his literary ventriloquism: the narrators and characters of his early short fiction include whites and blacks of virtually every level of education and social position. The most dramatic evidence of

Chesnutt's skill in juxtaposing dissimilar voices can be found in his celebrated collection of short fiction, *The Conjure Woman*. This set of seven stories is a narratological *tour de force* in which an educated white northerner, John, rhetorically engages the ex-slave yarn-spinner Julius. Chesnutt's ability to "speak" for John should cause no surprise—apart from race designation, the author shares interests and a common background with his white counterpart—but the accuracy with which he captures Julius's voice merits particular attention. In fact, one linguistic analysis of Chesnutt's use of dialect in *The Conjure Woman* concluded that the speech patterns were so precisely rendered that their exact provenance could be asserted.[31] Indeed, his meticulous attention to detail in representing the verbal expressions of narrators of such distinctly varied backgrounds and social positions engenders much of the tension that makes these stories so rich.

That a black writer would be noted for skillfully rendering voices as polarized as those of John and Julius should come as no surprise to students of African-American literature. Readers such as Henry Louis Gates, Jr., Houston Baker, and Susan Willis have argued convincingly that the black tradition is a kind of literary hybrid. Gates, for instance, suggests that "[African-American] canonical texts have complex double formal antecedents, the Western and the black" (*Signifying Monkey* xxiv). Usually, this double-voicedness, or what Gates calls a "two-toned" quality, of black fiction is dictated by audience, as when both Ellison's Invisible Man and Wright's Bigger Thomas speak a far different language to whites than they do to blacks. An incisive example of the practice can be found also in Charlie Russell's "Quietus":

> Randolph sits down and slaps a fist into his open palm: I blew, baby, I blew! If I don't ever blow another one, I blew that one. Though a college man, he still thinks in the language of the streets. In a less turbulent time he would tell you he is bilingual. (Hughes 347)

The rest of Russell's story depicts how his protagonist, much like Chesnutt in his role as author, does indeed speak in two languages, one when addressing his white employers and another when he is his own audience. The "double-voicedness" that typifies both Randolph in "Quietus" and much of Chesnutt's writing serves obvious pragmatic functions but also exacts a price: both Randolph and Chesnutt ultimately become objects of mistrust for their respective readers.

The same sort of dichotomy of voices might be found throughout *The Conjure Woman,* as John's refined narration surrounds and occasionally interrupts the carefully crafted dialect stories of Julius. In this way, Chesnutt literalizes the dichotomy, or double-voicedness, of black literature as articulated by Gates; that is, the author divides the narrative duties between a representative of the Western literary tradition and his counterpart, who speaks a form of black vernacular. This combination results in an uneasy narrative alliance that nevertheless engenders a provocative cultural and social dialogue.

But Chesnutt's ability to reproduce dialects and his deft handling of disparate voices represent only a fraction of the variety that characterizes his work. Writing about *The Wife of His Youth and Other Stories of the Color Line* (1899), Lorne Fienberg assesses the thematic and structural range of Chesnutt's fiction:

> In the arrangement of the nine stories in the collection, there is a ceaseless oscillation across boundaries: from present to past, from North to South, from freedom to slavery and back again. This fluidity, which is both structural and thematic, upsets the reader's assumptions about the dialectics of openness and enclosure which shape the characters' lives. (225)

Chesnutt's fiction does indeed move about geographically, historically, and socially, often within the same piece. His skill in representing various subject positions, the essence of what Fienberg calls "fluidity," derives from Chesnutt's ability to speak for such a broad range of characters: he captures the voices of slaves, slaveowners, free black witches, and northern liberals, to name a few, and he renders these voices without ever minimizing or ridiculing them. Unlike his contemporaries who idealized the antebellum South, including Thomas Dixon and Thomas Nelson Page, or who scourged it in the manner of Sutton Griggs, Chesnutt treats his characters—even those he must have disapproved of—with unusual respect and fairness.

What distinguishes Chesnutt from other writers of both races who comment on racial issues is, in fact, his ability to render the consciousnesses of unidealized black and white characters as they interact. He can, with equal skill, reproduce the voices of the talented-tenth types who populate "Mr. Taylor's Funeral," "The Wife of His Youth," and "A Matter of Principle"; the working-class laborers who achieve success through their tireless work, as illustrated in the protagonists of "The Partners" and "The Averted Strike"; and even trickster figures, including Julius and characters found in "Aunt Mimy's Son," "An Eloquent Appeal," and "A Roman Antique." Chesnutt peoples his fiction with an array of equally realistic white figures as well: the wealthy cotillion types of "Cartwright's Mistake" and "A Fool's Paradise"; the hard-working but not corrupt capitalists in "The Shadow of My Past" and "Walter Knox's Record"; the comic drunkards of "A Midnight Adventure" and "A Bad Night"; and even the literati in "A Grass Widow" and "Baxter's Procrustes." Chesnutt's short fiction, much of which has been neglected critically, explores without condescension or oversimplification a remarkable range of characters and voices.[32]

And, while Chesnutt's short fiction does not exclusively emphasize race issues, his works can be plotted along a continuum of racial identity. In general terms, that is, his writing often focuses on the formation and articulation of identity in relation to race, and the unique province of his literary skill is his ability to speak convincingly from virtually every point on that continuum without wallowing in his own biases. Writing about "The Wife of His Youth," William Dean Howells describes how effectively Chesnutt manipulates point of view and maintains narrative distance to achieve his literary success:

> Anyone accustomed to study methods in fiction, to distinguish
> between good and bad art, to feel the joy which the delicate
> skill possible only from a love of truth can give, must have
> known a high pleasure in the quiet self-restraint of the perfor-
> mance; and such a reader would probably have decided that
> the social situation in the piece was studied wholly from the
> outside, by an observer with special opportunities for knowing
> it, who was, as it were, surprised into final sympathy.
>
> Now, however, it is known that the author of this story is of
> negro blood. ("Mr. Charles W. Chesnutt's Stories" 699)

Howells's opinion that the author's race and allegiances are not
readily detectable from his fiction speaks to Chesnutt's command of diverse voices. It also reflects the tendency of readers,
even those as exceptionally skillful and well-intentioned as Howells, to welcome contextualizing data as a means of *situating*
themselves in relationship to Chesnutt.

Despite the extent to which Chesnutt and his works frus-
trate attempts to categorize him, he continues to be defined
almost exclusively in terms of an issue—racial prejudice—he
had hoped would become obsolete. Indeed, "critics have not
changed in their tendency to hoist him by the very 'color line'
that he wished so much to eradicate" (Terry 104). Much of
Chesnutt's literary production involves relationships between
the races, and often his characters have, like the author himself,
mixed blood. But when he is characterized, as he is in the first
sentence of William L. Andrews's introduction to *Collected Stories
of Charles W. Chesnutt,* as "the first African-American writer of fiction to enlist the white-controlled publishing industry in the service of his social message" (vii), a reader might protest. Such a
characterization suggests that Chesnutt's fiction serves exclusively to advance a racial agenda.

While Andrews's characterization of his subject would seem
to locate Chesnutt as an important social protester for racial
equality, perhaps even to the detriment of his craft, a second
irony in the shaping of his reputation is also at work. Although

Chesnutt voluntarily acknowledged his racial makeup, his place in African-American literature remains uncertain. Despite the author's reliance on black folk tradition, his use of dialect, and his frequent productions of protest fiction and nonfiction, many contemporary readers, including Dickson D. Bruce, Jr., point to "the ambiguous place Chesnutt occupies in black literary tradition" because his work was "both part of and removed from the main currents of black American literature during his day" (165). In fact, Chesnutt, according to Bruce, "was never committed to a distinctive black identity. His alienation from North Carolinians was striking. He certainly felt his own superiority to most black people around him. . . . Chesnutt wanted, above all, to be part of the American elite—an elite that happened to be white rather than black" (173). Such is Chesnutt's fate: counseled by Howells to temper the bitterness of his message,[33] he has also been called a "thoroughgoing assimilationist" (Bruce 173).[34]

Thus, Chesnutt occupies a uniquely precarious position in both American literature and African-American literature.[35] In curious fashion, however, the polarized responses to Chesnutt's alleged political slant indicate the degree to which he was successful in articulating multiple points of view. In fact, his inability, as Bruce would have it, to project a "distinctive black identity" suggests instead his ability to depict a plurality of both black and white characters rather than offering reductive generalizations about blacks or limiting his artistic expressions to a single, politicized voice. His skill in exploring varied perspectives, ironically, has inspired some energetic attacks on his reputation, often apparently motivated precisely *because* Chesnutt's work resists the unambiguously political messages late-twentieth-century sensibilities seem to favor. One recent reader, SallyAnn H. Ferguson, chides Chesnutt for being "a social and literary accommodationist who pointedly and repeatedly confines his reformist impulses" to efforts on behalf of those with mixed blood (109). As evidence of Chesnutt's own prejudice,

Ferguson cites Chesnutt's essay "What Is a White Man?" which includes this assessment of southerners' attempts to classify men by skin color:

> In view, therefore, of the very positive ground taken by the white leaders of the South, where most of these [black] people reside, it becomes in the highest degree important to them to know what race they belong to. It ought to be also a matter of serious concern to the Southern white people: for if their zeal for good government is so great that they contemplate the practical overthrow of the Constitution and laws of the United States to secure it, they ought at least to be sure that no man entitled to it by their own argument, is robbed of a right so precious as that of free citizenship: the "all-pervading, all-conquering Anglo-Saxon" ought to set as high a value on American citizenship as the all-conquering Roman placed upon the franchise of his State two thousand years ago. This discussion would of course be of little interest to the genuine Negro, who is entirely outside of the charmed circle, and must content himself with the acquisition of wealth, the pursuit of learning and such other privileges as his "best friends" may find it consistent with the welfare of the nation to allow him: but to every other good citizen the inquiry ought to be a momentous one, What is a white man? (6)

After quoting selectively from this passage, Ferguson offers a confounding gloss on the essay's message: "For Chesnutt, however, free citizenship for 'genuine Negroes' is apparently unworthy of argument" (110). This interpretation remarkably ignores the pervasive irony—perhaps *the* major trope of Chesnutt's work—of the passage, including Chesnutt's assertions locating "Negroes" outside "the charmed circle" and advocating that they trust in their "'best friends.'"[36] Chesnutt's experimentation with voices, combined with his naturally enigmatic authorial identity, makes him especially susceptible to misapprehension by those who seek affirmation of a specific ideology.

Chesnutt's unfortunate reputation may also be part of a larger pattern. Although African-American literature has generated extensive commentary in the past twenty-five years, some readers argue that it attracts a different *kind* of inquiry than that accorded to more entrenched, canonical works. In his introduction to *Black Literature and Literary Theory*, for example, Henry Louis Gates, Jr., explores what he sees as a dominant approach to black literature:

> For all sorts of complex historical reasons, the very act of writing has been a "political" act for the black author. Even our most solipsistic texts, at least since the Enlightenment in Europe, have been treated as political evidence of one sort or another, both implicitly and explicitly. And, because our life in the West has been one political struggle after another, our literature has been defined from without, and rather often from within, as primarily just one more polemic in those struggles. (5)

The result of this "curious valorization of the social and polemical functions of black literature," Gates justifiably laments, is that the black text is treated "as if it were invisible, or literal, or a one-dimensional document" (5–6).

Gates's perceptive analysis of the way black literature is read provides a useful framework for understanding why Chesnutt (although not specifically the subject of Gates's discussion) continues to be a misunderstood figure. Because of his position as the first major post–slave narrative black writer, Chesnutt developed a craft—that is, his very "literariness"—that makes him seem less a truthteller than writers such as Douglass and Jacobs, who rhetorically shaped their narratives to elicit a unified response. And if Chesnutt's texts are treated as "one-dimensional documents," like the majority of slave narratives, his rich plurality of perspectives and voices begins to lose dimension: his fiction does not easily fit under the rubric of what Petesch calls "literature of reportage." Chesnutt's reputation has certainly suffered because his writings have so often been read as polemics, and discussions of his work regularly seem far more concerned with the author's political or social attitudes than with the merit of his literary production. To some extent, of course, Chesnutt invites this sort of attention, declaring in his journal, for example, his "high and holy purpose for writing" to be a means of "elevating" white readers.[37] But any attempt to reduce the author's entire output to its political baseline ultimately belittles the rich diversity of his work.

Indeed, Chesnutt's writing may well be the most accomplished performance of what today we call multiculturalism. In modern critical parlance, that term typically refers to a group of writers or other artists, taken collectively, whose varied cultural and aesthetic perspectives form a panoramic account of the world around them. But the very nature of Chesnutt's work invites us to appreciate the texts of a single author in a context usually reserved for multiple authors. Few writers—even taken as a group—can claim to have so thoroughly represented the perspectives of such a broad range of the population. Chesnutt knew what it was to be a poor black man in the South during Reconstruction, and he knew life as a wealthy northern capitalist as well. His fiction reflects this diversity of experience, and his authentic reproductions of high-society literary banter—apparent in "Baxter's Procrustes" and "The Wife of His Youth"—are as compelling and precise as his rendering of a Fayetteville dialect.

Although Howells astutely recognized Chesnutt's "quiet self-restraint" as a writer, it is, paradoxically, Chesnutt's ability to speak so convincingly for such a broad range of subjects that makes his work resonate. The multitude of voices—most of them rendered with precision and compassion—in his fiction forms one of the most comprehensive explorations of identity to be found in American literature. And his adroit handling of the continuum of racial identity forces us to reconsider many of our notions of "race." Chesnutt's fiction, in fact, anticipates the concerns of many contemporary commentators, including Dominick LaCapra, who offers suggestive comments on the difficulties of writing about race:

> Indeed it is at present virtually impossible to write or say anything on the topic of race that is not in some way objectionable or embarrassing. This limitation applies particularly to those

who are not "people of color," for one's own existential or
"subject" position inflects what one says independently of the
propositional content of assertions. It is decidedly difficult to
overcome the tendency to privilege whiteness as the master-
text—the valorized and often unmarked center of reference—
and to identify the nonwhite as "other" or "different." (2)

The fluidity of Chesnutt's "existential or 'subject' position" no
doubt played a major role in engendering what Bakhtin might
call the *polyglossia* of Chesnutt's writing.[38] For although his work
often seems to conflate two language systems—standard American English and black vernacular—it is not a simple matter
to determine which, if either, is privileged, and which is the
"other." In fact, Chesnutt consistently destabilizes pat notions of
"otherness."

Indeed, Chesnutt's complex narrative strategies and elaborate masking devices contribute in no small part to the author's
current status as literary cipher. In a story such as "Her Virginia
Mammy," for example, he constructs a tale that invites attention
as an apparent endorsement of miscegenation, an extremely
controversial position for a turn-of-the-century black writer to
take. The work features an apparently white woman who refuses
to marry until she can confirm her "good" social ancestry; when
her suitor learns of her mixed blood, he marries her anyway
and keeps the information from her. But while the tale—which
might also appeal to audiences as a sentimental love story—
makes possible other readings, it essentially offers a satiric commentary on white readers who, like the female protagonist,
have developed a profound complacency about their racial
identities. Hence, Chesnutt challenges traditional reading positions, particularly those of his primarily white audience.

The extent to which Chesnutt unsettles the reader's position exemplifies the strikingly modern sensibilities of his fiction. His use of varied narrative constructions to articulate complex rubrics of identity reveals his skilled engagement with
issues and techniques we associate with our own era: he confronts without flinching the dynamics of race, gender, and class

interplay; he moves back and forth in time and venue, from the antebellum South to the industrial North, from the country to the city; and he manipulates point of view with such subtlety and rich complexity that his work anticipates the narratological deftness of Faulkner. Finally, one can perhaps best rely on Howells's assessment of Chesnutt's art as exemplified in *The Conjure Woman* and *The Wife of His Youth:*

> Mr. Chesnutt seems to know quite as well what he wants to do in a given case as Maupassant, or Tourguenief [*sic*], or Mr. James, or Miss Jewett, or Miss Wilkins, in other given cases, and has done it with an art of kindred quiet and force. He belongs, in other words, to the good school, the only school, all aberrations from nature being so much truancy and anarchy. He sees his people very clearly, very justly, and he shows them as he sees them, leaving the reader to divine the depth of his feeling for them. He touches all the stops, and with equal delicacy in stories of real tragedy and comedy and pathos. ("Mr. Charles W. Chesnutt's Stories" 700)

For Howells, Chesnutt belonged in the "good school, the only school" because, in his best short fiction, he demonstrated such considerable literary range and refused to promote a simplistic agenda of any stripe. Modern readers have, ironically, consigned him to a less certain standing for the same reasons.

2/ The White and the Black
. . . and the Limits of Authorship

Very near the beginning of *The Marrow of Tradition* (1901), Charles W. Chesnutt prepares the reader for the series of racially motivated injustices to come by having the novel's protagonist, a black doctor, rousted from his seat and forced to relocate to the "colored" car. The episode not only illustrates the fundamental inequality facing African Americans during and after Reconstruction—a period that "witnessed a snowballing of racist ideas and practices" (Bruce 2)—but also calls attention to the practical absurdities engendered by the Jim Crow laws. Here, a barely literate conductor possesses the authority to humiliate, and literally unseat, a cultured, highly educated man on the basis of his skin color. This scene strikingly exemplifies Robyn Wiegman's claim, in *American Anatomies: Theorizing Race and Gender,* that American "social hierarchies have been rationalized, in both senses of the word, by locating in the body an epistemological framework for justifying inequality" (2). The fictional doctor in *The Marrow of Tradition* is thus dispossessed of his position on the train (and in the social order) because of his apparent unwhiteness.

Chesnutt clearly recognized the value of this conceit, and he exploited railway car anecdotes to good effect in other works as well. In an essay published by the *Boston Evening Transcript* at about the same time *The Marrow of Tradition* appeared in print, for example, Chesnutt uses a similar set of circumstances to emphasize the inadequacies of distinguishing among people by means of race. The essay, "The White and the Black," relates how a conductor's misjudgment of a passenger's race had entangled the railroad in a lawsuit. In that case, the conductor had forced a white woman to ride in the colored car, and when her "palpably and aggressively white" son ("The White and the Black" 13) discovered the offense, he sued for damages. The case led Chesnutt to ponder the vagaries of race discrimination and reflect on a conversation he had once had with a conductor—while traveling between Washington, D.C., and Virginia—concerning the issue of classifying passengers according to their skin color:

> The American citizen, white or black, who has travelled all over the North and West, with only the private consciousness that his color affected his citizenship, is met at this gate to the Sunny South with a classification which puts a legal stamp upon the one as superior, upon the other as inferior.
>
> The conductor of a train has the power of an autocrat. He nods his Jove-like head, corrugates his high Caucasian brow and the Negro seldom argues, because there is no use in doing so.
>
> "How long," I asked a Virginia conductor, "has this Jim Crow car system been in operation?"
>
> "Since last July," he answered.
>
> "Does it work all right?"
>
> "Oh, yes."
>
> "Do the colored people object to it?"
>
> "No, they don't mind it. Some of them kicked a little at first—a nigger likes to show off, you know, put on a little airs; but I told 'em it was the law, and they would have to submit, as I had to. Personally I don't mean to take any chances; I've been hauled up in court once, or threatened with it, for not enforcing the law. I'd put a white man out of the colored car as quick as I'd put a nigger out of this one."
>
> "Do you ever," I asked, "have any difficulty about classifying people who are very near the line?"
>
> "Oh, yes, often."

"What do you do in a case of that kind?"

"I give the passenger the benefit of the doubt."

"That is, you treat him as a white man?"

"Certainly."

"But suppose you should find in the colored car a man who had a white face, but insisted that his descent entitled him to ride in that car; what would you do then?"

"I'd let him stay there," replied the conductor, with uncon-cealed disgust, which seemed almost to include the questioner who could suppose such a case.

"Anyone that is fool enough to rather be a nigger than a white man may have his choice. He could stay there till h-ll froze over for all I'd care." (13)

This passage has obviously relevant implications for readers of Chesnutt, particularly in regard to his lifelong devotion to studying the color line. The conversation exposes the fallibility of the Jim Crow laws in general while satirically examining the method of enforcement.

But if the railway episode from *The Marrow of Tradition* con-firms Wiegman's premise that social and cultural institutions rely unreflectively on what she calls "the epistemology of the visual" (8), Chesnutt's encounter with the conductor in "The White and the Black" enacts the subversive possibilities gener-ated by precisely such a reliance. For while the conductor in *Marrow* visually recognizes his passenger's "blackness"—a recog-nition that triggers his discriminatory act—the passenger in the essay (presumably Chesnutt himself) cannot be so readily clas-sified by race, suggesting that he is what in the late nineteenth century would have been termed a mulatto. The light-skinned Chesnutt (or his proxy) on the train thus personifies the "eva-sive and shadowy" materiality, to use Hortense Spillers's term, of the mulatto's presence in American social history. And if Bar-bara Johnson is right in claiming that the mulatto figure repre-sents "an allegory for the racially divided society as a whole, simultaneously un-American and an image of America as such" (252), then Chesnutt's two railway anecdotes dramatize those apparently polarized but finally complementary consequences of, or responses to, a social order based on racial taxonomies. In the first instance, the mulatto doctor is forced into exile, is subject, that is, to the caprices of an unjust legal and social system. The passage from *The Marrow of Tradition* quoted above, and indeed all of the novel, comments overtly on those injustices in an attempt to effect social change. But in the second case (which is, I would argue, far more representative of Chesnutt's short fiction), a figure of indefinite race identity exploits what Spillers calls the "cultural ambiguity" of mulattoes to expose the very flaws in the system that occasionally grant him social (and, in this case, literary) privilege.[1]

As a means of capitalizing on that "cultural ambiguity" in his writings, however, Chesnutt regularly plays loose and fast with legal and social restrictions, a strategy that occasionally strains his relationship with readers of his own time and ours. In his role as interlocutor in "The White and the Black," for example, he implicitly admits to having passed for white. Such an admission would not have been lost on a late-nineteenth-century reading audience, for whom, as Elaine K. Ginsberg notes in *Passing and the Fictions of Identity*, "the possibility that . . . 'whiteness' or ethnicity can be performed or enacted, donned or discarded, exposes the anxieties about status and hierarchy created by the potential of boundary trespassing" (4). In fact, Chesnutt's performance in "The White and the Black" explicitly confirms those "anxieties" by positing the existence of a black figure who passes for white, a figure Ralph Ellison would later call the "spy in the enemy's country."

Modern readers too have difficulty positioning themselves in relationship to the kind of "mulatto" texts Chesnutt often produced, texts which—like the figure who converses with the conductor in "The White and the Black"—refuse to identify themselves as black or white. Raymond Hedin argues, for instance, that Chesnutt's fictions, especially those found in *The Conjure Woman*, "often involved the narrative equivalent of 'passing,' with similarly inherent ambiguities":

> The black story had to look like a white story; it had to at least
> look like a story which was fully acceptable to the whites who
> heard it inside the text. If it became fully and equivocally
> acceptable, however, it ran the risk of losing its own identity; it
> would become a white story—as *The Conjure Woman,* for
> instance, is often taken to be. (195)

Questions of textual identity, especially in relation to figurings
of race, are indeed central here, and Hedin rightly notes the
"risk" inherent in the sort of delicate rhetorical gamesmanship
typical of Chesnutt's "race" stories: "even today," Hedin writes,
"many critics remain convinced that his stories passed over the
color line irretrievably" (196). Thus, while Henry Louis Gates,
Jr., is no doubt right when he asserts that "[r]ace is the ultimate
trope of difference" (*"Race"* 5), Chesnutt's fictional and nonfic-
tional constructs often obscure the boundaries between black
and white.

The exchange here between Chesnutt and the anonymous
conductor provides more than an incisive scrutiny of social
injustices. It also offers insights into several of the thematic patterns that pervade, and often govern, Chesnutt's fiction and
nonfiction writings throughout his career. His arrangement of
this anecdote plays on the mutability of identity, an issue central
to virtually all of his writings, but more pointedly satirizes those
who assert social taxonomics based on race. Conceding to a
light-skinned African American that "classifying" people is an
inexact science, for example, the conductor nevertheless rationa-
lizes his role in labeling passengers as members of one race or
another, with those whose characteristics mask an essential race
identity receiving "the benefit of the doubt."[2] But Chesnutt
chooses in this essay, and indeed throughout his career, to foreground explicitly the very doubts about race that so unsettle his
readers, including railway conductors.

Probing such sensitive topics required a deft touch for a
turn-of-the-century black writer, and "The White and the Black"
exemplifies some of the narrative strategies that typify Chesnutt's work, especially his tendency to present a divided account

of himself. There are in this brief anecdote three manifesta-
tions of Chesnutt. First, as an essayist he uses this encounter to
illustrate the logistical difficulties and the illogic that inevitably
attend attempts to enforce a policy of racism. Second, Chesnutt
functions as a *participant* in this scene as well, a position he
rarely takes in his fiction. As a presumably white figure, then, he
directly engages the conductor of the train, who also serves as a
character within this narrative frame. And third, he projects yet
another version of himself into their conversation by asking
about a hypothetical light-skinned black who apparently prefers
to sit with African Americans, a choice Chesnutt permanently
made when he publicly claimed black ancestry for himself.

The multiple incarnations of Chesnutt within this essay cor-
respond with the often protean narrative personae one finds in
his fiction, and his positioning of himself as narrator discloses a
great deal about his storytelling philosophies and techniques.
By relying on a hypothetical subject, for example, Chesnutt
masks himself (at least temporarily) and effaces his views on the
subject of discussion. Thus, the ironic subtext of the conversation—the conductor's willingness to confide his unreflective
racism to an educated and light-skinned black man—and not
Chesnutt's wounded sensibilities, serves to direct the reader's
focus.

In many ways this conversation also approximates the
uneasy relationship between Chesnutt and a turn-of-the-century
white reading audience unprepared for his ironic examinations
of their attitudes on race. The rhetorical attention Chesnutt
gives to *placing* himself in relation to the conductor in this passage exemplifies his authorial reticence—his comments no
doubt appear enigmatic to his companion—and his suspicion
of all who would "read" him. Despite having the breadth and
scope of his social power questioned, the conductor seems to
consider this conversation a form of pleasantry, at least until the
end. And we can also assume that Chesnutt was sitting in the
white car during this conversation. Not only would the anec-

dote make no sense otherwise, but the conductor's words—
"'I'd put a white man out of the colored car as quick as I'd put
a nigger out of this one'"—establish Chesnutt's location. The
conductor's disgusted reaction to a "questioner who could suppose such a case" likewise implies his reconsideration of what
he had assumed to be his white companion. If this scene thus
reflects Chesnutt's misgivings about his white audience, it also
makes clear why those readers might harbor their own reservations about *him,* and especially his attitudes toward them. Here,
after all, he's sitting in the *white* car, which we must take to mean
that he has at least temporarily accepted a position of social
privilege, presumably because of his light complexion, but then
he uses that very access to write a scathing (if entirely justifi-
able) satire on those who would judge him. This sort of delicate
(and rhetorically dangerous) relationship with his readers characterizes many of Chesnutt's writings, and it likewise provides
striking commentary on his authorial duality.[3]

As risky as it is, this strategy does allow him to explore the
boundaries of racial tension from a position of relative
anonymity. Unlike Frederick Douglass or other writers of slave
narratives, who embedded social commentary in fully described
personal experience, Chesnutt prefers to examine racially
charged situations like this one from a detached, apparently
impersonal perspective. Certainly, his account of the conversation with the conductor includes a fair amount of irony, mostly
directed at the attempts of his companion to justify an unten-
able position. But more importantly, Chesnutt does not choose
to reveal himself to the conductor as an enlightened avenger.
He may have exposed his own heritage by "supposing such a
case," but it is hard to imagine that the conductor was inspired
by this discussion to remove his interlocutor to the "colored"
car. Chesnutt clearly favors the low-profile stance of the realist,
one who quietly chronicles the world around him. While Douglass embraces, like Thoreau or Emerson, the more lyrical
possibilities of the first person, Chesnutt seems decidedly

Howellsian in his literary approach. In short, Chesnutt actively seeks to conceal himself behind his literary creations rather than foregrounding his life and experiences.

As evidence for this assessment of Chesnutt's career, one need only examine how he rhetorically and narratologically positions his storytellers, those who serve as his proxies in his fiction. Despite publishing more than sixty short stories and three novels during his life, in only five of these fictions did he make use of an "I"-narrator who serves as the story's protagonist. And of those five, only "The Shadow of My Past" (written after 1901)[4] merits serious critical attention. The other four—"A Bad Night" (1886), "A Metropolitan Experience" (1887), "A Midnight Adventure" (1887), and "Gratitude" (1888)—are brief, whimsically comic stories that appeared in newspapers or light magazines. Indeed, their comic tone is the most obvious characteristic common to the five short stories that use this narrative framework. While the most sophisticated of them, "The Shadow of My Past," infuses its serious social commentary with comedic elements, the other pieces rely on varying types of standard humor: "Gratitude" contains stock slapstick elements of physical humor, including the literal pants-kicking of an irritating salesman; "A Bad Night" and "A Midnight Adventure" feature narrators who dryly relate their drunken exploits and mishaps; and "A Metropolitan Experience" depicts the attempts of a young man to find (and define) the woman he loves in the confusing large city to which he has only recently moved.

These works, again with the exception of "The Shadow of My Past," appear at the beginning of Chesnutt's career, during the mid-1880s. That he subsequently rejected (or at least moved away from) this involved first-person narrative approach—with the one important exception occurring about 1901—suggests that his experimentation with various forms convinced Chesnutt of its unsuitability for him. Even "The Shadow of My Past," despite its first-person narrator-protagonist, is not so much an exercise in self-disclosure as it is an examination of the amorphous quality of identity. On the rare occasions when Chesnutt does use this most personal style of narration, he arranges to have his narrators effaced through a variety of methods, often involving the concealment or redefinition of the narrator's identity. Hence, those stories told in what traditionally has been a self-revelatory mode contribute to Chesnutt's career-long interest in the inscrutability of human identity.

His first-person narrator-protagonist stories have several elements besides their comic tone in common, the most provocative being the extent to which they explore shifting conceptions of identity. To be sure, Chesnutt exploits this theme often for comic purposes, but the stories fundamentally attest to his interest in the topic even at this early stage of his career. In "A Bad Night," for example, the narrator relates, in comically understated terms, how a night spent consuming Kentucky whiskey results in his feeling "extremely comfortable" (*SF* 273). The rest of the passage attests to his condition:

> In a fit of absent-mindedness I tried to open the door with my pocket knife for a while, but discovering my mistake, applied the latch-key and gained admittance. I hung, or meant to hang, my hat on a hook, but it fell on the floor and rolled over into a corner. I did not think it worthwhile to pick it up, as a slight feeling of languor stealing over me made me disinclined to any unnecessary exertion. . . . I meant to lie down on the lounge, but through some miscalculation or mistake, or misfortune, I missed the lounge and lay on the floor. My memory is a little indistinct about the matter now, but I remember I thought it would require a good deal of exertion to get up and lie down on the lounge, to say nothing of the possibility of another failure. (*SF* 273)

Because of this "miscalculation or mistake, or misfortune" (273), the narrator, Paul, falls asleep on the floor, where he is mostly concealed beneath a lounge chair. When his wife returns home, she sees "feet protruding from under the lounge" and concludes "that a burglar had secreted himself . . . with the intention of robbing the house when all the inmates were

asleep" (273). Through a series of comic misassumptions—all
of which conspire to obscure his identity—Paul is arrested and
forced to explain to the court how he "had been the innocent
victim of circumstances" (276). The first half of the story thus
comically describes how a drinking binge disrupts the narrator's
identity.

If "A Bad Night" initially exploits boozy disorientation for
light amusement, the story ultimately focuses on the ways in
which the narrator and his wife revise their impressions of his
identity, a theme crucial to Chesnutt's canon. His wife fails to
recognize Paul in his drunken incarnation, and his narrative
includes a collection of details that emphasize the now-protean
quality of his identity: when he is arrested, for example, he gives
a false name; near the end of the story, he studies himself in the
mirror to see if his "hair had not turned gray in a single night"
(*SF* 277); later still, after his incarceration, he says to his wife,
"'In me you see a nervous wreck, a blasted reputation, blighted
prospects, and a ruined life'" (276–77); and finally, after his
release from jail he remakes himself with a new suit and other
cosmetic changes, telling us that "the wretched creature who
had appeared in the Police Court would never have been recognized as the elegant Paul _____" (277). "A Bad Night,"
then, although not one of Chesnutt's more accomplished
works, anticipates his interest in the ways people construct,
revise, and understand their conceptions of themselves. This
topic reaches full flowering in *The Conjure Woman* (1899), *The
House Behind the Cedars* (1900), and *The Marrow of Tradition*
(1901), all of which include characters whose public personae
differ markedly from the ways they envision themselves and the
ways they are presented to the reader. By comically examining
the pressures that compel a businessman to rewrite his life, the
story also forecasts one of Chesnutt's most underrated works,
"The Shadow of My Past."

This notion of unstable or evolving identity not only pervades much of Chesnutt's fiction but also in many ways describes his own literary reputation. As a self-identified African

American[5]—he ponders in his journal whether he ought to attempt to pass, but rejects the idea—attempting to write himself into a mostly white literary tradition, Chesnutt often found himself pre- and mis-judged by white readers,[6] a topic he recapitulates to dazzling effect in "Baxter's Procrustes" (1904). His inability to earn a substantial living as a writer only magnified his initial mistrust of that audience's judgment.[7] Although use of a first-person narrator-protagonist might create expectations of a healthy dose of self-disclosure—of both the narrator and the author—Chesnutt's work with the narrative paradigm suggests that this obvious conclusion needs qualification. Each of his "I" narrator-protagonists presents multiple and constantly shifting conceptions of himself, and others. Ultimately, it is as if the author has engaged the reader in a sort of narrative shell game: distinguishing among and classifying in Chesnutt's fiction what Wayne Booth would call author, implied author, and narrator proves especially tricky. But this plurality of narrative identity does succeed in effacing the author, and Chesnutt remains as ambiguous a figure to the reader as he must have been to that Virginia conductor.

✑

Years after his earlier ventures into the first-person narrator-protagonist paradigm, at the height of his literary output—*The Conjure Woman, The Marrow of Tradition, The House Behind the Cedars,* and *The Wife of His Youth and Other Stories of the Color Line,* much of his short fiction, and his biography of Frederick Douglass all reached print between 1899 and 1902—Chesnutt produced his most successful example of the genre, "The Shadow of My Past." While many of his works feature examinations of identity, this story suggests that Chesnutt deliberately conceived and embraced the idea of fragmentation as a metaphor for post-Reconstruction American society. And although most of his examinations of that fragmentation explicitly portray black or mulatto protagonists, "The Shadow of My Past" considers the matter through the prism of a white narrator-protagonist,

Hal/Hank Skinner. Despite both its comic tone and the absence of literally black characters, this story nevertheless resonates as an allegory of racial identity.

"The Shadow of My Past" depicts how a "self-made man"—the term has special significance in this tale—self-consciously examines the construction of his own identity and subsequently reinvents his past. The story quickly becomes a personal archaeology, one which reveals that a man might indeed have more than one identity: although "my life in the city had been an open book," the narrator tells us, "my life before was a closed chapter; at least I had not opened it for thirteen years" (*SF* 293). This split grows even wider once his exploration of his past self shifts into full gear. Chesnutt's fascination with the implications of this figurative duality pervades the work, and he devises a narrative framework perfectly suited to amplify the story's consideration of those implications. The narrator, responsible for guiding us through this identity crisis, is also the protagonist; as he begins to doubt, and later to refashion, his own conception of self, the reader's position becomes increasingly uncertain. While the paradigm of first-person narrator-protagonist seems to demand a certain intimacy between narrator and reader, Chesnutt successfully obscures the narrating position by presenting an array of subjects of narration: the Hal Skinner who tells us the story; the mischievous but likable boy he believes he had been in his youth; the thoroughly disliked and possibly criminal Hank Skinner the townspeople remember; and, after his reinvention of himself, the Hal who is written up in the local press as "a matter of local pride" (*SF* 301). This plurality of identity might well prompt the reader to wonder which version is the "real" Hal.

The basic plot of "The Shadow of My Past" is a narrative literalization of the search for self-identity that plays so fundamental a role in much of Chesnutt's fiction. The protagonist and narrator, Hal, proposes to the daughter of his employer, Mr. Parker. The father's response, however, drives the plot: on his return from Europe in several months, Mr. Parker plans to travel to Hal's hometown, Greenville, and research the young man's background. As Hal's prospective fiancée explains, Mr. Parker "'has a theory that a man's character is a unit, and must be a harmonious unit; that if it is defective or weak at one point, or at any time in his life, it is marred all the way through'" (*SF* 292). Although Parker will not commence his inquiries for several months, the idea prompts the narrator to spend his vacation in Greenville to preview what his prospective father-in-law will discover: "It occurred to me," he writes, "that it might be well to anticipate Ethel's father's investigation and visit the old town and learn for myself whether I was remembered, and in what manner" (294). To those ends, Hal disguises himself—he becomes "'John H. Smith, Chicago'" (296)—so that, without revealing his identity, he can ascertain his own reputation.[8] Much to his dismay, the narrator's undercover detective work reveals, in a comically exaggerated manner, that the people of Greenville do *not* cherish the memory of Hal/Hank Skinner.

Both the narrative tension and the humor of "Shadow" derive from the disjunction between Hal's account of his youth and townspeople's version of the same events. In fact, their characterization of Hal's early life completely reverses his own conception of himself during that period. Chesnutt exploits the situational humor engendered by the narrator's smug confidence that his return will be greeted with affection and fond memories. Instead, each "witness" he speaks with describes a more wicked version of "Hank" than the last. While Hal speculates, for example, how "heartily" Mr. Gormully—his ex-employer and father to two children young Hank had wrestled with—"would laugh at the memory of my little 'scrap' with the children" (*SF* 294), the man instead announces his willingness "'to appear as a witness in the trial'" of the "'depraved'" Hank Skinner (296).

Further research into his past repeatedly confirms that the citizens of Greenville have a far different conception of Hal than the one he presents to the reader. Instead of recalling a disadvantaged but well-liked youth who had been victimized by circumstance, his erstwhile acquaintances remember him as the consummate villain, who in fact bears responsibility for various and far-reaching mischief:

> I collected elaborate details of my misdoings. . . . Not only was I made out the author of the misfortunes which had over-whelmed my family, but other mysterious crimes occurring about that time were imputed to me. People whom I had never known gravely bore witness to my precocious depravity. Such was my reputation as it would be gathered by my prospective father-in-law; who maintained that one serious moral lapse argued a permanently defective character. (*SF* 300)

Because Mr. Parker envisions identity as a coherent whole, the townspeople have the power to deny Hal both professional and personal contentment. Chesnutt thus reiterates in "The Shadow of My Past" his career-long interest in the social construction of a man's identity. The rest of the story confirms that notion, and also emphasizes the extent to which only some can exploit those very social conventions to rewrite, and presumably improve, that identity.

In a literalization of the concept of the "self-made man"—in which Chesnutt personally invested a great deal—Hal does successfully rewrite his own life before Mr. Parker hears it: in essence, he remakes himself, or, at the least, he remakes his reputation. The method by which Hal/Hank accomplishes this feat reveals both Chesnutt's deft comic touch and his more serious concern with the nature (and economics) of public identity. Although "the most retiring of men" (*SF* 300), Hal initiates "a campaign for publicity" (300) which redefines him in the public eye:

> Seizing every opportunity to speak, I began to develop forensic ability. During the fall I read a paper to the Chamber [of Commerce] on "The Relation of National Banks to National Prosperity," upon which I received many compliments. As my various successes were from time to time mentioned in the newspapers, I sent marked copies to Thomas Gormully, Esq.,

Editor of the *Greenville Torchlight*. A struggling weekly published my address in full—I confess I paid for the composition—accompanied by a short biography, prepared with an especial view to its reaching the eyes of the Greenville public, and so worded as to make clear my identity with the Hank Skinner who had formerly worked for the mayor. (301)

Thus, the narrator "composes" his own biography. And, while other Chesnutt fictions—including "Uncle Wellington's Wives" and "Cicely's Dream"—render the attempts of characters to remake themselves to improve their social positions, "The Shadow of My Past" differs from most of the author's works in that it features a narrator who *successfully* reinscribes himself into the social fabric. In many ways, then, the protean Hal/Hank serves as a proxy for Chesnutt, another inscrutable author trying to negotiate a relationship with an unpredictable audience. Both authors have a great deal at stake, after all, in their attempts to "sell" their fictions. But while Richard H. Brodhead has convincingly suggested that "by his twenties Chesnutt thinks of writing largely as a way *out*, a way to achieve a selfhood not bounded by his local scene" (20), Hank Skinner conceives of writing precisely as a way back *in* to his social community.

Despite its uniqueness in Chesnutt's fiction as an examination of successful identity-construction, "The Shadow of My Past" does rely on a tactic familiar to readers of Chesnutt and other African-American writers: the use of disguises or masks in the quest to find or construct one's identity. Often deployed in black writings, this strategy is apparent in the works of such diverse authors as Harriet Jacobs and Ralph Ellison, as well as throughout Chesnutt's works. Michael G. Cooke argues that the tradition of self-masking or self-veiling in black literature is inevitably harmful, resulting in versions of the "ex-colored man," James Weldon Johnson's phrase for the man who rejects his racial identity. For Cooke, the black raconteur Julius McAdoo of Chesnutt's *The Conjure Woman*, for example, is "the victim who knows and wryly, obliquely resists his fate, only to

embrace it and veil himself at last in a rush of instinctive sentimentality" (54). If Cooke's reading of *The Conjure Woman* discounts much of the complexity of Julius's characterization, his
commentary nevertheless reiterates a common notion that *all*
masking is necessarily a diminution of the self. Although there
are certainly Chesnutt works in which masking produces harmful results,[9] "The Shadow of My Past" and other stories emphasize instead the power to be derived from adapting one's identity to operative circumstances.[10] And although it's therefore no
easy matter to taxonomize Chesnutt's use of passing and masking in his fictions, many of his characters who mask themselves
thus bear at least a passing resemblance to their creator; in formulating identities for themselves they, like him, often try, in
the words of Julius in "Lonesome Ben," to "'make eve'y aidge
cut'" (*SF* 109). In that context, it seems appropriate that Chesnutt would rehearse this theme—the attempt to understand
and reshape one's identity—in his other fictions. In addition to
"The Shadow of My Past," several other works exemplify this
interest: "How He Met Her," "The Exception," and "A Bad
Night" all feature examinations (and usually reconstructions)
of characters' identities. While not emphasizing the anguished
search for identity one finds in such works as *The House Behind
the Cedars*[11] and "The Sheriff's Children," these stories represent Chesnutt's early (and usually comic) interest in the topic.

What separates "The Shadow of My Past" from his other fictional treatments of this theme is Chesnutt's ability in the story
to combine the comic tone characteristic of the lighter pieces
and the provocative search for identity typical of his novels and
serious short fiction. The extent to which the initially befuddled
protagonist-narrator pensively explores the construction of his
identity—by both himself and others—resonates throughout
this otherwise humorous tale. When he discovers, for example,
that his "friends'" stories share many key elements, Hal begins
to question the very fabric of his self-conception:

> Had I really been such a scoundrel as my old friends pic-
> tured me? Of course I had not poisoned my brother, or shot my

father, or burned my mother; but brushing aside these absurdities, had I been so much worse than other boys as to forfeit the toleration extended toward the faults of youth? Had I possessed no single redeeming trait? It was strange that they should all have misjudged me so greatly; and yet it would have been more remarkable that a sane person could have so greatly misjudged himself. A fool may not perceive his own folly, but a liar must know when he lies, and a thief when he steals. (*SF* 300)

Although the tone of this story remains comic even through this meditative analysis, the consequences of his sullied reputation threaten both his domestic life and his dream "of a public career. Could I hope for either with such a cloud hanging over me?" (300). It is the nature of this "cloud" that merits further consideration.

The story's title, "The Shadow of My Past," invites a plethora of interpretive associations relevant to the narrator's predicament and to Chesnutt's construction of an authorial identity. First, the phrase suggests that the narrator cannot escape the implications of his past actions, and that his future relies to a large extent upon his past: because of his prospective father-in-law's theory that a man's life is a holistic entity, these postulates are particularly true. The narrator learns in vivid terms that he carries the burden of his past—whether he participates in the formation of that past or not—into his professional and personal endeavors, a situation with which Chesnutt, a black writer, could readily identify. Yet another connotation of the word "shadow," however, is its slang usage. As any connoisseur of film noir knows, a "shadow" is a term that, in the twentieth century, has come to indicate a private detective who retraces the steps of a suspect in order to make or break a case against him or her. In that sense, "The Shadow of My Past" seems a particularly appropriate title. Hal becomes in effect his own shadow, responsible for piecing together his past from the recollections of his fellow townspeople: "I spent the remainder of the day," he writes, "in finding out all I could about myself" (*SF* 300). At one level, of course, the narrator merely wants to preview what Mr.

Parker will learn when *he* investigates. At the same time, however, this line reveals the narrator's (and Chesnutt's) earnest dissection of the concept of identity, and the epistemological frameworks that govern such conceptions. In fact, his efforts to learn about Hank Skinner—that Hal's younger self has a different name adds another layer to this examination of identity—force him to recognize the extent to which others have the power to define him.

More importantly, perhaps, the narrator's quest suggests his willingness to treat identity not as a fixed matter, but as a fluid, constantly shifting phenomenon, a conception of identity-formation that stands in direct opposition to Mr. Parker's theory that "a man's character" must form "a harmonious unit" (*SF* 293). Hal's realization of the protean nature of identity squarely aligns with Chesnutt's treatment of the theme in such works as "The Passing of Grandison" and "The Wife of His Youth."[12] In order to come to this conclusion, however, Hal must first shadow his past, a task that requires him to play the role of detective, and he pursues his earlier incarnation with a persistence that would do credit to any Hollywood gumshoe. In fact, several of the people he questions—in anonymity and under the guise of a pseudonym—about his former self assume he is a detective stockpiling evidence against the "'desprit character'" (*SF* 298) he had apparently been in youth.

But the term "shadow" has other, specifically relevant connotations for this work and the rest of Chesnutt's career as well. A shadow is, of course, primarily a dark reflection, and in "The Shadow of My Past" the narrator—the adult Hal Skinner—must confront the townspeople's conception of his past self—the juvenile Hank Skinner—as dark double. Their reading of his early life may be inaccurate, but it nevertheless forms a faint (though imperfect) representation of his past self that, if left intact, would ruin his personal and professional prospects. In that sense, the "shadow" of the title not only describes the darker elements of his past (and of the townspeople's memories) but also foretells (shadows forth) his future.[13] The narrator, then, wants to illuminate his shadowy past, but *only* if the illumination reveals to Mr. Parker that his "'career from the beginning has been a consistently worthy one'" (*SF* 293).

"The Shadow of My Past" thus depicts Hal's recomposition of his social identity in terms of shadow and light, black and white. After speaking with a few preliminary "witnesses" who detail his alleged youthful misdemeanors, for example, Hal tells us, "[m]y record was growing blacker and blacker" (*SF* 299). The absence of literally black characters here—the shadowy manifestation of Hank/Hal as remembered by the townspeople constitutes the story's sole dark figure—suggests that Chesnutt has recast his interest in race-identity issues in metaphoric terms. While "Cicely's Dream" and "The Sheriff's Children" fictionally render the literal struggles of African Americans to fashion personal and social identities in post–Civil War America, for example, this story recapitulates the same focus,[14] although without explicit mention of race.

Indeed, "The Shadow of My Past" forms Chesnutt's ideal allegory of identity formation, one in which the protagonist solely determines his own place in the social milieu.[15] While the white Hal is able ultimately to overcome the *figural* "blackness" of his record, though, other Chesnutt characters who attempt to script their own social positions cannot erase the *literal* "blackness" from their own pasts.[16] By contrast, Hal finally manages to reinscribe himself as a successful man—"the shadow of my past was lifted" (*SF* 302), he writes—and he concludes his narrative with a platitude about "the consequences of giving a dog a bad name. But the reverse of the proverb is also true, although it takes a little longer to make, and a little harder work to keep, a good name" (*SF* 302).

But even more telling here is the extent to which "The Shadow of My Past," which explicitly functions as a kind of "mulatto" story,[17] subverts readers' expectations. For if, as Ginsberg claims, "passing forces reconsideration of the cultural logic that the physical body is the site of identic intelligibility," it must also "challenge the essentialism that is often the foundation of identity politics, a challenge that may be seen as either threatening or liberating but in either instance discloses the truth that identities are not singularly true or false but multiple and contingent" (4). "The Shadow of My Past" represents, I want to argue here, a challenge formulated by Chesnutt to be seen as both threatening and liberating.

By insinuating that some *might* don the mask with positive effects—Hal transforms himself from "'desprit character'" to moral exemplar—this underrated story uses a white narrator-protagonist to articulate what Du Bois described as the black man's "double-consciousness, this sense of always looking at one's self through the eyes of others" (215). When Hal discovers the "black" record others attribute to him, he can (and does) re-write a "white" account of himself. In fact, in its own linguistic inversion of the white and the black, "The Shadow of My Past" confirms Donald A. Petesch's suggestion that "Chesnutt was an early 'spy in the enemy's country,' but his was not the 'darky act' of the protagonist's grandfather in *Invisible Man*. His was the act that presumed likeness, only to reveal the difference that was really likeness" (139).[18] But Chesnutt ultimately uses this guise of "presumed likeness" in "The Shadow of My Past" precisely to delineate the limits—and the very real differences—of authorship: whereas white or light-skinned characters (and authors) can overcome or reinvent their pasts, the fortunes of those with more tangibly black ancestry are relentlessly shadowed by the literal darkness of their skin.

3/ "Through My Leafy Veil"

Chesnutt's Narrative Witnesses

At the end of "The Bouquet," a story originally published in the *Atlantic Monthly* in 1899, a young black girl is prevented from putting flowers on the grave of her beloved teacher because the cemetery admits only whites onto (and presumably under) its grounds. The girl instead watches the funeral through the fence that guards the premises. This situation typifies Chesnutt's depiction of African Americans as outsiders, consigned to witness events—including those affecting primarily themselves—from afar. As Chesnutt's fiction makes clear, however, blacks are not the only ones to suffer from this sort of enforced marginalization. In one way or another, nearly all of his work features characters who exist on the margins of the social fabric: mulattoes, liberal whites in the South, mixed-race couples, and ex-slaves, among others. Often relating his fictions from the perspectives of these socially incidental characters—a telling gesture by a writer who was also a wealthy businessman and pillar of the Cleveland community— Chesnutt explores how various outsiders position themselves in an evolving, turn-of-the-century society. But his experimentation with narrative strategies led further: as a result of his shadowy subjects and his penchant for narratological subterfuge, Chesnutt also calls into question the very nature of interpretation, whether the subject is a literary text or a social one. Each of the stories considered in this chapter features a narrator who, although appearing as a character in the story he narrates,[1] remains peripheral to the action. By situating these "I"-narrators outside the central plot of the stories they tell, Chesnutt forces his readers to identify with the dislocated and disenfranchised, including several who, significantly, are not African American. These witness-narrator stories thus introduce a range of first-person narrators who tell their stories from the shadows. While most of them enjoy far greater social privilege than the little girl in "The Bouquet," they nevertheless share her angle of vision. For a host of reasons, these witness-narrators can only, like her, watch from the other side of the fence.

Despite the enhanced immediacy provided by the use of a first-person narrator, several generations of critics since the end of the nineteenth century have pointed out the potential shortcomings of the technique. Henry James offered perhaps the most damning assessment when he warned of the "terrible *fluidity* of self-revelation" (*Novel* 320). Other drawbacks include the tendency for readers to conflate narrator and author—a circumstance Poe dramatically encountered (and perhaps encouraged)—and the association with a romantic subjectivity that the "I"-narrator seems to invite. And if these conventional criticisms fail to discourage use of first-person narrators, black writers, according to Richard Yarborough, have had even more specific reasons to avoid that choice. In "The First-Person in Afro-American Fiction," Yarborough explores some of the reasons underlying the dearth of first-person narratives by black writers before World War II. "For many authors," he writes, "the self-justifying (and often therefore race-justifying) urge must have been so powerful that the very thought of using the first-person point of view (a mode of expression that blacks literally had to fight for) to create an openly fabricated voice must have appeared so irrelevant as to seem downright perverse" (111). More specifically, Yarborough speculates, black writers feared that use of the first-person perspective might also "negate the power of the authorial voice to evaluate and explain frequently victimized fictional characters" (115). This tendency in part relates to the central role in the development of black literature played by slave narratives, which demanded that authors subordinate individual experience to broader issues affecting the race as a whole.[2] Whatever the reasons, most early African-American writers of fiction—until Ellison, Himes, and others in the mid-twentieth century—relied almost exclusively on the more detached third-person authorial stance.[3]

Chesnutt does not completely conform to this pattern, however. As African-American literature in the late nineteenth century began to shift from the documentary literalness of slave narratives to the more figural representations of black life typical of fiction, Chesnutt experimented with a variety of narrative forms. Although Chesnutt narrates all three of his novels from a third-person detached point of view, *The Conjure Woman* tales and a handful of his other short fictions are told by "I"-narrators. But while Chesnutt occasionally used first-person narrators to position their own experiences at the center of the story—a narrative strategy discussed in the previous chapter—this chapter will analyze those works that involve an "I"-narrator whose story focuses, or at least seems to focus, on someone other than himself. In *Narrative Discourse: An Essay in Method*, Gérard Genette provides a useful distinction between these two primary types of first-person narrators:[4] "one where the narrator is the hero of his narrative *(Gil Blas)* and one where he plays only a secondary role, which almost always turns out to be a role as observer and witness" (245). Thus, the first category includes figures in American literature such as Huck Finn, whose own self-conscious moral development serves as a central component of his narrative. The second category, on the other hand, features narrators such as Nick Carraway, for whom Gatsby functions as the subject of narration. The Chesnutt stories discussed in this chapter, all of which belong in Genette's second category, depict narrators who observe—and usually attempt to assist—other characters as they undergo their own life-altering trials; in short, the works are told by benevolent, if often ineffective, witness-narrators.

Nine of Chesnutt's short stories use the witness-narrator paradigm, most of them dating from quite early in his career, six of them, in fact, from before 1890. Three of these works, "Appreciation" (1887), "An Eloquent Appeal" (1888), and "The Origin of the Hatchet Story" (1889), are very brief, but they reveal important tendencies that Chesnutt would later develop in more detail. The six more substantial examples include "Cartwright's Mistake" (1886), "A Grass Widow" (1887), "A Fool's Paradise" (1888), "Aunt Mimy's Son" (1900), "Baxter's Procrustes" (1904), and "Concerning Father" (1930). That his narratological experimentation led him to use this paradigm nine times in his fiction, nearly twice as often as the first-person protagonist narrator, implies his relative comfort with telling his stories from the fringe.

Chesnutt's partiality for witness narratives is partly explained by the rhetorical power such a strategy grants a black author interested in unseating the race prejudice at work in the United States. While narrators who also function as protagonists might offer compelling and highly personal accounts of their trials, the use of witness-narrators allows Chesnutt to engage readers' sense of reason as well as their emotions. In stories such as "Cartwright's Mistake" and "Aunt Mimy's Son," the witness-narrator often functions as a proxy for readers, a compassionate yet reasonable commentator on the injustices meted out to individual characters. And, perhaps most significantly for Chesnutt, each of these commentators—"readers" themselves—comes to recognize the inadequacy of his previously unexamined principles of interpretation. Chesnutt thus implicitly calls on his readers, most of whom were white, to reconsider the assumptions underlying their own conceptions of the world, and particularly, we might imagine, their understanding of race: for, in Chesnutt's writings, it is skin color that most often generates the sort of reductive judgment that these witness-narrators learn to question.

Balancing the demands of art with the desire to advance a social agenda generated a tension in Chesnutt's work throughout his career, but he was able at times to negotiate striking combinations of the two by means of deftly practiced narrative tactics, including the witness-narrator. A passage from his journals indicates the extent to which he would self-consciously embed social commentary in all of his writings: "The negro's part," he wrote in an 1880 entry, "is to prepare himself for social recognition and equality; and it is the province of literature to open the way for him to get it—to accustom the public mind to the idea; and while amusing them, to lead them on imperceptibly, unconsciously step by step to the desired state of feeling" (*Journals* 140). Chesnutt thus realized early in his literary career that if he were to reshape white readers' attitudes, he must approach his potentially provocative subjects with due care. Outraged rhetoric, he knew, would alienate those he hoped to inform and perhaps persuade. Although his motives in writing were never *exclusively* didactic, he chose to develop narrative strategies that, while entertaining and apparently conventional, often included meticulously camouflaged social commentary, as some readers have noted. William L. Andrews, for example, discusses one of the techniques Chesnutt uses in his attempt to adjust public attitudes: several "of Chesnutt's most memorable heroes," writes Andrews, "are confidence men . . . who lead their usually gullible victims 'imperceptibly' and 'unconsciously' to some ironic and unsettling revelation" (*Literary Career* 15). Andrews's description adroitly captures the essence of Chesnutt's "conjure" stories, which chronicle Uncle Julius's slick rhetorical manipulation of John and Annie, and the author's deft handling in that collection of his reading public. Although Andrews grants that Chesnutt's "mature work derives its distinctive artfulness" from this approach, the author's early fictions bear equally apparent marks of sophisticated rhetorical manipulation.

While many of his later stories, as Andrews argues, involve confidence men, Chesnutt's early witness-narrator stories often rely on building readers' trust through the use of likable and quietly reasonable narrators. This narrative stance can be partially explained by Chesnutt's own temperament. Andrews describes him as a "studious" man with "an introspective turn of mind" (7), a description Chesnutt endorses in an early journal entry in which he lists his qualifications for a writing career: "A fair knowledge of the classics, a speaking acquaintance with the modern languages, an intimate friendship with literature . . . and a habit of studying character" (*Journals* 139). It is no surprise, therefore, that some of his narrators share Chesnutt's "habit of studying character" and his artistic temperament—several, in fact, are writers and artists themselves who nevertheless think and express themselves in terms appropriate to men of business, a tendency common, of course, to Chesnutt as well.[5] The narrators of such works as "Cartwright's Mistake," "A Fool's Paradise," "A Grass Widow," and "Baxter's Procrustes" are successful businessmen and/or artists, whose actions and generally thoughtful commentaries on others' lives indicate temperaments defined by both fiscal conservatism and social compassion.[6] In short, the witness-narrators of these stories seem, at least initially, to serve as surrogates for Chesnutt himself.

But Chesnutt's sophisticated manipulation of narrative strategies and his often enigmatic authorial presence simply will not allow an uncomplicated conflation of him with his narrators. His intentions regarding the audience's response to those narrators remain cryptic at times, even inscrutable in their descriptions of the world around them. Despite the apparently liberal social views typical of these witness-narrators, for example, they nevertheless articulate or accept some startling opinions on African Americans. This tendency no doubt reflects, to some extent, Chesnutt's effort to increase the chances that his primarily white audience would come to identify with his narrators, and therefore be more willing to incorporate into their own reading the interpretive lessons learned by those narrators. While Chesnutt's social views are unambivalent in his nonfiction writings—which include such provocative titles as "Peonage, Or the New Slavery," "Obliterating the Color Line," and "The Future American: A Stream of Dark Blood in the Veins of

Southern Whites"—his fiction occasionally includes surprisingly stereotypical assessments of blacks.[7] In "Aunt Mimy's Son," for example, the narrator seeks advice from a white character, who offers a reductive description of African Americans: "'Negroes are like cats, you know. I don't mean the young Negroes, who like to wander, but the old generation, who cling to the old customs and the old places'" (*SF* 203). The narrator responds to this commentary by thanking his "kind informant" and following his advice. Later in the same story, the narrator witnesses a funeral "largely attended by colored people" and remarks on the "usual melancholy delight of their race in mortuary exercises" (207). Descriptions like these occur sporadically in Chesnutt's fiction, and they seem to indicate his conscious decision to appeal to his readership by using narrators who, while putatively sympathetic toward blacks, nevertheless rely on stereotypical or unexamined racial ideas. These narrators, in other words, might well have shared attitudes with their presumed audience, and such reader-narrator identification would offer Chesnutt another means of exposing the racism bred by precisely such uninterrogated assumptions. If the narrators of these works can come to revise their previously unquestioned views of the world, we might imagine, so too can the readers whom Chesnutt invites to identify with them.

Chesnutt's first-person witness-narrators share many other, less controversial characteristics. Of the stories considered in this chapter, only "Concerning Father" is narrated by a woman, and readers don't learn that narrator's sex until nearly halfway through the work. Indeed, the absence of gender-related issues makes the witness-narrator stories unique: by contrast, Chesnutt regularly uses gender concerns as a focus in fictions such as "Her Virginia Mammy," "Cicely's Dream," "The Wife of His Youth," and several of the *Conjure* stories. Similarly, the witness-narrator works seem initially to lack the author's usual emphasis on race. Chesnutt does not explicitly assign race identity to his witness-narrators, a strategy that Yarborough finds consistently throughout black literature. Many black writers use "colorless" voices in their fiction, he argues, partly in the hope "that the white reader would identify with the controlling or empowered consciousness in the text and thereby eventually come to share the author's views on the issues raised" (117). But Yarborough's comments only partially explain Chesnutt's decision to underplay race in these works.

Perhaps the most readily identifiable trait, in fact, common to virtually all of Chesnutt's narrators *and* characters, in both the short fiction and the novels, is their shared concern with economic matters. Other readers have noted this motif in *The Conjure Woman,* wherein issues of finance regularly govern the behaviors of both John and Julius, two figures thoroughly dissimilar in most other regards.[8] *The Marrow of Tradition* likewise portrays figures for whom financial interests predominate: after a railroad conductor compels the novel's protagonist, Dr. Miller, to relocate to the "colored car," for example, Miller contemplates, in explicitly economic terms, his new venue:

> It was an old car, with faded upholstery, from which the stuffing projected here and there through torn places. Apparently the floor had not been swept for several days. The dust lay thick upon the window sills, and the watercooler, from which he essayed to get a drink, was filled with stale water which had made no recent acquaintance with ice. There was no other passenger in the car, and Miller occupied himself in making a rough calculation of what it would cost the Southern railroads to haul a whole car for every colored passenger. It was expensive to say the least; it would be cheaper, and quite as considerate of their feelings, to make the negroes walk. (56)

Note that Miller's first reaction to his exile is not one of passionate objection, nor even a meditation on injustice. Rather, in typical Chesnutt fashion, he conceives of racism as an affront to business sense.[9]

This emphasis on money pervades the witness-narrator stories as well. "Baxter's Procrustes," for example, offers an extended commentary on the "value" of books; after the members of an exclusive book-collecting club learn they've been tricked into publishing a book "with nothing in it," they regain their sanguine dispositions only because of an auction in which the book—made up entirely of blank pages—secures for them "the highest price ever brought by a single volume published by the club" (*CS* 278). Financial concerns likewise suffuse the diary of the narrator in "A Fool's Paradise," who interrupts an account of his romantic pursuit of a young woman to confide his fears regarding a male friend: "(By the way, I hope he will not ask me for another loan before that time; he is not as prompt in his payments as I could wish)" (*SF* 321). Romance and finance are similarly bound up in "Cartwright's Mistake," in which the narrator explains his indifference to a "charming" young woman by admitting that another "had a first mortgage on [his] affections, and the arrangements had been made for a foreclosure shortly after her return in October" (316). The pervasiveness of these economic intrusions in Chesnutt's fiction might suggest both a literary strategy—other readers, including Lorne Fienberg and Trudier Harris, have noted the central role played by economics in black literature—and his own keen interest in financial matters. In an early journal entry, for example, Chesnutt writes, "I want fame. I want money; I want to raise my children in a different rank of life from that I sprang from . . . . But literature pays the successful" (*Journals* 154). Chesnutt seems ultimately to have decided, however, that literature did not pay *quite* enough, a conclusion foreshadowed in the experiences of his witness-narrators.

While these fiscally prudent, "colorless" witness-narrators certainly function as rhetorical mediators between the author and a white readership, they serve other, more complex purposes as well. One reason Chesnutt may have chosen to use a first-person narrator to relate someone else's story is that the format allows him to write from an outsider's perspective, for him a familiar position. That is, as a man of mixed blood, Chesnutt was, according to Andrews, "thought an unnatural racial hybrid by whites" and "a suspect social quantity to many blacks" (*Literary Career* 6). In an 1881 journal entry, Chesnutt expressed an acute awareness of his uncertain classification in society: "I am neither fish, flesh, nor fowl—neither 'nigger,' white, nor 'buckrah.' Too 'stuck-up' for the colored folks, and, of course, not recognized by the whites" (*Journals* 157–58). His witness-narrators share Chesnutt's sense of dislocation: despite not being victims of racial prejudice, these figures occupy ambiguous and shadowy roles in their own universes. Their efforts to sort through and make sense of social complexities in works such as "Cartwright's Mistake" and "Aunt Mimy's Son" often prove ineffectual, and they occasionally seem baffled by the events they relate.

In "Appreciation," for example, the narrator describes without comment the humiliating treatment of Pilgrim Gainey, an elderly black man recently returned from the North despite the better wages and more liberal social conditions he found there, at the hands of the white Tom Macmillan. After Macmillan knocks Gainey's hat off and "salute[s] him with a playful kick," he tosses the old man a plug of tobacco. Gainey's response, which ends the brief work, presumably provides the rationale for his return to the South: "'Now dat's what I calls 'preciation,' said Uncle Pilgrim, filling his mouth with the savory weed. 'I never had dat much terbacker give ter me all de time I wuz at de Norf!'" (*SF* 65). The narrator offers no final commentary on this situation, and thus anticipates several later witness-narrators who also "disappear" at the end of the stories they tell. "A Grass Widow," "A Fool's Paradise," and other stories likewise feature narrators left speechless by events they relate. The unwillingness of such narrators to comment on their own texts might reflect Chesnutt's early concern that his white readers, although putatively sympathetic to blacks, remained too often silent on important social issues. And that unwillingness (or inability) to comment may also represent Chesnutt's sincere bafflement regarding potential solutions to complex social issues.[10]

Whatever the motivation for its use, the narrative framework involving witness-narrators, which the author frequently uses to treat themes other than race relations, allows Chesnutt to dramatize the thesis that appearances often prove misleading, inaccurate, or superficial. This theme interested him throughout his career, partly because of his deep-seated awareness that the color of one's skin could determine a career or life, and he commented on it in both his fiction and nonfiction. In "What Is a White Man?" (1889), a response to political attempts to guarantee "that the 'all-pervading, all-conquering Anglo-Saxon race' must continue forever to exercise exclusive control and direction of the government" (5), Chesnutt points out the "manifest absurdity of classifying men fifteen-sixteenths white as black men" (6). In this essay he derides the use of race as a means of judging a person's worth. Other essays, including "A Plea for the American Negro" and "The Future American: What the Race is Likely to Become in the Process of Time," similarly catalog the overwhelming legal problems in *defining* "race," and the absurdities that result when social policy is constructed upon such an uncertain foundation. Because these essays and some of Chesnutt's fiction—particularly the novels and the stories collected in *The Wife of His Youth*—offer clear denunciations of race prejudice, Dickson D. Bruce, Jr., has argued that Chesnutt's work should be read "in light of his consistent objection to racial categories" (183). And, while these witness-narrator stories generally seem "colorless," many of them nevertheless recast in metaphoric terms Chesnutt's race concerns. Whether these works should be read as allegories of race or not, they actively question the superficial and sometimes inexplicable criteria people use to judge one another. In that sense, he objects to the type of categorization that results in dismissive or reductive assessments of complex phenomena, including the state of being human.

In "Cartwright's Mistake," for example, the narrator, Walton, overcomes his own aversion to the obese Cartwright when he learns that the man is "no mere vulgar bundle of adipose tissue" (*SF* 315). First appearing in the *Cleveland News and Herald* in 1886, the story explores the quirkiness of human interaction by tracing the romance of Cartwright and Florence Gaylord. Although her mother ridicules the suitor as "'ridiculously fat'" (315), Florence becomes enamored and agrees to marry Cartwright. Problems arise, however, when the prospective groom—using the pretense of an extended business trip—secretly seeks medical help to lose weight. When Cartwright returns as "a tall, symmetrical young man, without an ounce of superfluous flesh upon him" (319), Florence calls off the engagement, much to the bafflement of the narrator. While the story might be read as an allegory of racial prejudice—Cartwright is defined exclusively by his appearance—it works on a broader level to expose the inexplicability of human judgment.

One narratological explanation for the narrator's inability or refusal to comment upon the outcome of this affair lies in Chesnutt's use of what Dorrit Cohn calls "consonant self-narration." In *Transparent Minds: Narrative Modes for Presenting Consciousness in Fiction,* Cohn writes that this form of storytelling employs an "unobtrusive narrator who identifies with his earlier incarnation, renouncing all manner of cognitive privilege" (155). In other words, "Cartwright's Mistake" is told from the vantage point of an observer who, although recounting the past—in this case, the very recent past—has no greater knowledge or understanding now than he did while the events were unfolding. In this way, Chesnutt adapts his fiction to realism: the use of a consonant first-person narrator guarantees that we share Walton's perspective, and indeed his spontaneous reactions. Rather than having the narrative voice sort out the peculiarities of the events from a cognitively privileged position, Chesnutt forces us to confront the untidy situation as Walton perceives it. And, ultimately, even Walton disappears from his own text, which ends with a letter from Florence calling off the engagement: "We leave this morning on the early train, and I beg of you to release me from my engagement. It is difficult for me to express my meaning, but you are so different from what you were when we met and when we became engaged, that it is hard to realize that you are the same person" (*SF* 320). In ending the work with this letter, Chesnutt, as he does in other works, thus effaces (and in fact silences) his own narrator.[11]

By so doing, "Cartwright's Mistake" emphasizes the perilous nature of interpretation, pointing out that even an intelligent, sympathetic reader like Walton can be overmatched by a puzzling text, a theme to which Chesnutt provocatively returns in stories such as "The Passing of Grandison" and "Baxter's Procrustes." One rationale for weaving such a thesis into his fiction, of course, is his continued interest in persuading white readers to re-evaluate their judgments of blacks, but the story works as a commentary on the nature of interpretation as well. As in "The Passing of Grandison," and "Baxter's Procrustes," "Cartwright's Mistake" encodes Chesnutt's subtle indictment of a (white) reading audience too willing to rely on comfortable criteria for their judgments. Chesnutt returned frequently in his fiction to this vein of epistemological inquiry. "A Fool's Paradise," "Aunt Mimy's Son," and "An Eloquent Appeal" similarly depict witness-narrators who are forced to re-evaluate their interpretive skills when they learn that their initial assessments of people or situations have been startlingly inaccurate. In fact, another common element of these witness narratives is that the narrators all serve as readers of their own texts. That is, each narrator must interpret the significance of events he witnesses for himself, a task that overwhelms a few of them. In "Baxter's Procrustes," for example, Chesnutt comically deflates the narrator and his fellow book-club members who pompously misread Baxter's manipulation of them. And in "Aunt Mimy's Son," an otherwise bleak tale of a mother's tragic misreading of her son, Chesnutt uses humor to emphasize the extent to which the major characters misread what others have to say: when the narrator tells Aunt Mimy that her son sounds "bright" to have accomplished so much at such a young age, for instance, she responds by agreeing that her son is indeed several shades lighter than herself. The pun on the word "bright" both anticipates the more ominous miscommunications to come and lightly satirizes the notion of "passing," a topic not often treated comically early in the African-American literary tradition.

"A Fool's Paradise" constitutes an earlier treatment of similar interpretive inadequacies. Told in diary form over a ten-year period, the story follows the career of Ida, a beautiful young woman for whom the narrator, Paul Dunlap, develops an intense attraction. Although his initial proposal to her is rejected, he nevertheless remains her advocate as she experiences two unpleasant marriages, one contentious divorce and increasingly uncharitable gossip. Ultimately, Dunlap—who throughout characterizes himself as honest but relatively poor—comes into an inheritance and simultaneously has his second proposal accepted by Ida. Dunlap's diary ends with rhetorical questions—"Am I not the most fortunate of men? . . . What have I done to deserve such happiness?" (*SF* 329)—but a newsclip appended to the story announces his divorce from Ida on the grounds of her "drunkenness and gross neglect of duty" (329), the same charges from which Dunlap had previously defended her. By silencing the narrator's voice—the newsclip concludes the tale—Chesnutt subverts Dunlap's narrative authority and underlines his complete misreading of the situation. While Dunlap had been socially marginalized throughout his tale by relative poverty, he is finally pushed beyond the frame of, and excluded from, his own story. Like "Cartwright's Mistake," which ends not with the narrator's voice but by quoting Florence Gaylord's letter, this piece dramatizes the literalization of the narrator's outsider stance.

"Cartwright's Mistake" and "A Fool's Paradise" thus evolve narratologically in the same fashion. The narrators of these two stories live and function in their fictional worlds until the conclusion of each story, and then relinquish narrative control to other sources. Like Melville's *Billy Budd, Sailor*—which ends with a newspaper account that rearranges the events of the story, and a poem that contradicts the primary narrator's depiction of Billy's character—both stories feature narrators who disappear from their own texts and do not return. The refusal or inability of these narrators to offer final commentary upon their narratives suggests that Chesnutt has consigned them to permanent marginality, a status he perhaps felt approximated in some ways his own position as a black fiction writer in an American literary tradition. The stories work also to reiterate Chesnutt's satirical commentary on the interpretive skills of his white readers.

But the narrative strategies of these stories imply more than the disenfranchisement of the black intellectual. The conscious positioning of his witness-narrators as outsiders and the subsequent silencing of them have considerable implications for the study of Chesnutt's fiction. Despite their formal education, uniform intelligence, and reasonable demeanors, these "colorless" narrators find it difficult, often impossible, either to explain the actions of their subjects or to maintain their own narrative authority. This double failure of non-black narrators suggests that Chesnutt considered alienation (compounded by occasionally poor "readings") to be an equal-opportunity and universal state: the problem, as articulated in this set of stories, transcends the race issue. As in *The Conjure Woman,* Chesnutt uses his witness-narrator stories to foreground the hazards of interpretation.

Thus far my discussion has characterized these narrators' personal traits without considering what might be called the shared goal of their narratives. All of them seek to construct identity, either their own or their subjects'. In the case of "Baxter's Procrustes," identity—of both Baxter and his poem composed of "all margin"—becomes an absurd and abstract concept that calls into question the very nature of knowing. In the rest of these first-person, witness narratives Chesnutt has his "I"-narrators explore the parameters of personal identity in a shifting and uncertain *fin de siècle* world. While the enfranchisement of blacks remained a primary cause for Chesnutt throughout his life, his fiction and nonfiction also examine more broadly how the country struggled to remake itself. These works, and in fact all of Chesnutt's, consequently feature displaced characters working to adjust to the confusing social and cultural circumstances wrought by the Civil War, Reconstruction, and the turn of the century. In *The Marrow of Tradition* and *The House Behind the Cedars,* Chesnutt depicts the attempts of mixed-blood people to adapt to a culture that despises them from both sides; in *The Colonel's Dream* a transplanted northerner returns and fruitlessly tries to persuade the population of his southern home town to adapt to the new social and economic universe of the twentieth century. And in *The Conjure Woman,* John and Annie, two northerners, learn to cope with a culture they do not understand, a culture embodied in and "explained" by the inscrutable Julius McAdoo.

In Chesnutt's first-person, "raceless" stories the same goal is evident. Like the protagonist of "The Shadow of My Past," each of these narrators acts as a sort of detective who seeks to gain some understanding of himself and the world in which he lives by establishing and verifying the identities of his subjects. All too often, of course, these narrators prove *failed* detectives. In "A Fool's Paradise," for example, the last words of Dunlap's diary—"What have I done to deserve such happiness?" (*SF* 329)—suggest the extent to which Dunlap has misapprehended the nature of Ida. Chesnutt's detective-narrators also exist on the periphery of their own stories, and although consigned to the fringes, they apparently cherish their low profiles. The narrators of "Aunt Mimy's Son," "Cartwright's Mistake," "Appreciation," and "An Eloquent Appeal" all figuratively or literally step into the shadows at the conclusions of their narratives.

Chesnutt literalizes the outsiderness of these narrators in other ways as well. One strategy he regularly employs involves the spatial placement of his narrators in relation to the people and events which make up their stories. In effect, several of his witness-narrators gravitate so profoundly to the fringes that they function very nearly as voyeurs. "Cartwright's Mistake," for example, opens with the narrator sitting on a hotel piazza, "fol-

lowing with my glass the movements of a steamer in the offing"
(*SF* 315). Note how Chesnutt develops the narrator's interest in
what will prove to be the subject of his narrative: "As she
[the ship] disappeared around a distant bend of the shore, I
turned my head toward the left, from which I heard footsteps
approaching. My gaze rested upon the portly figure of a gentleman who stood a short distance from me, his hand resting on
top of the balustrade" (315). In this passage, the narrator's eyes
move from the ship to Cartwright, who serves as the object of
the narrator's gaze for the rest of the story. The narrator seems,
in short, constantly to be engaged in voyeurism, and Cartwright
proves a more interesting subject than the distant ship.

Chesnutt also arranges the spatial dimensions to construct his narrative situations in a manner that is strikingly
Hawthornesque. As in Hawthorne's *The Blithedale Romance* and
"Sights from a Steeple," Chesnutt often has his witness-narrators
concealed from the objects of their gaze. In "Cartwright's Mistake," for example, the narrator, Walton, overhears a conversation while sitting on one side of a "lattice-work, vine-covered
screen" that divides a pavilion. Lying on a chair, "the back of
which concealed the most of my body, while a mass of vines hid
my head from observation" (*SF* 317), Walton learns of Florence
Gaylord's affection for Cartwright. Note the similarity to the situation in "Aunt Mimy's Son," in which the narrator and his wife
approach a cemetery surrounded by a "fringe of trees and
bushes." Overhearing the sobs of their cook, Aunt Mimy, the
pair "drew softly near and peered through the bushes" (*SF*
207).

In both stories, as well as in other of these witness-narrator
works, Chesnutt separates his narrators from the people they
observe; secrecy thus becomes a major component of their narration. This strategy also serves as the central motif of *The House
Behind the Cedars,* as it examines the plights of a brother and sister with mixed blood who experience various degrees of success
by "passing." But where the novel seeks to *reveal* the hidden
nature of those who live behind the veil—presumably in an

attempt to accentuate the similarities between the characters and their readers—these first-person stories emphasize the narrators' attempts to remain concealed while depicting the situations of others' lives. Such a stance mirrors Chesnutt's position as a black writer of fiction: like Walton or the narrator of "Aunt Mimy's Son," Chesnutt—because of his literal blackness—describes and interprets the world around him from the relative shadows, particularly in terms of his fragile (and often dangerous) rhetorical position.

Chesnutt adds yet another layer of complexity to these narrative situations, one that calls for readers to examine self-consciously the texts before them: not only do his characters take refuge in bushes and behind screens, several of them engage in a sort of textual voyeurism. That is, each of them has access to the personal letters of those he watches. The narrators of "A Grass Widow," "Cartwright's Mistake," and "A Fool's Paradise" all study, with varying degrees of authorization, the correspondence of others. For most of Chesnutt's narrators, this textual voyeurism arises either by accident or from necessity, rather than as a result of indulging in the idle speculation or gossipy scrutiny that characterizes Hawthorne's Miles Coverdale.[12]

One of the best examples of this narrative strategy in the short fiction appears in a precursor to the "Uncle Julius" tales called "Aunt Mimy's Son." In that work the narrator—an early incarnation of the John who later appears in the stories of *The Conjure Woman*[13]—has his curiosity engaged by his cook, an ex-slave named Aunt Mimy, and the letters she regularly receives from her son. Through the son's letters to his mother, the contents of which she freely relays to her employer, the narrator learns of the exceptional achievements of her son—a representative of what William L. Andrews calls the "New Negro" (*Literary Career* 87)—in a variety of employments in the North.[14] In reality, however, the letters overstated the young man's accomplishments, and he ultimately returns in a "dissipated" condition, apparently having escaped from a northern prison; he soon thereafter dies. Although Aunt Mimy does not disclose that the dying man is her son, the narrator learns the truth when he witnesses the graveside misery of Mimy. Andrews sees "Aunt Mimy's Son" as a cautionary tale of "one southern black youth whose failure to resist the blandishments of the fast life in the North brings about a concomitant loss for the race as a whole" (87). Such a reading situates the story within a thematic pattern Chesnutt made use of early in his writing career, and one he drew on often thereafter. But the work might also be considered in the light of the author's framing strategies in other fictions, especially his witness narratives.

In "Aunt Mimy's Son," Chesnutt establishes several frames of reference that collide to reveal the importance of interpretation, and the failures of communication that often result from misreadings. The narrator "learns" the details of Mimy's son's career fourth-hand: the son writes to Mimy, who has a niece read his correspondence to her. Then Mimy interprets the contents of the letters in her conversations with the narrator. While she supposes her son is "'in de hotel business'" or "'runnin' one o' dem big railroads up dere in de No'th'" (*SF* 204) or has "'stahted a bank'" (205), we later learn that he had been employed as "'a hotel bell-boy, a sleeping-car porter, and an attendant in a gambling den'" (206). When the narrator finally has first-hand access to the letters—Mimy asks him to read the latest of the letters to her—he also interprets the writing for us: "It was written in a large hand, with some faults of grammar and spelling, but on the whole a creditable production. I did not think it quite a commercial hand, however, nor was the style that of a man accustomed to weighty affairs" (205). The narrator's literal reading of the letter, then, anticipates what his figural reading will later confirm: that the son's attempts to remake himself in the North—a goal achieved by Chesnutt—fail because of his inability to inscribe a satisfactory identity for himself; or that, like Chesnutt, who ultimately could not support himself by writing, the son simply cannot adapt his fictions convincingly enough to win over a predominantly white reading audience.

But if "Aunt Mimy's Son" enacts Chesnutt's literary anxieties, the story also reveals an ultimately paradoxical sense of his own identity, literary or otherwise. Mimy's son does seem to function, in some ways, as a proxy for Chesnutt, whose first works to earn national prominence, the dialect stories collected in *The Conjure Woman,* also featured what some might call "faults of grammar and spelling." In such a reading, the narrator of "Aunt Mimy's Son" assumes the role of a white literary critic suspicious of texts written in not "quite a commercial hand."[15] But in other ways, of course, the black figure in "Aunt Mimy's Son" clearly does *not* represent his creator; Chesnutt's class prejudice, a characteristic noted by more than a few readers,[16] no doubt prevented the author from casting himself as a barely literate criminal. The larger point I want to emphasize here is the crucial role played by interpretation (and indeed misinterpretation) in "Aunt Mimy's Son" and several of the other witness-narrator stories. Even putting race aside—often difficult when one contemplates his career—Chesnutt certainly recognized the profoundly subjective nature of language as a means of constructing and articulating identity. And if the acts of that construction were not complex enough, this and other witness-narrator stories, as well as works such as "Her Virginia Mammy," "The Wife of His Youth," and "The Web of Circumstance," also foreground the uncertainties involved in the very process of "reading."

This sort of approach has its risks, especially for an author interested in effecting social change. Chesnutt in large part offsets those risks, however, with his development of a reliable narrative figure who, while consistently engaging in what seem to be voyeuristic acts, could maintain a sympathetic, even philanthropic, demeanor. In contrast to Hawthorne's Miles Coverdale in *Blithedale,* who practices base and self-indulgent voyeurism, Chesnutt's narrators earn readers' trust and retain it. To insure his narrators' continued trustworthiness, Chesnutt thoroughly develops those narrators as benevolent figures whose first impulse is to assist the protagonists of their narratives. Despite occasionally entertaining themselves by spying on the events that shape other people's lives, his witness-narrators also evince genuine concern for their subjects, and attempt, though with varying degrees of success, to resolve what problems they can. In fact, their actions are often remarkably unselfish.

Furthermore, Chesnutt takes elaborate measures to reveal the discomfort that most of his narrators experience when they find themselves playing the voyeur; indeed, they often seem to feel trapped by circumstances they cannot overcome. Note, for example, how Walton apparently dislikes the voyeuristic situation he stumbles into:

> Of course the proper thing for me to do would have been to make my presence known. But she had already spoken, and I had already heard, and I spared her blushes by remaining quiet, hoping they would go away before burdening my conscience with any further weight of ill-gotten information. I could not now escape without being seen by them; the most I could do was to feign sleep, to provide against possible discovery. (*SF* 317)

Walton's benevolence and sensitivity are further revealed in his attempts to convey his "ill-gotten information" to Cartwright. He contemplates "the best way in which to give him the benefit of what I had heard, without disclosing too much, or the exact manner in which I had acquired my information" (*SF* 317–18). While the final clause of this statement is mildly unsettling in that the narrator demonstrates a propensity for concealment, his good intentions nevertheless remain clear. Chesnutt's own temperament no doubt informed the orientation of his witness-narrators to their subjects. But, finally, these works reveal his deep interest in manipulating point of view as a powerful tool in the construction of his fictions.

Most of the witness-narrator stories were written during what Andrews describes as Chesnutt's "apprenticeship" years, and some—most notably "Aunt Mimy's Son," which is narrated by the prototype of John—preview the direction and trajectory of his career. But neither Chesnutt's thematic concerns nor his

narratological sophistication developed in a strictly linear manner. These stories, in fact, feature complex rhetorical strategies
that compare favorably with the narrative situations in *The Conjure Woman*.

∽

   Perhaps the most complex and interesting exemplar of
Chesnutt's covert narrator can be found in "A Grass Widow," an
early work that superficially focuses on the fall of a young
woman. But despite the narrator's attempts to remain shrouded
behind the tale he tells, he finally reveals more about himself
than he does about his supposed subject. Although the story
was published in 1887, very early in Chesnutt's literary career, it
nevertheless foreshadows in many respects the author's ultimate retreat from full-time writing after his publication of *The
Colonel's Dream* in 1905. The story merits attention for its sophisticated narrative strategies, developing three separate narrative
voices, all emanating from the same person but representing
his thoughts at different times and in different contexts. Each
of these voices, responsible for the telling of what is essentially
the same story, interacts not only with its particularized story
but with the other voices as well. The narrative voices, then, are
not confined to the fictional frames they create. Rather, each
carries on a dialogue, along temporal and experiential lines,
with the other two voices and their stories. The resulting narrative interplay demands that readers constantly recalibrate their
idea of the narrator's position in, and relationship to, the
story.[17]
   While both "Cartwright's Mistake" and "A Fool's Paradise"
conclude with the effacement of their respective narrators,
Chesnutt apparently reverses the strategy in "A Grass Widow,"
which *begins* with a newspaper account. The inclusion of an official voice to initiate the story, rather than to end it, seems to
represent one of several modifications of the tactics generally
evident in those stories featuring witness-narrators. But the narrator of "A Grass Widow" also effaces himself at the end of his
story, although not by submerging his narrative presence

beneath a voice more official and authoritative. As in the other eight pieces that feature witness-narrators, Chesnutt chooses once more to dislocate the narrator's position in "A Grass Widow." The story nevertheless features some important modifications of the narrative paradigm outlined in the first section of this chapter.

"A Grass Widow" also brings into clearer focus Chesnutt's articulation of the writer's position in relation to the world in which he lives. The story opens with a newspaper report describing the corpse of a "dissipated" woman. Something in the description seems familiar to the narrator, Frank, and he responds to the newspaper's call for someone to identify the body. His identification of the woman, Mrs. Wharton, prompts a retrospective narrative of the events he presumes led to her dissipation. Frank knows her because, when he was a young man, Mrs. Wharton had stayed with him and his family, and in fact had tried, in spite of her marriage, to seduce him. She does ultimately persuade his brother George to leave his family and business for her, but Frank's discovery of the plot and confrontation of the couple at the train station (as well as the melodramatic news he brings of a catastrophic family crisis) result in his brother's decision to return to his family and send Mrs. Wharton on her way alone. The narrator of "A Grass Widow" adheres fairly closely to the pattern Chesnutt uses for his other witness-narrators. Frank is a college-educated, white narrator with an artistic temperament; he is a writer whose youthful self was engaged in producing a novel at the time of the events narrated. He maintains a mostly benevolent attitude towards the objects of his gaze, and he indulges, at times uncomfortably for the reader, a voyeuristic nature and a knack for concealment on several occasions. In short, "A Grass Widow" features what appears to be the typical Chesnutt witness-narrator.

The execution of the story, however, incorporates some substantial adjustments to the paradigm. In this work Chesnutt re-examines, for example, some troubling issues about the nature of narrative voyeurism, a few of which he only hinted at in "Cartwright's Mistake." While Frank—whose name suggests his disposition but not his handling of various situations—ultimately resolves the problem to good effect, he seems far more seduced by voyeurism than his counterparts in "Cartwright's Mistake," "Aunt Mimy's Son," or "Concerning Father." His first glimpse of Mrs. Wharton comes from behind a piazza on which "a climbing vine had been trained, forming a leafy screen, through which I could gratify my curiosity unperceived" (*SF* 333). Later, he indulges his voyeuristic tendency again when he overhears George and Mrs. Wharton discussing love, and his reaction is far less scrupulous than that of the narrator in "Cartwright's Mistake." Rather than moving away, or even expressing his discomfort with the situation, Frank tells us that "This conversation promised to become interesting. I kept quiet" (336). This statement reveals the extent to which Frank will suspend his ethical code, a penchant conspicuously absent in Chesnutt's other witness-narrators.

In other respects, too, Frank's story explores—and questions—some of the same issues that appeared in the other witness-narrator stories. For one, the youthful Frank conforms to the narrative pattern of textual voyeurism that Chesnutt establishes in "Aunt Mimy's Son" and "Cartwright's Mistake"; but while the narrators of those stories had *permission* to read others' correspondence, the narrator of "A Grass Widow" does not consult his brother George before reading a personal letter addressed to him. Furthermore, where Walton expresses his discomfort at finding himself trapped in a position of voyeurism— he contemplates and rejects for practical reasons several escape mechanisms—Frank responds quite differently to a similar situation:

> I sat down by the pile of luggage, and instinctively put my hand in my pocket for something to read—I remembered having stuck a newspaper in the inner pocket of the light overcoat which I had snatched up as I left the house. Instead of the newspaper I drew out a folded paper, which I opened with some curiosity, not remembering to have seen it before. I involuntarily glanced at the first few lines, when I became interested, and read the letter through (*SF* 340–41).

Rather than trying to avoid temptation, Frank plunges enthusiastically forward. His form of voyeurism—which calls attention
to his willingness, even eagerness, to indulge his curiosity—thus
differs markedly from that of other Chesnutt narrators.

Chesnutt may have emphasized the less pleasant elements
of voyeurism—an overweening curiosity and a disregard for
others' privacy, among others—to introduce his narrator as a
surrogate for the professional writer. Although related to the
people involved in this affair, Frank demonstrates a detachment
toward them that at times is unsettling. That he incorporates
Mrs. Wharton into his own novel and uses some of the conflicts
she causes to enhance his own fiction reveals the extent to
which his loyalties are divided. The way Frank prepares us for
what will come in his narrative suggests his willingness to treat
people close to him as characters, and also bears the stamp of
the story-maker at work. His foreshadowing includes, for
example, the information that while "affectionate and good-
tempered, George had one or two vulnerable points in his character and was easily tempted in certain directions" (*SF* 331). His
description of his brother's house and property also reveals his
conscious story-making: "A lane ran from the street to the
brook, which it crossed by a rustic bridge. I mention these details of the location of the house because they have an important bearing on my story" (331–32). This description foreshadows,
in fact, an accident involving the brook, the news of which effectively terminates George's romantic liaison with Mrs. Wharton.

Fittingly for such a self-conscious author-at-work, Frank
ends his narration by mentioning the story we'll never know,
the events that occur between Mrs. Wharton's failed acquisition
of George and her death:

> What kind of life she led, through what vicissitudes of fortune
> or misfortune she passed, how she sank step by step from
> respectability to shame, I never knew. The look on the marble
> face in the morgue; the mysterious death in the worst quarter
> of a great city; the shabby finery of her attire—these things fur-
> nished the outline of a story which the imagination may fill in.
> (*SF* 342)

Even though Frank knows the beginning and end of Mrs. Wharton's story, the transitional stage—perhaps because it is unknowable and smacks of scandalous romanticism—appeals to the story-maker in him. The curiosity that generated his voyeurism also energizes his revisionary construction of her story.

The use of a self-conscious writer as narrator likewise foregrounds some arresting narratological issues in the story. This framework forces the reader to consider the implications of Chesnutt's manipulation of the distance between subject and object, a distance not often found in first-person narratives. The actions of other characters hold a fascination for the narrator, and his relationships with them undergo several conceptual revisions: he often conceives of his associates as characters and therefore admits an interest in exploiting the logistical difficulties of their lives on artistic and intellectual grounds, regardless of personal concerns. After deciding to incorporate Mrs. Wharton into his novel, for example, Frank happily anticipates how her "grace and beauty would add immeasurably to the somewhat colorless abstraction which had hitherto done duty as the heroine of my novel" (*SF* 333). He continues to use Mrs. Wharton to characterize his fictional heroine, inserting, for instance, an equestrian scene in his novel because his human model rides so well. In a scene which ironically and subtly foreshadows Mrs. Wharton's attempts to convince George to run off with her, Frank also writes "up a runaway episode" because he witnesses his heroine expertly handling the reins of her horse.

Perhaps even more interesting, however, is the reciprocal effect the youthful author's fiction has on his understanding of what to him is a real-life situation. Once the inspiration for a fictional heroine, Mrs. Wharton undergoes a profound metamorphosis in Frank's eyes; his discovery of her unwholesome intentions—she nearly succeeds in convincing George to leave his wife and children—leads him to recast her in the melodramatic terms of his romantic prose. Rather than the heroine of his novel, she now becomes "[t]he wicked woman who . . . had wound her toils about [George's] weak nature, and a wife's love, a successful business career, even honor itself, had been thrown to the winds for a pretty face" (*SF* 341). In effect, the purple prose of his novel—which had been inspired by his (inaccurate) vision of Mrs. Wharton as a heroine—invades his interpretation of a "real-life" situation. Thus, Chesnutt explores, using complex narrative strategies, the constantly evolving interpretations of the two Mrs. Whartons—heroine and villainess—as constructed by the two Franks: the novelist who had only recently graduated from college and the mature, more detached narrator.

The complexity of "A Grass Widow" becomes even more pronounced when read in light of the narrative taxonomies described by Genette. The events that make up Frank's retrospective narrative are *diegetic*. Since the narrating act, according to Genette, always occurs one level removed from the events narrated, the mature Frank—who views Mrs. Wharton's body at the morgue—tells the story of his youthful encounter with the younger Mrs. Wharton from an *extradiegetic* level. But because the youthful Frank is also a writer, the events he composes—colored largely by his errant early interpretation of Mrs. Wharton—exist at a *metadiegetic* level, or what Genette calls "a narrative in the second degree" (228). In less daunting terms, the narrative of "A Grass Widow" explores the traditional boundaries of storytelling. While the framing technique in and of itself is not unusual, Chesnutt has achieved something distinctive by arranging to have the various narrative levels inform and modify each other.[18] Genette argues that one strategy for understanding the interplay of narrative levels requires that the reader distinguish between narrator and focalizer, or *"who is the character whose point of view orients the narrative perspective?* and the very different question *who is the narrator*—or, more simply, the question *who sees?* and the question *who speaks?*" (186). Although one might assume that these questions intersect in every first-person narration—that the "I" who sees is indivisible from the "I" who speaks—Genette suggests otherwise. One example he might cite is *Great Expectations*, in which the adult Pip, using language obviously beyond the scope of a child, describes the feelings and attitudes that the child Pip experienced. In narratological terms, the "I"-narrator, privileged by time and experience, is a different entity from his past self. Dorrit Cohn agrees with Genette on this issue: "In some respects," Cohn writes, "a first-person narrator's relationship to his past self parallels a narrator's relationship to his protagonist in a third-person novel" (143).

In Chesnutt's story, the mature Frank narrates his interaction with George and the youthful Mrs. Wharton through the consciousness of the inexperienced Frank: hence, the wildly divergent interpretations of the woman. Since narrator-Frank obviously knows the extent of her moral lapses when he begins the narration, his impressions of her as an innocent and admirable woman clearly originate in character-Frank's thoughts. This narrative arrangement, what Cohn calls *dissonant self-narration,* has "[a] lucid narrator turning back on a past self steeped in ignorance, confusion, and delusion" (145). Such a framework also describes Chesnutt's "A Fool's Paradise," featuring a disenchanted narrator who traces, in diary form, the naiveté of his earlier self. The opposite, in Cohn's terms, would be a *consonant self-narration,* a framework Chesnutt uses in "Cartwright's Mistake." There, the narrator enjoys no cognitive or experiential advantages over his past self; the narrator and the focalizer are the same person at the same time.[19]

In "A Grass Widow," Chesnutt makes use of narrative dissonance to examine the construction of identity, an issue that concerns him in all his works. By emphasizing the subjectivity of identity both for his narrator(s)—the two Franks—and the various incarnations of Mrs. Wharton, Chesnutt offers a telling commentary on the nature of interpretation. The narrator's reinscription of his own identity and that of Mrs. Wharton has as its source what should be the cognitively privileged location of the present. The people who interacted in the narrative proper no longer exist as such: Mrs. Wharton is dead and the mature

Frank is no longer the romantic novelist; instead, he has apparently embraced the more remunerative business world. But while the Frank who narrates these events is apparently many years older than the character Frank—the romantic prose that characterizes his youthful novelistic ambitions has given way to more conservative modes of expression—the two Franks share one significant trait. Where the youthful Frank unabashedly observes Mrs. Wharton from concealment, presumably for artistic purposes, the mature Frank concludes his narrative by effacing his involvement in the events he narrates:

> I wrote an unsigned letter to the undertaker, enclosing an amount sufficient to pay for her decent burial. I did not wish to appear personally in the matter, nor did I make my recognition of the body known to the public. She had long been lost to the world in which her early life had been passed. Better let her disappear, like a fallen star, in the darkness of oblivion.
> (*SF* 342)

These remarks suggest that Frank, too, has been lost to the romantic world in which *his* early life had been passed, exchanging the art-inspiring voyeurism of his youth for the shadows of discretion.

Thus Frank's narrative assumes what might be called circular form. By stepping into the narrative shadows—typically enough for Chesnutt's witness-narrators, he uses money to shield himself figuratively—the narrator consciously chooses to situate himself outside the frame of the story, a technique similar to the one Chesnutt uses in "Cartwright's Mistake" and "A Fool's Paradise." But he takes the paradigm one step further here. The story that begins with a newspaper account ends with Frank stepping back out of the frame of the narrative, an act that ultimately consigns him, like Mrs. Wharton, to "oblivion" (*SF* 342). Such a position might be taken to represent Chesnutt's articulation of the writer's circumstance in general. For, in the process of introducing the subtle nuances of black fiction to a white reading audience accustomed to the more polemical slave narrative tradition, Chesnutt, like the mature Frank—whose juvenile incarnation had dabbled in melodramatic prose before settling into the world of business—ultimately abandoned his writing career for the more tangible rewards of commerce. Although Chesnutt initiated a tradition of African-American fiction, which more firmly took root during the Harlem Renaissance and blossomed into the diverse works of Hurston, Wright, Ellison, and Baldwin, he has been consigned mainly to the shadows of that tradition by contemporary readers.

"A Grass Widow," then, traces the development of a narrator who very much anticipates Chesnutt's own career in literature. While the younger Frank is a passionate devotee of his calling, the more mature narrator, like the experienced Chesnutt, has chosen to withdraw from the field; like Chesnutt, too, the mature Frank has evolved into a businessman, and apparently a successful one. And although a young Chesnutt wrote that literature "pays the successful," he learned that pecuniary success does not often come to those who tell their stories from behind a "leafy veil."

4/ Negotiating Belief and Voicing Difference

In "Post-Bellum—Pre-Harlem," an essay he published near the end of his life, Chesnutt rejected an earlier suggestion that *The Conjure Woman* (1899) constituted a novel, insisting instead that the book be read as "a collection of short stories in Negro dialect."[1] Although he no doubt accurately assessed the genre of his work, one can easily understand the rationale for calling the work a novel. The seven frame tales collected in the book trace the evolution of three primary characters—Ohio businessman John and his wife Annie, who have recently resettled in North Carolina, and Julius, an ex-slave coachman—in a strikingly novelistic manner. Novel or not, though, Chesnutt apparently did not consider *The Conjure Woman* to be his last word on the subject. He composed a total of fourteen stories using the same characters and narrative arrangement,[2] one that typically features Julius's rendition of a magic-imbued slave tale enclosed within the framework of John's empirically grounded narration, as Annie listens and reacts to the two storytellers and their colliding world views. Despite considering the series exhausted as early as 1889,[3] only two years after its inception, Chesnutt frequently revisited it in later years and in fact did not publish the final installment until 1924–25. While the classification of the conjure tales may be fundamentally a subordinate issue, I want to stress how those fourteen stories combine to fashion a telling narrative of

Chesnutt's evolving philosophies and writing strategies. Written over a period of nearly forty years, Chesnutt's conjure tales thus play out in near-epic style his own anxieties and hopes about race, geography, economics, and history. Read chronologically, these dialogues between the two narrators, John and Julius, negotiate a new, if not entirely resolved, relationship between two previously isolated (and occasionally warring) American voices: the black and the white, the rich and the poor, the North and the South. The currency of their negotiation is belief, and the two voices, openly suspicious of what the other has to say early in the series, ultimately come to listen more meaningfully to each other.

Although this narrative paradigm has been associated primarily or even exclusively with the seven stories of *The Conjure Woman*—"The Goophered Grapevine" (originally published in *Atlantic Monthly* in 1887), "Po' Sandy" (*Atlantic Monthly* 1888), "Mars Jeems's Nightmare" (*Conjure Woman* 1899), "The Conjurer's Revenge" (*Overland Monthly* 1889), "Sis' Becky's Pickaninny" (*Conjure Woman* 1899), "The Gray Wolf's Ha'nt" (*Conjure Woman* 1899), and "Hot-Foot Hannibal" (*Atlantic Monthly* 1899)—Chesnutt reproduces essentially the same framework in ten other fictions. "Dave's Neckliss" (*Atlantic Monthly* 1889), "A Deep Sleeper" (*Two Tales* 1893), "The Dumb Witness" (unpublished until Render's collection but probably written before 1897),[4] "Lonesome Ben" (*Southern Workman* 1900), "A Victim of Heredity" (*Self-Culture Magazine* 1900), "Tobe's Tribulations" (*Southern Workman* 1900), and "The Marked Tree" (*The Crisis* 1924–25) involve the same set of characters as in the *Conjure Woman* tales.[5] In addition, Chesnutt uses a version of the same narrative arrangement—though with different characters—in three other stories, all written early in his career: "Tom's Warm Welcome" (*Family Fiction* 1886), "McDugald's Mule" (*Family Fiction* 1887), and "A Virginia Chicken" (*Household Realm* 1887). The latter three seem to have been the prototypes for the conjure stories,[6] but they differ from their progeny in significant ways. For one, both "I"-narrators in the prototypes are white, although they do, like John and Julius, come from different social and economic planes.[7] This chapter will focus primarily on *The Conjure Woman* but will also take into account the other seven works in which Chesnutt has John and Julius share narrating duties.

While Chesnutt clearly hoped to tap into the local color writing market with *The Conjure Woman* in order to exploit what William L. Andrews calls "the curiosity of northern readers about social idiosyncracies and economic conditions in the New South" (*Literary Career* 42), he had other compelling reasons for designing the conjure stories as frame tales. In using a dual-narrator structure and in consolidating (and updating) many conventions of the plantation tradition—conventions popularized by such writers as Joel Chandler Harris and Thomas Nelson Page[8]—Chesnutt made several astute judgments.[9] By drawing on such a well-established literary tradition, he enjoyed the considerable advantages of working in a genre his late-nineteenth-century readers found familiar and comfortable. That familiarity accorded Chesnutt precisely the situation he needed to produce fictions that satisfied both of his literary desires.[10] He could gain a modest measure of popular acclaim, essentially for the only time in his career, by fulfilling the superficial expectations of a readership captivated by the quaintly exotic nature of the conjure tales while simultaneously he infused those stories with the subversive (and thus instructive) implications that make the conjure tales so distinctive. He was able to appropriate a format typically wielded for what Robert M. Farnsworth calls "Southern white propaganda" designed "to establish a nostalgically sentimental picture of slave-master relations prior to the Civil War" (*CW* v) for altogether different purposes: to emphasize the humanity of African Americans, to call attention to the brutal and ongoing consequences of slavery, and to delineate the racial and cultural terms of a national, post–Civil War reconciliation and regeneration.

Just as important, Chesnutt's use of the frame-tale structure also offers a thorough and significant commentary on his conception of authorship. The frame narration in many ways signals Chesnutt's own divided authorial identity and, more broadly, foregrounds his interest in issues of representation. By splitting the narrative duties between two such polarized figures as John and Julius, Chesnutt regularly capitalizes on multiple narrative levels, a strategy that, according to Shlomith Rimmon-Kenan, "often enacts a doubt about the possibility of reaching reality and constituting a self" (105).[11] For Chesnutt, the very act of composing fictions of identity had to be envisioned through the prism of his own conflicting loyalties and anxieties,[12] and his two narrators embody those competing interests throughout the series. John and Julius thus "speak" both for and about their author.

A transplanted northerner, John suggests just how out of his element he is when he describes his new home at the beginning of "The Goophered Grapevine," the first story in the series. Told that this southern town, Patesville, had a thriving business community, he confides to the reader that

> [t]his business activity was not immediately apparent to my
> unaccustomed eyes. Indeed, when I first saw the town, there
> brooded over it a calm that seemed almost sabbatic in its rest-
> fulness, though I learned later on that underneath its somno-
> lent exterior the deeper currents of life—love and hatred, joy
> and despair, ambition and avarice, faith and friendship—
> flowed not less steadily than in livelier latitudes. (*CW* 4)

His inability to "read" the town—even though the subject is business, a topic he knows well—prepares us for his failure in the series to comprehend the ex-slave, Julius, he finds on the property he intends to buy. Because Julius's stories typically explore the costs and benefits of magic (generally provided by Aunt Peggy, the conjure woman for whom the collection is named) for an assortment of slaves living in North Carolina, John cannot always grasp Julius's nuanced renderings of southern life, especially in regard to race. In that first story, Chesnutt foreshadows John's perplexity about his new context when

Julius tells him "'dat dis yer ole vimya'd is goophered,'" and John, "not grasping the meaning of this unfamiliar word" (*CW* 11), has to ask for a definition of the term.

Thus the goopher, or magic, Julius so habitually positions at the center of his stories forms a metaphoric barrier that separates the two narrators for most of the series. Since magic has no place in the empiricism that dominates John's philosophy when we first meet him, he discounts most of what he hears. Julius's mixed-genre narratives framed by John's skeptical commentary create a recurring structure that emphasizes the extent to which the white narrator cannot believe: because Julius's stories involve the empirically unprovable, John has license to reject everything Julius tells him, including details concerning the horrors of slavery.[13] But as the series progresses chronologically, the relationship between the narrators alters. Ultimately, John evolves from someone who does not know the meaning of the word "goopher" into a man who willingly follows Julius's advice on how to counteract a spell. Hence, the narrative of these conjure stories, from "The Goophered Grapevine" (1887) to "The Marked Tree" (1924–25), suggests that the two warring belief systems articulated by Chesnutt's narrators finally converge in what might be called mutual understanding.

The stories of *The Conjure Woman* and others that employ the same or similar framing devices feature a narratological dialogue between two narrators who each identify themselves as "I." Because of the intimacy engendered by this narrative structure—a duo of first-person narrators "reading," commenting on, and thus shaping each other's stories—outside readers might choose to project their insights onto one of the primary spokesmen. Much of the critical commentary on *The Conjure Woman*, in fact, has been devoted to attempts to isolate which of the two voices Chesnutt primarily identified with. Eugene Terry, for example, argues that "it is Julius's voice to whom the reader—the third listener—must give his attention if he would hear the author's meaning" (125). David Britt, Robert M. Farnsworth, Valerie Babb, and Lorne Fienberg similarly envision Julius as Chesnutt's proxy, an encoder of subversive messages on race issues. Other readers, including R. V. Burnette, Donald Gibson, and Dickson Bruce, have argued quite the opposite: Bruce, for example, unambiguously locates Chesnutt's sympathies with his white narrator John "because, in terms of background and temperament, he felt himself to be a man like his narrator, regardless of color" (183). Both sides of this debate advance valid, if not quite satisfying, characterizations of the two narrators, and therein lies compelling testimony to Chesnutt's subtle manipulations of the narrative levers.[14]

But the real power of these dual-narrator stories derives from Chesnutt's ability to force us constantly to reshuffle our own constructions of what these co-narrators have to say to each other and to us. Through the use of multiple narrative voices, that is, Chesnutt compels readers not only to examine what each narrator says, but also to explore the interaction between the voices. Hence, while the author does offer "ironic and sometimes satirical" assessments of John (Terry 124), such a strategy does not automatically conflate Chesnutt's attitudes with those of Julius. Indeed, one need only look to "The Wife of His Youth," "A Matter of Principle," or "The March of Progress" to find characters who seem to be proxies for the author—they belong to the same club, have the same interests, are, like Chesnutt, schoolteachers or lawyers, etc.—and yet suffer emphatically ironic and satiric treatment. Similarly, Burnette's assertion that "the paternalism and condescension in John's relationship to Julius were, in fact, a part of Chesnutt's psychological makeup" (442) does not lead convincingly to the same critic's conclusion that "it was upon the shoulders of John, the white narrator, that Chesnutt's moral motives fell" (452). Rather, one might more productively envision both narrators as reflecting and articulating Chesnutt's complex attitudes, though neither, it seems, does so exclusively.

In many ways the conjure stories represent the zenith of

Chesnutt's dexterity in his literary handling of dissimilar voices. In them, the author combines many of the narrative stances and strategies found in his other fiction. In terms of voice, for example, Julius speaks in a manner reminiscent of the characters in such early dialect stories as "How Dasdy Came Through," "Aunt Lucy's Search," and "A Limb of Satan." The other narrator, John, bears a remarkable similarity in speech patterns and demeanor to figures in "A Bad Night" and "A Metropolitan Experience." And in terms of the narrator's position within the text, the conjure tales build on their predecessors as well. Like the narrators of "Cartwright's Mistake" and "A Grass Widow," John functions as a mostly sympathetic witness or observer to the action. Plotted on a continuum of Chesnutt's career, then, these stories combine the narrative elements typical of the author's first-person works, while the use of an empirical-minded and detached commentator anticipates in many ways the more Howellsian narrative positioning found in *The Wife of His Youth* (1899).

As Chesnutt's most accomplished effort, *The Conjure Woman* has generated a spate of commentary—much of it incisive and useful[15]—but an investigation of its critical history reveals that little consensus has been reached, even as to the rubric that ties these works together. The title of the collection, for example, suggests that Aunt Peggy, the most frequently appearing conjure woman, might form the axis around which these stories revolve, and yet she appears in only five of the seven. In the other two, "Po' Sandy" and "The Conjurer's Revenge," supernatural duties devolve to other characters. Similarly, of the seven other conjure stories, "The Dumb Witness" and "The Marked Tree" make no mention of Peggy, and the former relies for its plot more on stubbornness than on goopher. Thus, Peggy is present in ten of the fourteen conjure stories, and her importance to the plots of those ten varies widely.[16]

Some commentators, including Robert Bone,[17] emphasize the thematic importance of the transformations that take place in these fictions. In his reading of *The Conjure Woman,* Bone focuses on "the metamorphosis found at the center of each conjure tale" (83), and indeed nearly all of the stories include some sort of transformation. In several stories a conjurer changes slaves into a variety of animals, including a mule, a hummingbird, and a wolf; this recurrent element, recalling Harris's "Uncle Remus" tales, affirms the debt these works owe to the conventions of the folktale and local color traditions from which Chesnutt gleaned conceptual frameworks for his stories.[18] "Mars Jeems's Nightmare," the conjure tale in which Chesnutt comes nearest to revealing his own advocatory impulses, transforms the master of the plantation into a slave so that he might better understand the horrors over which he rules. But the type of transformation varies from story to story, and in some no physical alterations occur at all. "Dave's Neckliss," for example, dramatizes not the supernatural transformation but the psychological deterioration of a slave who finally hangs himself in a smokehouse because he comes to believe that he is a ham.[19] A less gruesome example appears in "Hot-Foot Hannibal," where Aunt Peggy wields her goopher not to transform anyone but merely to cause the titular character to have literally hot feet, a problem so distracting that he loses his favored position with both the masters and his romantic interest.

The way the magic is used in these works, in fact, disallows pat taxonomies. It is tempting, of course, to envision Chesnutt using goopher as a means of empowerment for slaves in their otherwise powerless position within the economic and social hierarchy of the antebellum South.[20] "Sis Becky's Pickaninny" and "Mars Jeems's Nightmare" do indeed dramatize how goopher could at least temporarily enable slaves to thwart the cruel vagaries of their white masters, while "Po' Sandy" depicts Tenie's ill-fated attempts to offer the same relief to her husband. But goopher does not always shift the scales of power in favor of African Americans. "A Victim of Heredity" and "The Goophered Grapevine" both have Aunt Peggy helping white men, one of whom is a slaveowner. Even more surprising, several of these works—including "The Conjurer's Revenge," "The Gray Wolf's Ha'nt," and "Hot-Foot Hannibal"—explore the harmful uses of goopher, as black characters use magic as a weapon against one another. Chesnutt might well be emphasizing the limited resources of power for slaves: in turning to goopher, they enlist an unpredictable and often dangerous ally. Still, it is difficult to codify these conjure stories solely on the basis of magic as a source of power. In the complexity of Chesnutt's treatment of magic and other folktale elements, the conjure stories address themes and issues found much later in the works of contemporary black authors such as Toni Morrison and Charles Johnson, whose novels display an American version of magic realism.

Chesnutt's "goopher" stories particularly anticipate Morrison's *The Song of Solomon* and *Beloved* in that, like those novels, Julius's tales often foreground questions of family identity and reconstruction. As in *Beloved,* for example, the African Americans depicted in the conjure stories have so few avenues for redress that they can only turn to conjurers, an often unreliable source of help, in their attempts to form or preserve their families, a thematic concern that pervades all of Chesnutt's fiction. "Po' Sandy," "Sis Becky's Pickaninny," and "The Gray Wolf's Ha'nt" all depict randomly cruel masters who without qualm separate black families for financial gain. Chesnutt's interest in formulating (and reformulating) the concept of the family resonates throughout the frame stories that make up *The Conjure Woman:* in "Hot-Foot Hannibal" Julius apparently tells his story as a means of reuniting John's sister-in-law and her estranged fiancé. Eugene Terry argues that "Chesnutt undercuts his own book with this last tale" and that the work represents the author's "failure of nerve" manifested by "bringing stereotypic, hot blooded young white lovers together" (124). But such a reading discounts the high value Chesnutt places on family identity throughout his oeuvre.[21]

Like issues pertaining to family, economics also plays a crucial role in the conjure fictions, as it does in other Chesnutt works. Many commentators point, in fact, to economic concerns as the unifying motif pervading the consciousnesses of the two narrators, and both Julius and John do conform to Julius's metaphoric characterization of a financial-minded slaveowner in "Lonesome Ben": "'Mars Marrabo wuz,'" Julius tells his audiences, "'one er dese yer folks w'at wants ter make eve'y aidge cut'" (*SF* 109). Indeed, although John often stresses the foreignness of Julius's views compared to his own, the two figures share a deep interest in all things financial, a point Lorne Fienberg confirms: "both the narrative frame and the tales of Chesnutt's collection," he writes, "are permeated by the signs of the marketplace and by the concern for economic value" (165). Eugene Terry similarly decries Julius for the way "the sufferings of his people become the scrip with which he makes his meagre purchases of honey and suits and grapes" (115). But David Britt rightly counters by suggesting that in only one of the seven *Conjure Woman* stories does Julius gain anything of substantial economic value. In the others, he achieves some markedly nonfinancial goals: he arranges the reunification of a white couple; he manages to keep his nephew in John's employ; and he maneuvers to acquire a new meeting place for his church group. Thus, the two narrators do engage in a sort of commerce with one another, but the nature of that engagement seems to me more complicated than matters of mere financial profit and loss (although those are not incidental concerns for either John or Julius). The two characters and storytellers build their relationship through an elaborate barter system. And, while John seems at times preoccupied with his financial maneuvering, and Julius's narratives catalog the dehumanizing consequences of a system in which blacks became little more than commodities to be bought and sold, I want to suggest that both figures invest more in their dialogue than they might admit. Nevertheless, as a rubric or motif, economics proves a less-than-consistent key to these works.

Perhaps the defining feature of this narrative paradigm is, after all, the extent to which Chesnutt constantly reworked it.

The narrative partnership between John and Julius underwent extensive revisions throughout the nearly forty years that Chesnutt used it. Any attempts, therefore, to offer a definitive account of so amorphous a paradigm quickly devolve into qualifications: Aunt Peggy does appear in *most,* but not all, of these tales; transformations of one sort or another occur in *almost* all of them; economics *usually* plays a crucial role for both John and Julius, but the goals for both at times seem to shift; a condemnation of slavery is evident on *several* occasions, although the series does feature a few apparently "contented" slaves. None of these elements, then, can by itself serve as the linchpin that connects all fourteen dual-narrator stories.

The only common element to all of these works, in fact, is the narrative presence of John and Julius, whose voices combine and compete to form a unified, if constantly shifting, whole. Chesnutt's remarkable evolution of this narrative format speaks to his keen awareness of the mutability of his own social, cultural, and literary worlds. The conjure stories in many ways form a bridge between Reconstruction and Modernism: the works look backward to the black folklore that engendered the series in 1887 and forward to the Harlem Renaissance already taking shape in 1924–25, when "The Marked Tree" reached print. In addition to these temporal links, the stories also traverse geographic and psychological chasms one associates with Chesnutt. John and Jules often represent contending economic, racial, and philosophical notions—all, like the two narrators, very much in flux—of a still-developing, multiracial America. This narrative paradigm, in short, is composed of a variety of dichotomies. But because Chesnutt revises the interaction of voices as the series progresses, one might reasonably argue that his purpose in using the format can only be appreciated when viewing the entire corpus of John/Julius narratives. And ultimately, Chesnutt eliminates (or at least renegotiates) some of these dichotomies, both in terms of theme and, provocatively, in the voices of his two narrators.

One of the most striking paradoxes of this narrative

partnership is that Chesnutt uses a conventionally humorous frame narrative to encase some profoundly gruesome plots. The often ghoulish stories Julius tells coexist with the tone of comic tolerance that characterizes John's commentary. The incongruity of the comic frame for the usually unpleasant content of Julius's tales has not elicited much comment. Indeed, Chesnutt's fiction in general does not often prompt discussions of humor. William Dean Howells, for example, suggests that Chesnutt's *The Marrow of Tradition* (1901) is characterized chiefly by "a courage which has more justice than mercy in it. The book is, in fact, bitter, bitter. There is no reason in history why it should not be so, if wrong is to be repaid with hate, and yet it would be better if it was not so bitter."[22] In several of Chesnutt's shorter works, however, that bitterness is tempered, and at times eclipsed, by the author's use of situational humor. In "The Passing of Grandison," for example, Chesnutt depicts the comic inability of a plantation owner's lazy son to free one of his father's slaves in a desperate, if elaborate, attempt to impress his lover.

While "Grandison" is an apparently light-hearted story of almost vaudevillian character,[23] Chesnutt's humor usually reveals a much more complex and often dark vision of human nature, a tendency that is most apparent in his "goopher" stories. Often, the disbelief of the white characters engenders much of the humor in these works. Uncle Julius slyly attests, for example, to the measure of Aunt Peggy's authority in this passage from "Hot-Foot Hannibal": "'En w'iles Mars' Dugal' say he did n' b'liebe in cunj'in en sich, he 'peared to 'low it wuz bes' ter be on de safe side, en let Aun' Peggy alone'" (*CW* 219).

Julius's understated narrative style, apparent in the passage cited above, provides only one source of the richness of these stories. Another, and perhaps richer, vein is the narrative frame Chesnutt uses to establish a recurring conflict between the refined disbelief of the white, empirically grounded narrator and the rhetorically suspicious magic stories of Uncle Julius. In a 1931 essay published both in *Colophon* and in W. E. B. Du

Bois's *The Crisis,* Chesnutt discusses this framing technique, especially in regard to *The Conjure Woman,* which he describes as

> a collection of short stories in Negro dialect, put in the mouth of an old Negro gardener, and related by him in each instance to the same audience, which consisted of the Northern lady and gentleman who employed him. They are naive and simple stories, dealing with alleged incidents of chattel slavery, as the old man had known it and as I had heard of it, and centering around the professional activities of old Aunt Peggy, the plantation conjure woman, and others of that ilk.
>
> In every instance Julius had an axe to grind, for himself or his church, or some member of his family, or a white friend. The introductions to the stories, which were written in the best English I could command, developed the characters of Julius's employers and his own, and the wind-up of each story reveals the old man's ulterior purpose, which, as a general thing, is accomplished.[24]

There is much more ambiguity in these stories than Chesnutt suggests here; in fact, the reader is often left to wonder, like the bemused narrator, just what "ulterior purpose" these involved fictional constructs "reveal."

The belief systems of these two men are as disparate as the language each uses to express his thoughts, and it is this gulf of understanding that Chesnutt examines in his fiction. In "Tobe's Tribulations," a story originally published in *Southern Workman* after the appearance of *The Conjure Woman,* John tells us that Julius's

> views of life were so entirely foreign to our own, that for a time after we got acquainted with him his conversations were a never-failing source of novelty and interest. He had seen life from what was to us a new point of view—from the bottom, as it were; and there clung to his mind, like the barnacles to the submerged portion of a ship, all sorts of extravagant beliefs. The simplest phenomena of life were to him fraught with hidden meaning—some prophecy of good, some presage of evil. (*SF* 99)

Thus, John conflates Julius's economic status—the "bottom"—

with his "extravagant beliefs," or goopher, and he is able therefore to maintain his skepticism. Disbelief for John becomes a
mark of class distinction.

What emerges in these stories, then, is a series of rhetorical
struggles between the benevolently devious Julius and the skeptical narrator, whose articulate expressions of doubt make him
a suitable proxy for both the wary *fin de siècle* reading audience
and the superficially nonbelieving plantation owners.[25] John's
oft-articulated cynicism about the tales—"'I was old enough,
and knew Julius well enough, to be skeptical of his motives'" (*CS*
88), he confides to the reader at the end of "Hot-Foot Hannibal"—invites turn-of-the-century white readers to identify with
him. Thus, John's presence and indeed his almost predictably
cynical commentary on Julius's narratives may very well reassure
white readers who might likewise be skeptical of *Chesnutt's*
motives. And, John's dependence on reason in order to dismiss
the tacit indictment of white Americans manifest in the tales of
Julius serves another purpose as well. Chesnutt may have hoped
that those white readers who, while putatively against race prejudice, embraced John's measured resistance to Julius's version
of social history, might follow John's lead once more at the end
of the series. For, ultimately, John's attitudes shift significantly
by the end of "The Marked Tree."

In response to the narrator's disbelief early in the series,
however, Julius begins the process of reformulating his listen-
ers' opinions on such subjects as race relations in the South by
attaching morals to several of his tales, including this one from
"Mars Jeems's Nightmare":

> "Dis yer tale goes ter show," concluded Julius sententiously,
> as the man came up and announced that the spring was ready
> for us to get water, "dat w'ite folks w'at is so ha'd en stric', en
> doan make no 'llowance fer po' ign'ant niggers w'at ain' had
> no chanst ter l'arn, is li'ble ter hab bad dreams, ter say de leas',
> en dat dem w'at is kin' en good ter po' people is sho' ter pros-
> per en git 'long in de worl'." (*CW* 100)

Despite John's ironic response to the inevitable rhetorical manipulation—"'that was powerful goopher. . . . I am glad, too, that you told us the moral of the story; it might have escaped us otherwise'" (*CW* 101)—he agrees to rehire Julius's nephew. And by relenting, he demonstrates that he too has gained something from this narrative transaction. Although he continues to be plagued by an unambitious employee, John enjoys access to a first-class raconteur and, perhaps more importantly, is the direct beneficiary of Julius's machinations in at least two of the stories. In "Sis' Becky's Pickaninny," Julius's tale of the supernaturally aided reunification of a mother and her child appeals to the superstitious nature of the narrator's wife, Annie, and succeeds in lifting her "settled melancholy" (*CW* 132). And, in "Hot-Foot Hannibal," Julius plots to reconcile John's sister-in-law and her fiancé by inventing a goopher story that recounts the melodramatic consequences of deferring true love.

Mutual benefits aside, the central ambiguity of this series of Chesnutt's short fiction lies in whether Julius believes in the supernatural events he describes or is merely using them to manipulate his northern employers, particularly the more sympathetic (and apparently more superstitious) wife of the narrator. In the best of these stories, Chesnutt creates a comic tension by juxtaposing Julius's deadpan accounts of the occult with John's ironic, but ultimately uncertain, responses. The narrator's characteristic reserve is evident in this summary of Julius's narratives:

> Some of these stories are quaintly humorous; others wildly extravagant, revealing the Oriental cast of the negro's imagination; while others, poured freely into the sympathetic ear of a Northern-bred woman, disclose many a tragic incident of the darker side of slavery. (*CW* 40–41)

This commentary on Julius's stories not only reveals much about John's reading skills, but also emphasizes the importance of his wife, Annie, to this series of works.

It is only through the Annie, in fact, that the disjunction in belief between John and Julius can be mediated, at least for most of the series; only Annie, of the internal audience, gets beyond the improbable supernatural elements to what Julius really has to say. She functions as interpreter, broker, buffer, and guide, not only between the two men but between Julius's fictions and the reader. Like us, she cannot quite discount the tales as pure works of imagination as her husband does, nor can she fully commit to accepting the yarns as truth, either literal or metaphoric. But in her thoughtful consideration of the tales, Annie develops with Julius what Farnsworth calls "a community of feeling" because "the woman's heart reaches much further toward Uncle Julius's world than does the man's mind or social conscience" (*CW* ix–x). John, too, comments on his wife's empathetic listening skills when he characteristically seeks an empirical explanation for her "sympathetic ear" in "Lonesome Ben": "My wife," John tells us, "came from a family of reformers, who could never contemplate an evil without seeking an immediate remedy" (*SF* 114).

But Annie proves a more sophisticated reader and listener than John realizes. "Po' Sandy," a story the narrator would probably classify as "wildly extravagant," explores her developing reading skills and serves as an early clue to the narrative design of the entire corpus of conjure stories. The frame of the story involves the narrator's desire to dismantle a shack on his property in order to use the lumber to build a kitchen for his wife. When Julius learns of this prospect, he spins a yarn that relates the ill-fated attempts of the slave Sandy and his wife, a conjure woman named Tenie, to stay together. Rather than separate from his wife, Sandy agrees to be turned into a tree, and he subsequently is chopped down and taken to the lumbermill. It turns out that the shack destined for demolition is, according to what the narrator calls Julius's "gruesome narrative" (*CW* 60), all that's left of Sandy, who continues to haunt the building. This detail is enough to convince Annie that she wants all new lumber for her kitchen. "'What a system it was,'" she says after listening to the story, "'under which such things were possible'" (60). When John questions "'the possibility of a man's being turned into a tree'" (60), Annie's response demonstrates that she, like Julius, can wax inscrutable: "'Oh, no,' she replied quickly, 'not that'; and then she murmured absently, and with a dim look in her fine eyes, 'Poor Tenie!'" (60–61).

The punchline of this "gruesome" story is the narrator's discovery that Annie has given permission to Julius and his church to use the shack as a meeting place:

> "What are they going to do about the ghost?" I asked, somewhat curious to know how Julius would get around this obstacle.
>
> "Oh," replied Annie, "Uncle Julius says that ghosts never disturb religious worship, but that if Sandy's spirit *should* happen to stray into meeting by mistake, no doubt the preaching would do it good." (63)

This conclusion is typical of both Chesnutt's humor and his use of Annie, whose reading of Sandy's misfortunes differs markedly from that of her husband. This contrast serves to provide readers with two discrete interpretations of Julius's narrative, but also exposes some of the inadequacies intrinsic to her husband's interpretive framework, relying as it does on the strictly empirical. Indeed, she becomes one more narrative device by which the author complicates our reading of what appear to be simple ghost stories.

At the beginning of "The Gray Wolf's Ha'nt," the penultimate tale in *The Conjure Woman,* Chesnutt emphasizes the refinement of Annie's already-perceptive reading skills as a means of deflating John's absolute faith in rationalism and for subtler reasons as well. When John attempts to entertain his wife by reading philosophy to her—"'"The difficulty of dealing with transformations so many-sided as those which all existences have undergone, or are undergoing, is such as to make a complete and deductive interpretation almost hopeless"'" (*CW* 163)—she interrupts pointedly: "'I wish you would stop reading that nonsense'" (164).[26] She suggestively uses the same word here ("nonsense") to rebuke her husband for his philosophical excesses as she uses to express disappointment with Julius's overly contrived tale in "The Conjurer's Revenge." Annie thus functions as an impartial listener, and she solidifies her position as the unacknowledged arbiter between John and Julius (and the two inflexible world views they repeatedly delineate).

The final tale in the 1899 collection epitomizes the extent to which Annie's role within Chesnutt's framework evolved. Because "Hot-Foot Hannibal" concludes the original edition of *The Conjure Woman,*[27] it perhaps represents what Chesnutt thought would be his final word on the series; although he expressed relative indifference regarding the order Houghton, Mifflin chose for the conjure tales, he did suggest that "'Hotfoot [*sic*] Hannibal' winds them up well" (*Letters* 113). In that light, the story varies the paradigm established by its predecessors in remarkable ways, the most telling of which is that Annie has transformed from listener to co-conspirator. Annie intuits Julius's motives for telling his tale of love deferred, and she joins his plot to reunite her sister Mabel with her fiancé by arranging a "chance" meeting between the two on the road. Equally interesting, however, is that John thus becomes the isolated figure of the three; of all audiences for this last tale, only he cannot decode the "meaning" of Julius's text.

Taken together, the elements of Chesnutt's narrative frame in the conjure stories enable him to maintain a distance not present in *The Marrow of Tradition,* the novel Howells rightly calls a bitter work. Although most of these stories have at their core an indictment of slavery and the greedy, mean-spirited whites who established that system, the injustices depicted are more subtly conveyed than in his longer prose works. By choosing to speak in more than one voice—that is, by using embedded narratives—Chesnutt filters his work through a variety of perspectives, a strategy that provides his reader with a more fully developed understanding of the events narrated and their implications. And by mixing in another personified layer of interpretation in Annie, he offers his readers a kaleidoscopic vision of complex issues and ideas. But ultimately Chesnutt seems to have concluded that even Annie, acting alone, could not effect a lasting mediation between the polarized belief systems articulated by John and Julius. The post–*Conjure Woman* publication of other conjure stories attests to Chesnutt's apparent belief that the dialogue composed by his two narrators had not yet satisfactorily resolved itself.

In fact, the seven additional conjure stories not appearing in *The Conjure Woman* provide some of the most dramatic revisions of the series-long referendum on belief that transpires between John and Julius. The first salient fact and biographically significant datum one notices, for example, belies the idea that Chesnutt confined his writing of dialect stories to the early stages of his career. Three of these seven works appeared in 1900, and a fourth was published in 1924–25. Each of these other works stands on its own as a significant contribution to the Chesnutt canon, and some of them differ markedly in crucial details from the works collected in 1899: "The Dumb Witness," for example, seems at first to feature the same frame until it becomes apparent that John has usurped Julius's rights of authorship. Julius tells John his narrative offstage—we do not read Julius's version—and John *summarizes* for us, minus the dialect, the story as he reshapes it:

> Some of the facts in this strange story—circumstances of which
> Julius was ignorant, though he had the main facts correct—I
> learned afterwards from other sources, but I have woven them
> all together here in orderly sequence. (*SF* 156)

Thus, John narrates the entire story, a shift of perspective that robs us of Julius's considerable storytelling skills.[28] John cannot completely elide Julius from the storymaking process, however: Julius still does manage to supply the story's coda.

Similarly, "Tobe's Tribulations" and "Lonesome Ben" also differ from the expected pattern of these dual-narrator works. In the second, Julius fails to achieve his material goal, perhaps the only time in any of the fourteen stories featuring him that such an outcome can be confidently asserted. But the more interesting of the two works, "Tobe's Tribulations," diverges from the pattern in an even more provocative manner. In this tale, Julius's narrative concludes the larger story. While John introduces the work in the accustomed fashion, he offers no commentary at the end of the story. Hence, this work allows Julius to provide closure, for him an unfamiliar narrative position. Equally interesting, John's voice does not assume its usual role in shaping the story. Because "Lonesome Ben" and "Tobe's Tribulations" were published in 1900, a year *after* the works collected as *The Conjure Woman,* we might reasonably infer from Chesnutt's modifications of this paradigm that the author intended to shift the thematic direction of his series as well. In other words, if his goal were merely to cash in on the success of his collection, why fundamentally alter the format?

Indeed, Chesnutt most dramatically re-envisions the dual-narrator stories in a work, "The Marked Tree," that appeared twenty-five years after *The Conjure Woman.* Although Chesnutt's literary production waned after *The Colonel's Dream* in 1905, he nevertheless resurrected the conjure series in 1924–25 by publishing "The Marked Tree," a tale that incorporated not only the same narrative framework, but also many of the themes found in his earlier efforts. In it, Julius describes how an understandably embittered slave, Phillis, had put a curse on an oak tree that stood in front of the master's family house. Since that time, the family has been decimated, its members all dying mysteriously after contact with the tree. Through his tale Julius implicitly advises the narrator to remove the stump of the tree as a means of averting a like tragedy befalling his own family.

Chesnutt suggests throughout "The Marked Tree" that his heretofore dueling narrators have begun to share common ground. As in "Sis' Becky's Pickaninny" and "Hot-Foot Hannibal," Julius has no apparent economic motive for spinning this yarn. Even more important, though, is the way Chesnutt subtly conflates the positions of the two figures in this story. A cousin from Ohio asks John to find for him "a suitable place for a winter residence" (Brodhead 194) in North Carolina. An outsider for most of the series who gradually acquires familiarity with southern habits and culture through Julius, John now *becomes* the inside man himself, helping a northerner navigate the perils of North Carolina real estate. He thus plays a role familiar to Julius.

The plot of Julius's narrative centers around John Spencer, son of the plantation owner, and Isham, son of the slave Phillis. The fates of the two sons metaphorically converge in an oak tree linked with the Spencer family: ""'Dis fambly has growed an' flourish' wid dat tree,'"" Julius quotes Alex Spencer as saying, ""'an' now dat my son is bawn, I wants ter hab him christen' under it, so dat he kin grow an' flourish 'long wid it'"" (Brodhead 198). But Alex Spencer's eventual sale of Isham in order to afford a more lavish wedding for his own son cultivates Phillis's hostility:

> "When de young ma'ied folks came back f'm dey weddin' tower, day had de infair, an' all de rich white folks wuz invited. An' dat same night, whils' de big house wuz all lit up, an' de fiddles wuz goin', an' dere wuz eatin' an' drinkin' an' dancin' an' sky-larkin' an' eve'body wuz jokin' de young couple an' wushin' 'em good luck, Phillis wuz settin' all alone in huh cabin, way at de fah end er de quarters, studyin' 'bout huh boy, who had be'n sol' to pay fer it all." (Brodhead 201)

After her own son is killed as a result of a fight with his new owner, Phillis "marks" (or curses) the tree so that the entire Spencer line dies as well.

But while the "marked" tree thus represents the violent division of John Spencer and Isham—white and black sons born on the same day—the *telling* of the story fuses the fates of Julius and John, Chesnutt's black and white narrative "sons." Perhaps the most startling element of this piece, in terms of what Chesnutt had done in others of these stories, is that John ultimately, and unreservedly, believes Julius's supernatural tale. In the previous thirteen Uncle Julius stories, remember, John has sustained an ironic distance from not only Julius but also the material he presents, whether fictive or not. Equally significant, the narrator's wife, Annie, who had acted as a sort of intermediary between the two men in the past, is virtually absent in this story—that is, the narrator directly connects with Julius here without any outside mediation. This development may suggest that Chesnutt, justifiably bitter about race relations for much of his career, still saw some hope for amelioration. If an educated white northerner can learn to believe the "goopher" stories of an ex-slave raconteur, then perhaps there is a chance to bridge the cultural and sociological gaps that separate the races. "The Marked Tree" stands as Chesnutt's final word in the conjure series, and it suggests that he was finally able to reconcile the two voices used in the series: the studied articulateness of the narrator and the rhetorically incisive dialect of Uncle Julius.

Ultimately, however, it is the inscrutability of Uncle Julius that makes all of these stories resonate. Although his untutored dialect suggests a lack of sophistication, he masterfully blends fantasy and reality, and he infuses into the world he creates a full range of humor, from slapstick to satire. Despite his employment as a coachman, Julius maintains a benevolent control over his northern employers—after, that is, his initial attempt to scare them back North in "The Goophered Grapevine"—and he uses storytelling as his method of enforcement. The combination of humor and the occult found in his narratives provides a thorough and entertaining—if sometimes uncomfortable—account of the world as he knew it. The use of a figure such as Julius, who bears superficial resemblance to a host of late-nineteenth-century stereotypical black characters in the works of Thomas Nelson Page or Joel Chandler Harris, has its risks.[29] But Chesnutt handles potentially explosive issues, including race, with delicacy and complexity, as Andrews notes in his introduction to *Collected Stories of Charles W. Chesnutt*: "Still, whether for good or for ill, the consistent use of hoodoo practice by the black characters of *The Conjure Woman* enabled their creator to endow these men and women with a variety of desires and needs that call attention to their diverse, nonstereotypical humanity" (xi). Whether Julius believes in the more supernatural elements of these stories or not, it is clear that goopher is a powerful weapon when used by an expert.

By dividing the narrative duties, which results in an ongoing dialogue, Chesnutt endows these stories with a thematic and narratological fluidity. The dialogue thus exists in a constant state of flux as the two primary voices converge and, ultimately, shape one another. While the two narrators finally begin to listen to what the other has to say, implicitly promising that their "conversation" will fruitfully continue, Chesnutt does not suggest that all of the racial and cultural oppositions embodied by the two men have been magically merged. Rather, these stories—in addition to their substantial literary merit—describe the value of ongoing personal and cultural negotiation.

৻৵৹

Because it establishes the terms of our readership of this extended rhetorical debate between John and Julius, "The Goophered Grapevine" seems the logical story to examine in depth. It introduces the three major characters, and it comes as close to typifying the series as any work in this protean cluster of fictions. The story also emphasizes the inscrutability of Julius for both the inside readers—John and Annie—and us. And as the revisions of "The Goophered Grapevine" suggest, Julius's character has something of an amorphous quality even for Chesnutt.

The first of the conjure tales (or rather the opening tale of *The Conjure Woman*) catalogs how a plantation owner, Mars Dugal' McAdoo, hires Aunt Peggy, a free black woman living nearby, to put a spell on his vineyards as a means of preventing the local slaves from stealing his grapes. Peggy's spell causes anyone who eats the grapes to die within one year. Just the threat of this magic convinces the locals to leave the vineyards alone, until Henry, a recently acquired slave who has not been warned of the spell, eats grapes from the vines. Since Henry possessed no knowledge of the goopher, Aunt Peggy decides to spare him by putting a protective spell on him, but one that inextricably links his fortunes to those of the vines themselves. When the crop thrives in summer, Henry therefore thrives, but when the off-season saps the vines of their strength, Henry is likewise weakened, as Julius explains:

> "When Henry come ter de plantation, he wuz gittin' a little ole an stiff in de j'ints. But dat summer he got des ez spry en libely ez any young nigger on de plantation; fac', he got so biggity dat Mars Jackson, de oberseah, ha' ter th'eaten ter whip 'im, ef he did n' stop cuttin' up his didos en behave hisse'f. But de mos' cur'ouses' thing happen' in de fall, when de sap begin ter go down in de grapevimes. Fus', when de grapes 'uz gethered, de knots begun ter straighten out'n Henry's ha'r; en w'en de leaves begin ter fall, Henry's ha'r 'mence' ter drap out; en when de vimes 'uz bar', Henry's head wuz baller 'n it wuz in de spring, en he begin ter git ole en stiff in de j'ints ag'in, en paid no mo' 'tention ter de gals dyoin' er de whole winter. En nex' spring, w'en he rub de sap on ag'in, he got young ag'in, en so soopl en libely dat none er de young niggers on de plantation could n' jump, ner dance, ner hoe ez much cotton ez Henry." (*CW* 23–24)

The spell thus conflates Henry's physical well-being with the cycles of growth, dormancy, and regeneration of the grapevines. This conflation also prepares the ground for a highly metaphoric discussion of the economic ruthlessness inherent to the slave system.

A typical slave owner in Chesnutt's works,[30] Dugal' McAdoo—for whom, Julius explains, "'it ha' ter be a mighty rainy day when he could n' fine sump'n fer his niggers ter do, en . . . [it] ha' ter be a monst'us cloudy night when a dollar git by him in de darkness'" (*CW* 24)—notes this pattern of deterioration and renewal, and he devises a scheme by which to profit from Henry's fluctuations of strength and energy. During Henry's vibrant season, the spring, the slave's physical vigor and robustness make him a valuable commodity, one which McAdoo sells for a large sum; and then, in the fall when Henry seems on the brink of death, the slaveowner reacquires him for a significantly smaller amount, thus profiting on the seasonal difference in Henry's net worth. This plan works so well that McAdoo is able to purchase another plantation from his proceeds on Henry alone. But this successful enterprise eventually comes to an end when McAdoo, the victim of his own greed, takes advice on how to make his crops even more lucrative from a Yankee confidence man: the crops and Henry ultimately die.

Thus Julius's embedded narrative about Henry's fate literalizes the conflation of African Americans and property, in this case transforming a black man into the very land he works. For here, Henry becomes literally a part of the crop McAdoo cultivates, harvests, and profits from every season. Henry functions as another form of currency by which this plantation owner does his business, and the story thereby offers John an incisive commentary on the treatment of blacks (and the economics of slavery) in the Old South. Julius rearticulates this conflation several times in "The Goophered Grapevine," including his sly revision of a familiar aphorism to explain McAdoo's rationale for pampering Henry in the off-season:

> "He tuk good keer uv 'im dyoin' er de winter,—give 'im w'iskey ter rub his rheumatiz en terbacker ter smoke, en all he want ter eat,—'caze a nigger w'at he could make a thousan' dollars a year off'n did n' grow on eve'y huckleberry bush." (*CW* 27)

And Julius emphasizes the conflation of Henry and the land once more with this wry description of how the Yankee's role in McAdoo's bad fortune with his crops inspired the plantation owner to assemble, with deep enthusiasm, a regiment to fight in the Civil War: "'Mars Dugal' tuk on might'ly 'bout losin' his vimes en his nigger in de same year. . . . He say he wuz mighty glad dat wah come, en he des want ter kill a Yankee fer eve'y dollar he los' 'long er dat grape-raisin' Yankee'" (*CW* 32). The embittered McAdoo envisions his loss as strictly financial, and he plans to repay the debt by killing other Yankees. The story thus consistently measures black human life in naked economic terms.[31]

But beyond merely offering a moralistic account of the insensitivity of whites in their treatment of blacks, Julius's story also indicates the degree to which Aunt Peggy proves less than a constant ally to her people. She willingly aids McAdoo—her motives, like everyone else's, are apparently economic—in his quest to intimidate grape poachers, suggesting that even the supernatural world cannot escape the crass economics of the marketplace. And, according to Julius, Peggy also "'went out ridin' de niggers at night, fer she wuz a witch 'sides bein' a cunjah 'oman'" (*CW* 15). Although she helps slaves in others of these stories, always for a price, Peggy is established in this first narrative as a dangerous and amoral ally, and not as some sort of just rescuer. And the goopher itself is introduced not as a means of redressing wrongs visited on blacks but as a method of enforcement for the white plantation owner and his authority. Hence, Julius does not seem to envision goopher as a weapon of social protest. In fact, the extent to which the magic is linked metaphorically with economics becomes apparent when he describes how McAdoo "'peared ter be bewitch' wid dat Yankee'" and his promise to double McAdoo's profits (28–29).

His inclusion of goopher as a storytelling device introduces a kind of literary referendum on the question of belief for Julius's readers: John, Annie, and us. We quickly recognize that, despite the rhetorical maneuvering and the economic motivations that characterize both narrators, their belief systems diverge sharply. For Julius's narrative in many ways directly comments upon what John has told us in his introduction to the story. John opens the work, for example, by relating how he had decided to move south on the advice of a doctor, "in whose skill and honesty I had implicit confidence" (*CW* 1). Thus we learn of John's faith in science, a belief system Julius scorns twice in his account of Henry's cycle of de- and re-generation. The first time occurs when Peggy's goopher claims two unwary victims, deaths the "'[w]'ite folks'" attribute to "'fevuh, but de niggers knowed it wuz goopher'" (17). Julius similarly expresses *his* disbelief when narrating the inability of a plantation owner to explain Henry's deterioration:

> "He sent fer a mighty fine doctor, but de med'cine did n' 'pear ter do no good; de goopher had a good holt. Henry tole de doctor 'bout de goopher, but de doctor des laff at 'im." (25)

While John scorns the idea of goopher in almost all of the conjure stories, Julius here establishes the parameters of his own beliefs, and science occupies in his philosophy roughly the same position of irrelevancy as that to which John relegates magic in his universe of belief.

The frame and the embedded story thus comment on and revise each other, a pattern that persists throughout the series. When Julius concludes his account of how the vineyard came to be goophered, John and Annie form a primary audience, and a type of chorus, albeit a discordant one. John expresses, for example, what comes to be his customary skepticism about Julius's narrative: when Julius warns him that the vines will probably not survive long, John says, "'But I thought you said all the old vines died'" (*CW* 33). Annie, however, occupies the middle territory between Julius's occult explanations for events and John's reliance on strict empiricism and logic: "'Is that story true?' asked Annie doubtfully, but seriously, as the old man concluded his narrative" (33). This depiction of her attitude—she can question Julius "doubtfully, but seriously"—reveals the economy of Chesnutt's narrative skill. With three words he captures the essence of her philosophy, which is a kind of hybrid of the two narrators'. Her mediation of their divergent philosophies proves so successful that by the time Chesnutt wrote "The Marked Tree," her perspective had already become internalized in Julius and John. Hence, her presence is unnecessary in that final story of the series, wherein the two narrators come to believe one another.

But in this first story Annie functions as a surrogate for much of Chesnutt's audience, in that she lacks the certainty of perspective her two companions profess. Like us, she cannot commit to either man's explanation of events. She is established in the series, then, as the only character who has access to both the empirical universe her husband articulates and the supernatural world conjured up by Julius. She therefore has the responsibility of judging each story on its own merits, rather than dismissing all of them, as John does, on principle, and she regularly exercises her status as a free-agent reader: at the end of "The Conjurer's Revenge," for example, Annie sides with her husband when she tells Julius that the tale "'is n't pathetic, it has no moral that I can discover, and I can't see why you should tell it. In fact, it seems to me like nonsense'" (*CW* 127). She takes the opposite tack at the end of "Sis' Becky's Pickaninny," the conclusion of which features a disagreement between husband and wife over the merit of Julius's narrative. When John calls the work an "'ingenious fairy tale,'" Annie responds, "'Why, John! . . . the story bears the stamp of truth, if ever a story did'" (159). Hence, like the outside reader, Annie occupies a position of flux within the dynamic of the series-long debate between John and Julius.

While Annie seems to validate our own uncertainty about the stories being told, Chesnutt reinforces the reader's sense of dislocation or flux with his refusal to establish a tangible setting for "The Goophered Grapevine." Note how pointedly the story denies outside readers specific information: when, for example, John first describes his prospective new home, he tells us that it is "a quaint old town, which I shall call Patesville, because, for one reason, that is not its name" (*CW* 3). Appearing as it does in the first of *The Conjure Woman* series, this statement aggressively calls attention to the work as *fiction*. The author similarly chooses not to divulge specifically when the story occurs. We learn only that "[i]t was a sufficient time after the war for conditions in the South to have become somewhat settled" (2). Chesnutt thus refuses to allow his readers to establish a comfortable temporal or geographic relationship with the text; in short, he forces those readers, virtually all of whom would have been accustomed to the far more literal and grounded literary representations crafted by writers of slave narratives, to rethink their attitudes in regard to "black" writing. This unsettled and unstable reading position also derives in part from the extent to which the embedded narratives insist on exploring what Eric Sundquist calls "[t]he marginal world between redaction and invention" and "the marginal world between slavery and freedom" (360). For Sundquist, *The Conjure Woman,* and particularly Julius's narratives within the larger frames, "became a probing theoretical statement about the transition between oral and literary forms in African American culture" (361).

Sundquist has a point. But the interplay between the two frames also charts the transition between reading positions for the audience(s) of these narratives. It reifies the intersection of two traditionally exclusive belief systems, and forces the reader, like Annie, to occupy what Hawthorne might describe as the space between. Hence, Chesnutt's continuing revisions of his narrators' relationship as the series progresses contribute to our sense of the fluidity of this dialogue. Perhaps the most dramatic evidence of this designed instability is that Chesnutt revised "The Goophered Grapevine" more than ten years after its initial publication and before it appeared as the first story in *The Conjure Woman.* The work initially published in the *Atlantic Monthly* in 1887—which introduced the characters and established their roles for the entire series—underwent fairly extensive revisions, which substantively alter our understanding of the conjure stories to follow.

The most provocative change, according to R. V. Burnette, involves Chesnutt's reclassification of Julius's race identification: originally a "venerable-looking colored man" (*AM* 254) in the 1887 version, Julius transforms into a "venerable-looking colored man" who "was not entirely black" (*CW* 8–9) by the time *The Conjure Woman* collection reached print in 1899. While Burnette rightly points out some of the thematic implications of these revisions—mostly having to do with the author's interest in mulattoes—he ultimately concludes that this transformation of Julius into a "not entirely black" man confirms the notion that Chesnutt was advocating the assimilation of light-skinned blacks into white society. Burnette attributes this revision, then, to the author's desire to placate his white audience: "As a result of this conviction," writes Burnette, "the Uncle Julius stories, despite their frequently impressive craftsmanship, were abandoned, as Chesnutt opted for a different strategy and subjects that confronted racial issues more directly" (453). But Chesnutt did *not* abandon the series—he wrote four of the Uncle Julius stories after the publication of *The Conjure Woman*—and therefore the revisions of "The Goophered Grapevine" must have had a different motive.

By altering his work, Chesnutt destabilizes even further the reading position of his audience, who collectively are forced to reassess their perceptions of the entire series. Another of the revisions adds a scene at a literal crossroads, a place where John and Annie are "in doubt as to the turn to take" (*CW* 7). This scene prepares us for the figurative crossroads Julius's tales will make all his readers—both inside and outside of the narrative frame—confront by the end of the series.[32] But the transformation of Julius particularly resonates because it seems so perfectly to capture the essence of the stories: the inside storyteller—who constructs tales that relate the transformations of his characters—undergoes a metamorphosis of his own at the hands of *his* creator. And we are left to wonder, like John, just what Julius means, and perhaps, which Julius means it. By the end of "The Marked Tree," however, *both* of the narrators have had their philosophical positions reshaped by the other. Ultimately, the debate between John and Julius might more profitably be envisioned as an evolution of ideas and beliefs rather than an articulation of Chesnutt's fixed philosophy. In a series that includes fourteen stories and spans more than thirty-five years—from the publication of the initial story to the appearance of "The Marked Tree"—the works collectively suggest that belief is a commodity that can only be acquired gradually. "The Goophered Grapevine" establishes the terms for this acquisition, but, as Chesnutt's revisions of the first work in the series attest, even those terms are subject to retroactive renegotiation.[33]

5/ Speaking For (and Against) Each Other

The Inside Narratives

When a lynch-mob confronts Sheriff Campbell of Branson County at the door of his jail to demand that he turn over a black prisoner, the sheriff refuses, but not before asserting the dual impulses of his personal and professional selves: "'I'm a white man outside,'" he tells them, "'but in this jail I'm sheriff'" (*CS* 140). Chesnutt returns to this divided-self motif later in the same story, "The Sheriff's Children," when the sheriff's mulatto son, the prisoner so precariously lodged in the jail, explains his urge to escape despite no longer wanting to live: "'It is the animal in me, not the man, that flees the gallows'" (145). Both protagonists thus characterize themselves by emphasizing their own duality, an emphasis that typifies much of Chesnutt's short fiction in two ways. First, identity functions here—as it does in much turn-of-the-century African-American literature—as a primary thematic concern, with many of Chesnutt's characters striving to construct or reconstruct their sense of self in a society remaking itself following the Civil War. Second, the author uses a divided or asymmetrical narrative structure in several works as a means of illuminating the social and cultural situations confronting African Americans (and women) during the late nineteenth century. Partly because his works regularly feature characters who, for various social and personal reasons, "mask" themselves or are masked by others, Chesnutt chose not to tell their stories through the medium of a single, unified voice.[1] Instead, he devised a narrative framework that combines the advantages of a detached perspective with the immediacy of an eyewitness account.

While a third-person narrator introduces each of the ten stories in this group—listed below, with dates of publication— Chesnutt embeds within that frame a personal narrative by a character (generally an African-American woman) who relates an extended tale in her own words.[2] Often told in dialect, these emotionally charged first-person accounts force readers to confront more immediate and powerful "inside" narratives.[3] At least one character—and as many as three—in each of these works relates her story directly to the reader: the "inside" narrators thus *compose* a substantial text of their own lives within (and often against) the social and cultural contexts established by the more detached "outside" narrators. In this asymmetrical narrative partnership, the primary narrators in many ways represent the mainstream, largely white community, and their renderings of characters embroiled in "color line" issues, while usually sympathetic, are highly detached, and often ironic. Hence, Chesnutt erects a sort of "master" narrative, one that presumably epitomizes the attitudes of a white reading audience toward African Americans. The "inside" tales, in contrast, foreground other, traditionally less empowered, voices, especially those of blacks and women. These inside narratives interrupt and thus reshape the pat conceptions regarding blacks that are intrinsic to the master social narrative of the late nineteenth century in America. Chesnutt experimented with this narrative paradigm quite early in his career, and he used it regularly to explore what would become familiar thematic ground.[4] Ten of his stories conform to this rubric: "The Fall of Adam" (1886), "Aunt Lucy's Search" (1887), "The Sheriff's Children" (1889), "A Limb of Satan" (before 1900), "White Weeds" (date of composition unknown),[5] "The Wife of His Youth" (1898), "Her Virginia Mammy" (1899), "Cicely's Dream" (1899), "The March of Progress" (1901), and "The Doll" (1912).

Chesnutt's choice of an imbalanced narrative structure for these stories seems particularly fitting given the extent to which his protagonists, like Sheriff Campbell and his son, have to struggle against their *fin de siècle* society to reconstruct their splintered identities. As a means of examining the broader process of social reconstruction, each story depicts the attempts of black families to form or re-form in a turbulent cultural context. "The Fall of Adam" and "Aunt Lucy's Search," for example, both depict black characters seeking to rebuild communities, although the two works approach the topic from vastly different angles of vision. The first story comically infuses folklore into the Bible as a preacher tries to explain to a skeptical congregation how African Americans figure in the "family" of God. The second story—which in both plot and narrative structure anticipates the more sophisticated "The Wife of His Youth"—melodramatically renders a woman's quest to locate each of her children following the Civil War. "A Limb of Satan" is a humorous account of the tenuous reunion of a cranky old man and his equally ill-tempered grandson. And "White Weeds" chronicles the deterioration of a marriage after a man receives an anonymous (and hence not definitive) letter alleging that his bride has black ancestry.[6]

This chapter will in large measure focus on the other six fictions that share this "divided" narrative paradigm; each of them likewise foregrounds familial relationships as thematic linchpins. In "The Doll," for example, a successful black businessman's confrontation with his father's murderer forces him to choose between personal revenge and social and family responsibility; in "Her Virginia Mammy," a black mother who has spent her life searching for her long-lost daughter must ultimately deny their relationship in order to protect the young woman's marital prospects; and, in "Cicely's Dream," the protagonist falls in love with an amnesiac she has nursed back to health only to lose him when the past reasserts itself in his life.

These stories have obvious thematic and stylistic similarities, but none so pronounced as their shared interest in genealogy, an issue which, according to Kimberly W. Benston, resonates throughout African-American literature:

> For the Afro-American, then, self-creation and reformation of a fragmented familial past are endlessly interwoven: naming is inevitably genealogical revisionism. All of Afro-American literature may be seen as one vast genealogical poem that attempts to restore continuity to the ruptures or discontinuities imposed by the history of black presence in America. (152)

If Benston is right about black literature forming "one vast genealogical poem," then Chesnutt contributes his best stanza with this group of stories, in which he emphasizes the crucial role played by storytelling in the healing (or overcoming) of "ruptures" engendered by "a fragmented familial past." While he gestures toward re-imagining the American family in broader, more multiracial terms throughout his career, fictions such as "Her Virginia Mammy," "Cicely's Dream," and "The Wife of His Youth" represent his most thorough and ambitious contemplations of these issues.

Even the very act of *preserving* one's family, however, can sometimes produce those "ruptures," a theme Chesnutt dramatizes to impressive effect in "The Doll," published in *The Crisis* in 1912. The plot depicts the attempts of a successful black barber, Tom Taylor, to reconcile his responsibilities to his daughter with the chance to avenge his father's murder. When the murderer—Colonel Forsyth, now a southern politician—comes to Taylor's barbershop one day and narrates his crime in excruciating detail while being shaved by Taylor, the reader might recall Melville's "Benito Cereno." One major difference, however, is that, unlike the beleaguered captain of Melville's story, Forsyth has *chosen* to put himself under the razor of his victim's son; in fact, he tells his tale precisely to prove to a northern associate, Judge Beeman, that blacks are fundamentally submissive, even under circumstances as extraordinary as listening to the murderer of one's father revisit his act. Blacks, Forsyth tells Judge Beeman, "'are born to serve and submit. If they had been worthy of equality they would never have endured slavery. They have no proper self-respect; they will neither resent an insult, nor defend a right, nor avenge a wrong'" (*SF* 406). When Beeman objects to this dismissive classification, Forsyth's response sets the stage for the story's conflict: "'Come downstairs to the barber shop,'" he tells the judge, "'and I'll prove what I say'" (*SF* 406).

Colonel Forsyth then delivers his version of the killing in a fairly long embedded narrative, told expressly to prove that African Americans, as represented by Tom Taylor, will not avenge an egregious wrong:

> "The girl [Tom's sister] was guilty of some misconduct, and my mother reprimanded her and sent her home. She complained to her father, and he came to see my mother about it. He was insolent, offensive and threatening. I came into the room and ordered him to leave it. Instead of obeying, he turned on me in a rage, suh, and threatened me. I drew my revolver and shot him. The result was unfortunate; but he and his people learned a lesson. We had no further trouble with bumptious niggers in our town." (*SF* 408)

The manner in which this embedded narrative functions within the larger context of the story conforms for the most part to the narrative paradigm Chesnutt uses in earlier fictions. One character, here Colonel Forsyth, has the opportunity to articulate his own story in his own words. In two crucial areas, however, "The Doll" differs radically from the other stories to be considered in this chapter.

The first difference lies in Taylor's response to Forsyth's narrative. While "Her Virginia Mammy," "Cicely's Dream," and "The Wife of His Youth" feature at least two quoted embedded narratives of substantial length, "The Doll" changes the pattern. Although the story includes Taylor's response to Forsyth—given immediately following the colonel's performance—it is not articulated by Taylor himself; instead, the narrator summarizes Taylor's version:

> The barber had heard the same story, with some details
> ignored or forgotten by the colonel. It was the barber's father
> who had died at the colonel's hand, and for many long years
> the son had dreamed of this meeting.
> He remembered the story in this wise. . . . (*SF* 408)

As summarized by the narrator, Taylor's account of the episode between his father and Forsyth, with only a few minor exceptions, "had been much as the colonel had related it" (409).

Rather than focusing (as Faulkner would more than twenty years later in *Absalom, Absalom!*) on competing accounts of the same event, then, "The Doll" instead examines the *effects* of Forsyth's two actions—the killing of Taylor's father and the subsequent retelling of it. Thus, the primary narrating voice devotes most of the remainder of the story to relating Tom's mental struggle over whether or not he should kill Forsyth. Despite the obvious appeal of revenge, such a course, the barber realizes, would have far broader consequences than determining his own fate: the shop, "a medium of friendly contact with white men, would be lost to his people" (*SF* 411); his employees would lose their livelihood; and, most important, his daughter, of whom he is reminded by the sight of her doll he has promised to fix, would lose her father.[7]

The second way "The Doll" diverges from the narrative pattern typical for this cluster of stories has to do with the authority seemingly granted Forsyth's account. While the other stories using this narrative paradigm give voice, in effect, to the traditionally voiceless, "The Doll" permits a profoundly unsympathetic figure to express himself through an embedded narrative. That is, Chesnutt usually empowers the downtrodden and isolated among his characters—friendless ex-slaves, unmarried white schoolmistresses, mulatto outlaws—by having them speak convincingly and movingly for themselves. But here, a successful southern white politician who "had ridden into power on his hostility to Negro rights" (*SF* 409) enjoys direct access to readers. Why, one might ask, would Chesnutt give voice to an unreconstructed oppressor? The narratological and rhetorical structuring of "The Doll" might provide some answers.

By focusing on the effects of Forsyth's account, Chesnutt thereby foregrounds the readers of the colonel's narrative, including Tom Taylor, Judge Beeman, and the outside audience. As narratee, Taylor enlists the reader's sympathy as a reasonable man pushed to the brink by the brutality enacted (and later narrated) by Forsyth. Despite Taylor's ability to maintain a stoical demeanor, Forsyth's narrative nevertheless triggers in Tom an emotional turmoil with which the reader might easily empathize:

> The colonel's eyes were closed, or he might have observed the sudden gleam of interest that broke through the barber's mask of self-effacement, like a flash of lightning from a clouded sky. Involuntarily the razor remained poised in midair, but, in less time than it takes to say it, was moving again, swiftly and smoothly, over the colonel's face. (*SF* 407)

Taylor plainly does not conform to Forsyth's paradigm of the "submissive Negro"—the colonel is obviously the story's *worst* reader—and this passage captures how acutely he does resent a wrong. Forsyth's claim that blacks "'have no proper self-respect'" (*SF* 406) is emphatically refuted by Taylor's subsequent response to him. Like Dr. Miller in *The Marrow of Tradition* (1901), Taylor effectively prioritizes his responsibilities and emotions, thereby establishing him in the reader's mind as the more civilized participant in this "debate."

Should the reader need more prompting, Chesnutt includes another internal reader, and one clearly established as a proxy for his turn-of-the-century audience. As his title implies, Judge Beeman is professionally well qualified to weigh the merits of each man's actions, and as a political intimate of Forsyth and a frequent customer of Taylor's, he projects an aura of impartiality.[8] Beeman's reaction is, in fact, so central to Chesnutt's purpose in the story that the judge's thoughts essentially conclude the story: "The judge was not sure that the colonel had proved his theory, and was less so after he had talked, a week later, with the barber" (*SF* 412). Hence, Chesnutt focuses attention here on the second narratee (or internal reader) of Forsyth's narrative, who seems to endorse, albeit tepidly, Taylor's position. Although perhaps not a newly converted champion of liberal race doctrines, Beeman nevertheless acknowledges his serious reservations about Forsyth's "theory" of blackness. Thus, the effect these events have on Beeman— resulting in a tentative comprehension of the black man's behavior—might well epitomize the effect Chesnutt hoped to reproduce on his supposed white reading audience. By the 1912 publication of "The Doll," Chesnutt had resigned himself to a certain pragmatism on race matters, and the grand ambitions he announced in an early journal entry to "elevate" white readers seem to have given way to this more realistic objective.[9]

Between Taylor's thoughtful and deliberate reaction to Forsyth's narrative and Beeman's impartial judgment, Chesnutt rhetorically overwhelms the voice he had apparently privileged at the beginning of this story. By depicting how two reasonable men, one white and the other black, respond to Forsyth's application of "theory," the author induces his readers to reconsider their own positions on race. The story has perhaps even more of an edge, though. By arranging the narrative elements in this way, Chesnutt has also emphatically dramatized how African Americans at the turn of the century were virtually silenced. For whether one recognizes the heroism of Taylor's restraint or not, it is clear that *any* action he takes—even verbal—while Forsyth sits in his barber chair will result in dire consequences for the barber and his family. In this way, "The Doll" anticipates *Their Eyes Were Watching God,* Hurston's account of a strong black woman who struggles against the recurrent efforts by a variety of sources—her husbands, the female community, the white judicial system—to silence her.

Although Taylor cannot avenge his father's murder nor even verbally confront the murderer, Chesnutt nevertheless makes clear that he is the best reader in the story. For Taylor not only intuits the purpose of Forsyth's narrative, he alone fully comprehends the cultural milieu in which he must formulate a response to that narrative. Thus, Taylor's very inaction—which the colonel mistakenly reads as confirmation of his "theory" and which seemingly accounts for Beeman's lukewarm dismissal of that theory—instead constitutes a man's deliberative, even heroic resolve to keep his family intact, a theme one finds throughout Chesnutt's fiction.

The remaining Chesnutt stories of this narrative type similarly emphasize the importance of creating and maintaining family bonds, but they treat the theme from a much different perspective. While "The Doll" and "The Sheriff's Children" explore issues of family from predominantly masculine positions, seven of the eight other stories focus on how late-nineteenth-century American women, both black and white, work to remake or protect their families. Indeed, Chesnutt locates feminine perspectives at the core of "The Wife of His Youth," "Her Virginia Mammy," "Cicely's Dream," "The March of Progress," "White Weeds," "A Limb of Satan," and "Aunt Lucy's Search."[10]

"Her Virginia Mammy," for example, examines just how complex identity-construction could be for a late-nineteenth-century woman with an uncertain family history. Like other Chesnutt fictions, the story explores race issues, but it suggests that while women must struggle, like men, to fashion personal and family identities during (and after) Reconstruction, the two sexes envision their problems in significantly different terms. First published in *The Wife of His Youth* (1899), the story features Clara Hohlfelder, the adopted daughter of German immigrants who refuses to marry until she can verify the worthiness of her blood family. "'You know I love you, John,'" Clara tells the man who has just proposed to her, "'and why I do not say what you wish. You must give me a little more time to make up my mind before I consent to burden you with a nameless wife, one who does not know who her mother was'" (*CS* 115). Clara's refusal to marry a man of "pure" blood—his ancestors include "'the governor and the judge and the Harvard professor and the *Mayflower* pilgrim'" (116)—derives from her fear that she comes from common stock.

While the light-skinned Clara dreads the possibility of having coarse ancestry, she never considers the true case: she is a mulatta. Clara ultimately meets the woman—Mrs. Harper, really her mother—who can answer her genealogical concerns. But when Mrs. Harper learns that Clara's marital hopes depend upon the purity of her blood, she does not refute her daughter's mistaken guess that the older woman is her "Virginia mammy." In another writer's hands, such a plot might easily devolve into mawkish sentimentality, but Chesnutt manipulates the story in such a way as to minimize the importance of the pair's coincidental discovery of one another after so many years of separation. Instead, he focuses on the way Clara and Mrs. Harper deliver their own stories to each other, forming what Susan Fraiman calls "a long, caressing conversation in which the two women piece together their common past" (446). But this scene has bite to it as well, which becomes clear when Mrs. Harper ultimately and purposefully subverts the conversation: by choosing to omit one crucial detail of her own story—her real relationship to Clara—she consciously permits her daughter to form an inaccurate conception of her race identity. Mrs. Harper's selfless act thus allows Clara to marry and therefore to build a family, at a huge cost to herself and her own dreams of family reconstruction.

By focusing on how Clara and Mrs. Harper exchange and reshape one another's narratives—and especially the latter's reluctant affirmation of her daughter's mistaken genealogical beliefs—Chesnutt examines the construction of family from a less literal perspective than elsewhere in his fiction. Through the telling of her carefully crafted narrative, which she modifies *in medias res* for Clara's benefit, Mrs. Harper *composes* a family for her daughter, even at the exclusion of herself. Rather than rely on literal "blood" connections—as an ex-slave, she had seen her own union condemned by her husband's prestigious slave-owning family—Mrs. Harper (and later John) instead expands the very notion of family, translating a genealogical construct into a linguistic one. In thus fashioning a more inclusive model of family, one that takes its form from the narrative exchanges that lie at the heart of the stories in this cluster, Chesnutt establishes a trope that likewise informs "Cicely's Dream," "The March of Progress," and "The Wife of His Youth."

Despite the maudlin nature of the plot, Chesnutt infuses "Her Virginia Mammy" with rich ironies, and in a context one rarely associates with irony. Throughout a story that initially appears to conform to the stereotypical "tragic mulatto" paradigm,[11] Clara's actions and words provide a darkly comic foreshadowing of what the reader comes to learn. Clara teaches dancing, for example, to a class of black pupils, although the decision to do so has not been an easy one, as the narrator points out: "Personally she had no such prejudice, except perhaps a little shrinking at the thought of personal contact with the dark faces of whom Americans always think when 'colored people' are spoken of" (*CS* 119). Once she accepts the class, her views grow more expansively liberal, and she tells John, "'I hardly think of them as any different from other people. I feel perfectly at home among them'" (121).

Other characters' comments similarly generate dramatic irony. Early in the story, for example, Clara's suitor attempts to placate his lover's "blood" concerns by telling her not to brood on the subject to the exclusion of life's pleasures: "'It is a fine thing, too,'" John says, "'to be able to enjoy the *passing* moment. One of your greatest charms in my eyes, Clara, is that in your *lighter* moods you have this faculty'" (*CS* 121, emphasis added). Chesnutt here puns on passing, a term often used in reference to African Americans who choose to live as white, and a subject about which few authors make such jests.[12] In addition to foreshadowing the culmination of the plot, these subtle (and almost uncomfortably comic) ironies also emphasize the extent to which Mrs. Harper's genealogical lie, when combined with Clara's light-colored skin, will insure that the young woman enjoys a future made up exclusively of "passing moments."

Mrs. Harper also articulates ironies—clearly with more self-consciousness than Clara or John demonstrates—by using the same term in consecutive sentences to reify vastly different realities. When Clara asks about her blood parents' backgrounds, for example, the older woman replies, "'Your father was a Virginia gentleman, and *belonged* to one of the first families . . . [and] Your mother—also *belonged* to one of the first families of Virginia'" (*CS* 127–28, emphasis added). The second use of "belonged" has, of course, a more literal connotation here, one that reveals Mrs. Harper's past status as a slave. Finally, the story's most piercing irony comes after Mrs. Harper has delivered Clara's incomplete (and therefore misleading) family information, confirming the young woman's fantasy that she comes from "pure" bloodlines: "'I knew it must be so,'" Clara tells Mrs. Harper, who must want either to giggle or scream at her daughter's profound misreading of her heritage, "'Blood will always tell'" (127). Here Clara's fragile psyche is protected, in fact, precisely because "blood" (Mrs. Harper) will not "tell."

Despite this ironic treatment of the heroine, the story ends with the betrothal of this racially mixed couple, an event which William L. Andrews suggests took "the question of miscegenation out of the realm of abstract moral prohibition and made it a matter of personal ethical decision" (*CS* xv).[13] The person who must decide this question, however, is neither Clara nor Mrs. Harper, but John, the man who willingly chooses to marry a woman with black ancestry. Although no one expresses the idea openly, and Clara certainly misses the signposts, John clearly recognizes that Mrs. Harper and Clara share bloodlines:

> Then she [Clara] told him Mrs. Harper's story. He listened attentively and sympathetically, at certain points taking his eyes from Clara's face and glancing keenly at Mrs. Harper, who was listening intently. As he looked from one to the other he noticed the resemblance between them, and something in his expression caused Mrs. Harper's eyes to fall, and then glance up appealingly. (*CS* 130)

Despite his recognition of the family resemblance, John neither reveals his understanding to Clara nor cancels the engagement.

This passage partly illuminates the web of Chesnutt's complex thematic and narrative intentions. The two women inextricably linked by blood but separated by circumstance are once more reunited here symbolically when Clara takes on the telling of Mrs. Harper's story. In the retelling, Clara becomes a surrogate narrator for her mother, and simultaneously reveals her true genealogy to John, who "reads" both the story itself and the subtext Clara cannot decode. "Her Virginia Mammy" thus ultimately suggests that both extremes of the racial polarity—a Boston Brahmin and an ex-slave—can place the idea of "family" on a higher plane than race or "blood." And while Clara's obsession with the past forces Mrs. Harper and John to mislead her, Chesnutt seems here to devalue the importance of the past as a shaper of identity. Standing in marked contrast to Morrison's *Song of Solomon,* Walker's *The Color Purple,* and Griggs's *Imperium in Imperio,* among many other works by black writers that insist on the importance of tracing one's roots, "Her Virginia Mammy" stresses instead the advantages to be derived from *de-emphasizing* ancestry.

It seems likely, in fact, that John speaks for the author when he offers, long before learning of Clara's true heritage, this rebuttal to her concerns about her bloodlines:

> "We are all worms of the dust, and if we go back far enough, each of us has had millions of ancestors; peasants and serfs, most of them; thieves, murderers, and vagabonds, many of them, no doubt; and therefore the best of us have but little to boast of. Yet we are all made after God's own image, and formed by his hand, for his ends; and therefore not to be lightly despised, even the humblest of us, least of all by ourselves. For the past we can claim no credit, for those who made it died with it. Our destiny lies in the future." (*CS* 118)

Significantly, although John had outlined this position while still under the impression that Clara's ancestry was "merely" common, he does not renounce this idealistic philosophy once he recognizes the truth.

Faced with the imminent marriage of John and Clara at the conclusion of "Her Virginia Mammy," modern readers have noted the potentially subversive qualities of the work. It might easily be read, as Andrews suggests, as an endorsement of miscegenation, a dangerous position for a turn-of-the-century black writer to take. In another recent reading, Fraiman foregrounds the importance of gender in "Her Virginia Mammy," a story which, while "most overtly a tale of racial identity," is "also a tale of *female* identity. I suggest a reading that focuses less on black-white relationships than on mother-daughter relationships, less on race than on generation and gender. Such a reading should not diminish but, on the contrary, heighten our attention to race in this story; in Chesnutt the issues of gender and race overlap with and serve to amplify one another" (444). Fraiman's discussion of "Her Virginia Mammy" positions the work within a matrix of *both* gender and race, a locus that is dramatically apparent as well in "Cicely's Dream" and "The March of Progress."[14]

But while Fraiman is right in seeing "Her Virginia Mammy" as an important and neglected work that encases the author's sensitivity to the importance of gender in identity-construction, it is also one of Chesnutt's most pointed metacritical commentaries on his readers, both of his own day and ours. The story's ironies collude to establish Clara—whose name ironically suggests racial purity—as the proxy for late-nineteenth-century white readers. Like Sheriff Campbell in "The Sheriff's Children," Clara is a benevolent but befuddled reader of the world around her, especially when confronted with texts that challenge her preconceived notions of blackness (notions that insist, for instance, that an older black woman must be "mammy" rather than "mother").

Unlike the sheriff, though, Clara is protected from the consequences of her misreading, leading to what might seem to be a happy ending for her. Yet it is precisely within the nature of that protection that Chesnutt calls the story's ending—and benevolent white readers' sense of self—into question. For Clara's happiness and ability to carry on with her life come only at enormous cost: her enforced and continuing ignorance of the most intimate details of her personal—and racial—history. Through the deceived but content Clara, Chesnutt thus mocks the very idea of a secure identity, thereby warning that the racial complacency of even the most sympathetic white reader may well have hidden costs. In a story whose "happy" ending likely would have appealed to readers with unexamined assumptions about racial identity, then, Chesnutt dramatically embeds an incisive satire of those readers. Just as provocative, though, is the manner in which Chesnutt calls attention to the very nature of the family formed at the end of "Her Virginia Mammy." For by the conclusion of the story, the apparently progressive John has suddenly transformed into an ominously magisterial presence. As Clara celebrates her newfound identity—"'Clara Stafford,' mused the girl. 'It is a pretty name'" (*CS* 130)—John immediately usurps it: "'You will never have to use it,'" he tells her, "'for now you will take mine'" (130). Even Clara, not the most astute of readers, seems to intuit her husband's intentions here when she laments, "'Then I shall have nothing left of all that I have found'" (130). And John's final act in the narrative—he puts "his arm around [Clara], with an air of assured *possession*" (130, emphasis added)—resonates forebodingly with the diction of slavery. Thus, while John appears entirely satisfied with the outcome of events, the two women pay differing but profound costs for the formation of this particular family.

If the optimism raised by Clara's impending marriage is tempered by the price at which she achieves it, the other stories which highlight feminine perspectives articulate still more pessimistic readings of their characters' chances of creating or preserving their families. "Cicely's Dream," for example, might easily be read as an answer to "Her Virginia Mammy," in that both consider interracial love. But while the latter story concludes with a marriage, the former depicts how Cicely, a young black woman, must confront the grim consequences of her falling in love with a white man, although the circumstances of the story collude to hide his race from her until it is too late. The plot has Cicely finding a badly wounded young amnesiac of indeterminate race—an adult *tabula rasa*—in the field near her house, and, with her family's help, nursing him back to physical health. Since he has lost his memory and other brain functions, she also has the rare opportunity of constructing an identity for him. In an inversion of what Reconstruction generally meant for blacks, here an African-American woman is enabled to posit an identity for a white man.

Chesnutt sets "Cicely's Dream" in the South during a time of political and social regeneration, and his story mirrors that process on a far more personal level. He focuses on how Cicely re-creates John—her family names him after John the Baptist—as an ideal mate for herself, and John becomes a masculine double of his benefactor. In typical fashion for his canon, Chesnutt here highlights the extent of this doubleness by focusing on voice:

> As time went on Cicely found that he was quick at learning
> things. She taught him to speak her own negro English, which
> he pronounced with absolute fidelity to her intonations; so
> that barring the quality of his voice, his speech was an echo of
> Cicely's own. (*CS* 176)

Not surprisingly, the story emphasizes the degree to which these two characters share speech patterns. For Chesnutt, voice and identity often overlap, and in "Cicely's Dream" the author contrives an inverted tale of "passing," as a white man who speaks "negro English" is accepted into the black community. John's learned identity (and his impending marriage to Cicely) is finally displaced only when he has contact with another voice from his past.

Ultimately, John is "restored to reason and to his world" (*CS* 185) by listening to the embedded narrative of his long-lost fiancée, who just happens to be Cicely's white teacher, a transplanted northerner named Martha Chandler. Martha's moving narrative, ostensibly of how she came to teach blacks in the South, penetrates the fortress of his amnesia and strips away Cicely's reconstructive efforts. In her farewell address to the schoolchildren and their families, Martha's story—purportedly an autobiographical one, which begins "'I want to tell you how I came to be in North Carolina'"—evolves into a tribute to her lost love:

> ". . . so that if I have been able to do anything here among you for which you might feel inclined, in your good nature, to thank me, you may thank not me alone, but another who came before me, and whose work I have but taken up where *he* laid it down. I had a friend,—a dear friend,—why should I be ashamed to say it?—a lover, to whom I was to be married, as I hope all you girls may some day be happily married. His country needed him, and I gave him up. He came to fight for the Union and for Freedom, for he believed that all men are brothers. He did not come back again—he gave up his life for you. Could I do less than he? I came to the land that he sanctified by his death, and I have tried in my weak way to tend the plant he watered with his blood, and which, in the fullness of time, will blossom forth into the perfect flower of liberty."
> (*CS* 185)

In effect, John—or Arthur, the name by which Martha knows him—is the subject of narratives by two women who love him. First, Cicely recreates him as a black companion for herself, and then Martha's eulogy of him as a valiant martyr for freedom reawakens his dormant memory. But the story concludes by defining him once more in relation to a woman: "From that moment his memory of the past was a blank until he recognized Martha on the platform and took up again the thread of his former existence where it had been broken off" (*CS* 185). His identity within the context of the story, therefore, remains completely a feminine (and linguistic) construct.

Chesnutt's narrative construction of the story in many ways mirrors that of "Her Virginia Mammy," in which Clara and Mrs.

Harper compose family identity through the exchange of their stories. While "Cicely's Dream" initially follows that pattern with the personal narratives of Cicely and Martha, the two stories differ in one provocative way. Indeed, the very telling of Martha's story, which allows her to refashion her family by restoring the narrative of her fiancé's past, interrupts *Cicely's* own successful composition of a family bond for herself and John. A literal embodiment of the past—and, suggestively, a white past—thus overwhelms Cicely's voicing of the present and the future in a way that evokes the central tension of "Her Virginia Mammy." But recognizing the potential ruptures that would result from her own role as an incarnation of her daughter's history, Mrs. Harper chooses to shield Clara from the past and its consequences. Although "Cicely's Dream" renders Cicely's ultimate loss of John, it, like "Her Virginia Mammy," nevertheless hints at the optimistic message that, if not for a confrontation with the burden of the past, a young, black, turn-of-the-century woman might very well succeed in forcefully *articulating* her own place in the world.[15]

Cicely ultimately cannot reinscribe herself into a happier position in the world, but her story typifies this cluster of works in that they all resonate with the voices of characters seeking to form or preserve a more broadly defined sense of family. While all of Chesnutt's fiction might be said to explore family relationships, this group of stories suggests a more inclusive idea of family, one that seeks to erase or at least to moderate the barriers that separate men and women, blacks and whites. Ultimately, stories such as "Cicely's Dream," "Her Virginia Mammy," "The Doll," and "The Wife of His Youth" argue that the formation and maintenance of identity is a tricky business, and a constantly shifting one. For in them, Chesnutt has blacks and whites and mulattoes speaking for themselves and for the "other," and these furtive couplings of voices result in a set of truly multicultural texts. Here, he allows a host of diverse and insistent voices to construct identity for themselves and their families. By interweaving personal identity with genealogy and language, Chesnutt traces out the human family tree, whether those branches bear fruit or are victims of blight.

∽

After listening to the story of a woman who has searched for her husband for twenty-five years, the protagonist of "The Wife of His Youth," Mr. Ryder, "stood for a long time before the mirror of his dressing-case, gazing thoughtfully at the reflection of his own face" (*CS* 110). With this scene, Chesnutt literalizes a recurrent theme in his fiction: the search for identity that so many of his characters undertake often culminates in self-reflection. In this case, listening to another's story compels Ryder to ponder his own sense of identity and is but the first step for him in acknowledging a past he had perhaps hoped to escape. The woman's story prompts him to reconstruct his past, through the development of his own storytelling skills, and it also allows him to embrace the future. The result is an apparently optimistic work, and one of the most narratologically subtle of Chesnutt's career.

"The Wife of His Youth" best exemplifies the Chesnutt stories that mediate between the dialogue of "I"-narrators he uses to structure *The Conjure Woman* and the monologic, usually ironic and detached perspectives that characterize stories like "A Matter of Principle" and "The Passing of Grandison." While the former create a dialogue of voices within the fictional construct of the story itself, the latter—told by an anonymous and omnipresent narrator external to the action he narrates—reflect Chesnutt's use of a Howellsian realistic narrative strategy. In "The Wife of His Youth" Chesnutt combines the two narrative strategies by using a detached, gently ironic external voice to handle most of the narration while significant portions of the story are delivered by the two protagonists in their own voices. The story dramatically illustrates Chesnutt's deft handling of radically different voices, a skill he honed through his attention to detail in his dialect works. But while in *The Conjure Woman* he emphasizes the extent to which Julius and John often fail to listen to one another, "The Wife of His Youth" seems to suggest that apparently irreconcilable voices can not only understand each other but can come together to form an harmonious chorus.[16]

By the time "The Wife of His Youth" appeared in the *Atlantic Monthly* (July 1898), Chesnutt had already accumulated more than thirty publications. His early successes—especially "The Goophered Grapevine," "Po' Sandy," and "Dave's Neckliss"— had earned him a reputation, but one that he found confining: he was known as a dialect writer.[17] Despite his eagerness to expand his literary repertoire, he did not rashly abandon his formidable skills in presenting an array of voices, including dialects. The immediate result of Chesnutt's energies in this new direction became the title piece of his collection of mostly non-dialect works published in 1899, *The Wife of His Youth and Other Stories of the Color Line.* As the title suggests, each of the stories in the collection purports to examine racial issues of the time, a focus that resurfaces throughout Chesnutt's canon. All of his novels—*The House Behind the Cedars, The Marrow of Tradition,* and *The Colonel's Dream*—treat the interrelationships of the races, and his one biography is of Frederick Douglass. In addition, he often explored the topic in his nonfiction as well, in essays such as "The Disfranchisement of the Negro," "Obliterating the Color Line," and "The Future American: A Stream of Dark Blood in the Veins of the Southern Whites."

A conscious departure from his dialect frame stories, "The Wife of his Youth" addresses many of the same issues, although finally it offers one of his more ameliorative explorations of the race question. As in *The House Behind the Cedars* and "A Matter of Principle," Chesnutt focuses less on white oppression than on the prejudice and discrimination within the African-American community. The protagonist of this story, Mr. Ryder, is "dean" of a society of African Americans that has come to be known as the "Blue Veins." The purpose of this organization— which Andrews suggests may have had as its source the Cleveland Social Circle, Chesnutt's own club—"was to establish and maintain correct social standards among a people whose social condition presented almost unlimited room for improvement" (*CS* 102). That the Blue Veins' membership is composed of "individuals who were, generally speaking, more white than black" (102), the narrator ironically attributes to accident. Despite the opportunities for divisive commentary, however, the narrator's depiction of these Blue Veins—a group of light-skinned, well-educated African Americans with whom Chesnutt had much in common—remains gently ironic.

Indeed, "The Wife of His Youth" features a primary narrator who might most accurately be described as a wry but sympathetic commentator whose role as ironist diminishes as the voices of his characters gain strength. By the midpoint of the story, in fact, he becomes as much of an arranging presence as a narrator, and he devotes most of his energy to orchestrating the embedded narratives of the two protagonists. Thus, Chesnutt gradually effaces his primary narrator until the voices of his characters finally articulate their own identities without any external mediation from the narrator. In this way, the author fashions one of his best realistic fictions: the narrator merely directs the reader's attention to vital information rather than attempting to interpret events and actions for his audience.[18] Early in the story, however, the narrator establishes the tone by undercutting the pretensions of Mr. Ryder and the other members of the "Blue Vein" club.

Encased in this mildly critical treatment of those who would re-draw racial boundaries in their own favor is a remarkably sentimental love story. While Mr. Ryder prepares a marriage proposal to a young, light-skinned widow named Mrs. Dixon—a proposal he plans to deliver publicly at a Blue Vein function that evening—his meditations are interrupted by an elderly ex-slave named 'Liza Jane. She has come to him seeking help in locating her long-lost husband, separated from her by the random cruelty of slavery. She has been looking, she tells Mr. Ryder, for "Sam Taylor" for the past twenty-five years, but without success. Even the epitome of snobbery, Mr. Ryder, cannot easily dismiss the loyalty and determination of this woman.[19] At the Blue Vein dinner that evening, Mr. Ryder repeats to his guests the woman's story, onto which he grafts an apparently hypothetical conclusion. Suppose the man she seeks had since raised himself to a respected position within the community, he wonders aloud. He further asks them to suppose that the man has learned that his wife, whom he thought dead, had been seeking him for all those years. And, finally, Mr. Ryder asks, "'suppose that perhaps he had set his heart upon another. . . . What would he do, or rather what ought he to do, in such a crisis of a lifetime?'" (*CS* 112). After his guests tearfully respond that this hypothetical man ought to acknowledge her, Mr. Ryder introduces to them the wife of his youth.

Chesnutt spends nearly half of the story establishing the daunting odds that this long-separated couple must overcome to achieve their reunification. He takes great pains to emphasize the extent to which 'Liza Jane embodies precisely what Mr. Ryder has spent most of his adult life trying to avoid. She violates the two primary unwritten principles that the Blue Veins have formulated, that members be light-colored and of free birth. As an ex-slave, she obviously fails the latter criterion, and as to the former, the narrator offers a definitive description: she is "very black,—so black that her toothless gums, revealed when she opened her mouth to speak, were not red, but blue" (*CS* 106). This physical description of 'Liza Jane captures Chesnutt's meticulous handling of imagery: Mr. Ryder, the dean of a club that allegedly permits into their society no one who "was not white enough to show blue veins" (102), ultimately acquiesces to the most intimate society possible with a woman so black that her gums appear blue. The description also emphasizes the physical disparity between 'Liza Jane and Ryder, whose "features were of a refined type," and whose "hair was almost straight" (103).

In addition to the profound difference in appearance between the two, Chesnutt likewise stresses the social impediments to their reunion. 'Liza Jane delivers her speech to a man who, the narrator tells us, lamented the "growing liberality" in social matters that had forced him "to meet in a social way persons whose complexions and callings in life were hardly up to the standard which he considered proper for the society to maintain" (*CS* 105). Indeed, the narrator suggests that as "one of the most conservative" members of the Blue Vein Society, Ryder had become "the custodian of its standards, and the preserver of its traditions" (103). To that end, Ryder hopes his social ball for the Blue Veiners "would serve by its exclusiveness to counteract leveling tendencies, and his marriage to Mrs. Dixon would help to further the upward process of absorption he had been wishing and waiting for" (105).

While their differences in social station and appearance seem overwhelming, the profound contrast in voice most emphatically divides Ryder and 'Liza Jane early in the story. Chesnutt arranges to have them speak in what appear to be two different languages. Ryder's diction and vocabulary do not differ materially from that of the articulate and well-educated narrator, as evidenced by this passage in which the dean of the Blue Veins describes his feelings on the race question:

> "I have no race prejudice," he would say, "but we people of mixed blood are ground between the upper and the nether millstone. Our fate lies between absorption by the white race and extinction in the black. The one does n't want us yet, but may take us in time. The other would welcome us, but it would be for us a backward step. 'With malice towards none, with charity for all,' we must do the best we can for ourselves and those who are to follow us. Self-preservation is the first law of nature." (*CS* 105)

This passage, constituting the first instance in which the protagonist is quoted in the story, establishes Ryder's voice: his polished, elevated language nevertheless calls attention to the obvious philosophical shortcomings of the speech, as well as its utter(ed) hypocrisy.[20]

Compare Ryder's elevated diction to the dialect of 'Liza

Jane, whose speech elicits from the elite Blue Veiner an attitude of "kindly patronage" (*CS* 107): "'scuse me, suh,'" she tells him, "'I's lookin' for my husban'. I heerd you wuz a big man an had libbed heah a long time.'" In order to dramatize even more emphatically the disparity in locution of these two characters, Chesnutt juxtaposes 'Liza Jane's speech with Ryder's reading aloud of Tennyson's poetic descriptions of feminine beauty: Ryder wonders whether the woman to whom he will propose more nearly resembles "'A daughter of the gods, divinely tall'" or "'a part of joyous Spring'" (*CS* 105–6). The scene his ex- and future wife walks into, then, establishes a context of verbal expression that apparently excludes her from his milieu.

Paradoxically, however, 'Liza Jane effectively penetrates Ryder's hypocrisy through her compelling account of her search for "Sam," as told in her own voice:

> "Den de wah broke out, an' w'en it wuz ober de cullud folks wuz scattered. I went back ter de ole home; but Sam wuz n' dere, an' I could n' l'arn nuffin 'bout 'im. But I knowed he 'd be'n dere to look fer me an' had n' foun' me, an' had gone erway ter hunt fer me."
>
> "I's be'n lookin' fer 'im eber sence," she added simply, as though twenty-five years were but a couple of weeks, "an' I knows he's be'n lookin' fer me. Fer he sot a heap er sto' by me, Sam did, an' I know he's be'n huntin' fer me all dese years,— 'less'n he's be'n sick er sump'n, so he could n' work, er out'n his head, so he could n' 'member his promise. I went back down de ribber, fer I 'lowed he'd gone down dere lookin' fer me. I's be'n ter Noo Orleens, an' Atlanty, an Charleston, an' Richmon'; an' w'en I'd be'n all ober de Souf I come ter de Norf. Fer I knows I'll fin' 'im some er dese days," she added softly, "er he 'll fin' me, an' den we'll bofe be as happy in freedom as we wuz in de ole days befo' de wah." (*CS* 108)

This moving description of 'Liza Jane's physically and emotionally devastating odyssey inspires in Mr. Ryder a personal odyssey of his own. But in order for him to complete his journey he first must undergo a step-by-step process that emphasizes the importance of voice in forming or re-forming identity, both individual and family. He successfully completes the first stage of his conversion back to "Sam Taylor" when he listens to 'Liza Jane's narrative. He accomplishes the second when he, like Clara of "Her Virginia Mammy," takes on the telling of another's story, by repeating 'Liza Jane's story to the Blue Veins. "The Wife of His Youth" goes beyond "Her Virginia Mammy" in that while the protagonists of the latter trade narratives, no final merger is possible because the mother withholds a crucial piece of information, and the daughter cannot "read" her mother's subtext: Mrs. Harper thus remains "Mammy" rather than "Mother." But Mr. Ryder and 'Liza Jane fully share their stories, and their lives become once more intertwined, their family restored.

Their reunification demands more, however, than merely Ryder's willingness to listen to his long-lost wife: he must also acknowledge his past self. Along with accepting his past—and the consequences of that acceptance—Ryder embraces an earlier incarnation of himself, and one that must be particularly painful for a Blue Vein to admit. This reversion manifests itself in a very public shift of voice as he retells 'Liza Jane's story to the Blue Vein Society:

> He then related, simply but effectively, the story told by his visitor of the afternoon. *He gave it in the same soft dialect, which came readily to his lips,* while the company listened attentively and sympathetically. For the story had awakened a responsive thrill in many hearts. There were some present who had seen, and others who had heard their fathers and grandfathers tell, the wrongs and sufferings of this past generation, and all of them still felt, in their darker moments, the shadow hanging over them. (*CS* 111, emphasis added)

This passage stresses the ways Chesnutt brings together several polarities. First, 'Liza Jane's dialect springs readily to Ryder's lips; the years he has spent subordinating the speech patterns of his youth slip away as he narrates his wife's story. Second, the usually distant and snobbish Blue Veiners who pride themselves on their "lightness" suddenly discover a broader community of feeling while listening to a story that highlights their "darker moments."

But Ryder does not commit himself fully even by speaking her story. He takes a final step in that direction by offering a "hypothetical" exploration of Sam Taylor's options. By recasting his own life into these apparently speculative terms, Ryder can function as narrator, and thereby create a distance from his past self from which to study this confusing array of issues. In putting the case to his guests, Ryder once more emphasizes the polarities that separate 'Liza Jane from her hypothetical husband:

> "Suppose that he was young, and she much older than he; that he was light, and she was black; that their marriage was a slave marriage, and legally binding only if they chose to make it so after the war. Suppose, too, that he made his way to the North, as some of us have done, and there, where he had larger opportunities, had improved them, and had in the course of all these years grown to be as different from the ignorant boy who ran away from fear of slavery as the day is from the night." (*CS* 112)[21]

After stressing these additional polarities—in age, in color, in training, and in geography—Chesnutt bridges them by having Ryder acknowledge, at the urging of the Blue Vein Society, the wife of his youth, an act that also affirms his own identity.

The juxtaposition of these two narratives likewise reveals that Chesnutt has reversed the verbal hierarchy that the early parts of the story had established, a strategy he uses in *The Conjure Woman* and "The March of Progress" as well.[22] Because much of the story until the appearance of 'Liza Jane's embedded narrative is focalized through Ryder's perspective, readers might also tend to adopt his attitude of condescension toward the apparently illiterate old woman who shows up at his door.

But when we witness, or rather "hear," how 'Liza Jane's embedded narrative is a far more persuasive social commentary than
the polished hypocrisy of Ryder early in the story, we have to re-
evaluate our notions of "articulateness." Confronted with 'Liza
Jane's powerful narration of her own life, in which she lays bare
the profound commitment of her quest in her own compelling
voice, readers might suddenly find themselves dislocated. Mr.
Ryder does, of course, find himself dislocated, or rather *relocated,* after listening to her stirring oration. Indeed, her story
triggers the events that ultimately result in the two protagonists
working toward reunification by trading and finally combining
narratives in a complex matrix of identity-building that culminates in the two figures creating one shared life-narrative.

The very telling of 'Liza Jane's story allows Ryder to recapture a powerful voice of his own. Gone is the suave hypocrisy
that characterizes his speech early in the story. It has been
replaced by Ryder's forceful "old" voice, a conversion which
suggests that true articulateness need not spring from social
refinement. And when Ryder's voice begins to revert to dialect,
his audience of Blue Veins—moved to tears by his compelling
evocation—are more affected, the reader might speculate, than
they would have been by the high-brow poetry he had originally
planned to read.

Chesnutt self-consciously positions storytelling at the center
of "The Wife of His Youth" as he does in *The Conjure Woman.* But
where Julius appears on the scene as raconteur, Mr. Ryder
becomes a storyteller as a means of reconstructing his past. His
successful transformation has a direct and proportionate relationship to 'Liza Jane's influence, as Lorne Fienberg notes in
"Charles W. Chesnutt's *The Wife of His Youth:* The Unveiling of
the Black Storyteller": "Ryder's narrative ends where 'Liza Jane's
began, with an acknowledgment of identity, but it is much more
than a confession. His skillfully enacted drama of self-revelation
calls upon the Blue Veins to examine and redefine the founda-
tions of their own exclusivity" (225). Once more, Chesnutt's

meticulous structuring of his fiction is apparent. Where 'Liza Jane had announced her identity to open her embedded narrative, Ryder closes the story (and his own embedded narrative) with a definitive assertion of his long-suppressed identity and a commitment to share the rest of his life with the woman from his past.

Ryder's final acknowledgment of his wife and his own identity affirms Chesnutt's conflation in this work of the many polarities that inform most of his canon. As in *The Conjure Woman,* he places two dissimilar voices in dialogue. But where the first collection emphasizes the tension between the two culturally polarized voices and only hints at the possibility of mutual understanding, "The Wife of His Youth" suggests that the rift need not remain permanent. When the twain do meet, as they do in the reunion of Mr. Ryder and 'Liza Jane, other polarities are similarly reconstructed: the old and the new, the light and the dark, the rich and the poor, the North and the South. In "The Wife of His Youth," Chesnutt acknowledges the existence of the barriers that so often separate the characters in his other works, but here he refuses to grant final authority to those barriers.

'Liza Jane and Ryder overcome these barriers in part because they are permitted to articulate their own identities with little mediation from the primary narrator. By the end of the story the narrator's early ironic tone has subtly diminished, and his role is finally defined by his absence. The characters themselves narrate most of the last third of the story, with the primary narrator commenting only briefly on their situation, as in the penultimate paragraph of the story:

> He turned and walked toward the closed door of an adjoining room, while every eye followed him in wondering curiosity. He came back in a moment, leading by the hand his visitor of the afternoon, who stood startled and trembling at the sudden plunge into this scene of brilliant gayety. She was neatly dressed in gray, and wore the white cap of an elderly woman. (*CS* 113)

But the final words of this story about rediscovering one's voice and identity—"'Permit me to introduce to you the wife of my youth'" (113)—are appropriately spoken by Ryder.

"The Wife of His Youth" thus foregrounds voice as an essential component of identity, particularly for African Americans. The story examines how Mr. Ryder rediscovers himself only through coming to terms with his past voice, and then merging that voice into a union with that of his once and future wife. The story also suggests that to acknowledge, perhaps even to embrace, one's heritage can be both heroic and fortunate. Like "Her Virginia Mammy," "Cicely's Dream," and "The March of Progress," "The Wife of His Youth" has at its heart the exchange of narratives by two characters. But the transactions in the other works are ultimately interrupted or suspended, suggesting Chesnutt's acknowledgment that his linguistic model of family—while certainly a promising one for an author interested in erasing racial boundaries—could not ultimately overcome the pressures of American social history. It is only in "The Wife of His Youth," the sole story in this cluster populated exclusively by black characters, that the exchange results in a true and lasting family dialogue between long-separated voices.

But even this apparently optimistic message must be tempered by our awareness that Ryder seems ultimately to sacrifice a great deal. While it is tempting to celebrate without reservation the reunion of this long-suffering woman with the husband of her youth, the conclusion of the story resonates with less happy implications. The seemingly inevitable remarriage interrupts, for example, the protagonist's upcoming union with the woman he *currently* loves, in a manner that strikingly recalls the events in "Cicely's Dream." Perhaps even more troubling, though, is the extent to which a reunion with 'Liza Jane represents for Ryder a sort of re-immersion in slavery, or what early in the story the narrator derisively calls a "servile origin" (103). Thus, even the most "optimistic" of Chesnutt's re-imaginings of the American family has its barbs. Although works such as "The

Doll," "Her Virginia Mammy," "Cicely's Dream," and "The Wife of His Youth" reflect his desire to explore the possibilities of a more inclusive notion of family, one that seeks to erase or at least to moderate the barriers that separate men and women, blacks and whites, Chesnutt cannot finally bring himself to write a story that enacts those possibilities.

6 / Shortening His Weapons

The More Detached Voice of Realism

I n "A Psychological Counter-Current in Recent Fiction,"
W. D. Howells advises Chesnutt the writer to eschew "the
cheap graces and poses of the jester" (882) before offering
this assessment of *The Marrow of Tradition* (1901): "He
does, indeed, cast them all from him when he gets down to his
work, and in the dramatic climaxes and closes of his story he
shortens his weapons and deals his blows so absolutely without
flourish that I have nothing but admiration for him" (882).
One can easily see the attraction for Howells. For, while one of
the strengths of Chesnutt's work is his ability to assume a range
of voices, some of his best mature short fiction emanates from
a fixed and effaced narrative position, a style that recalls in
many ways the fiction of Howells and James. This chapter will
focus on those Chesnutt stories that rely on single-voiced or
"monologic" narrators—that is, traditional third-person narrators. In each of the works discussed, Chesnutt locates the storyteller both physically and emotionally outside the narrative he
tells, a stance that often subordinates political and social commentary to more aesthetic concerns. This group of stories, as a
consequence, has significantly more substantive comedy—as
distinguished from the brief humorous pieces Chesnutt produced in the 1880s for *Puck* and *Tid-Bits*—than any other type
of his writing.

While only a few of these stories rely on overt humor, they

deploy the full force of the irony Chesnutt developed in other fictions. The sharp-edged ironic tone of works such as "A Matter of Principle" and "Uncle Wellington's Wives" emphasizes the distance between narrator/author and subject matter, perhaps reflecting Chesnutt's growing realization of the distance between himself and his mostly white reading public. The narrative detachment apparent in these works, without reversing or negating the author's usual thematic concerns, heralds a shift in bearing on Chesnutt's part. Like other realists of his day, the author in these works allows the action to deliver the message, with little or no narrative commentary. As Myles Raymond Hurd suggests, "Like Henry James, [Chesnutt] chooses 'showing' over 'telling' to attain desired responses" in "The Passing of Grandison" and other mature fictions (83). This group of stories collectively advances a wry, often understated assessment of a complex world as seen through the eyes of a writer who, unlike Chesnutt the social reformer who had penned "The Sheriff's Children" and "Cicely's Dream," seems more interested in describing his universe than in changing it.[1]

Eighteen of Chesnutt's stories feature this single-voiced third-person narratological paradigm, although nearly half of them remained unpublished in Chesnutt's lifetime. Of those that did reach print during the author's life, five were collected in *The Wife of His Youth and Other Stories of the Color Line* ("The Bouquet,"[2] "A Matter of Principle," "The Passing of Grandison," "Uncle Wellington's Wives," and "The Web of Circumstance"), and five appeared in various journals: "Uncle Peter's House" (1885), "The Sway-Backed House" (1900), "The Partners" (1901), "The Prophet Peter" (1906), and "Mr. Taylor's Funeral" (1915). Sylvia Lyons Render collected the other eight in *The Short Fiction of Charles W. Chesnutt* (1974). Their approximate dates of composition are given parenthetically: "How He Met Her" (before 1890), "The Averted Strike" (before 19 May 1899), "Stryker's Waterloo" (between 1888 and 1899), "Walter Knox's Record" (between 1899 and 1901), "The Kiss" (after Sept. 1901), "The Exception" (after Sept. 1901), "A Miscarriage of Justice" (after Sept. 1901), and "Jim's Romance" (after Sept. 1901). Of these last eight, then, at least five and possibly as many as seven were composed in 1899 or later.[3] But while Chesnutt did seem to favor this third-person narrative paradigm later in his career—seven of these fictions were produced after 1901—he had experimented with this detached realistic stance throughout his writing life. Ultimately, the chronology of Chesnutt's narratological development remains as enigmatic as his vision of the world in which he lived.[4]

Among Chesnutt's stories using traditional third-person, detached narrators, "The Passing of Grandison," "Uncle Wellington's Wives," "A Matter of Principle," and "Mr. Taylor's Funeral" exemplify the highly stylized ironic prose and detached tone of these works, whose narrators typically excel at offering urbane assessments of character. In "Mr. Taylor's Funeral," for example, the disappearance of the heretofore reliable Taylor for more than a month convinces his wife and friends that some tragic misfortune has befallen him. When Taylor wanders in during his own "funeral," however, the narrator wryly explains his extended absence in a passage typical of Chesnutt's ironic wit:

> It might be said, in passing, that Mr. Taylor never explained his prolonged absence very satisfactorily. He did tell a story, or rather a vague outline of a story, lacking in many of the corroborative details which establish truthfulness, about an accident and a hospital. As he is still a pillar in the Jerusalem Methodist Church, and trying hard to live up to the standard set by his funeral sermons, it would be unbecoming to do more than suggest, in the same indefinite way, that when elderly men who have been a little wild in their youth are led by sudden temptation, when away from the restraining influences of home, to relapse for a time into the convivial habits of earlier days, there are, in all well-governed cities, institutions provided at the public expense where they may go into retreat for a fixed period of time, of such length—say five or ten or twenty or thirty days— as the circumstances of each particular case may seem to require. (*SF* 269–70)

As this passage illustrates, one effect of this increased narrative distance is a tone far different from the stridency of the voices that narrate Chesnutt's novels and his more melodramatic short fiction.[5]

Although a lighter tone figures prominently in his third-person narratives, Chesnutt had not abandoned social commentary altogether. Indeed, such works as "The Passing of Grandison," "Uncle Wellington's Wives," and "A Matter of Principle," while manifestly funny, embed potentially controversial themes, including issues of miscegenation and race prejudice. Two of these detached-narrator fictions explicitly feature the kind of social protest one might expect from the author of *The Marrow of Tradition* and *The Colonel's Dream:* "The Web of Circumstance" bleakly catalogs the circumstances, mostly having to do with racial injustice and flawed communication, that collude to send an innocent black man to prison; "The Bouquet" offers a similarly grim portrayal of the persistent social inequalities facing African Americans at the turn of the century. Both stories prove as unblinking and solemn in their assessments of social conditions for blacks as any works by Chesnutt. Taken together, in fact, these detached-narrator works showcase Chesnutt's breadth of range in both theme and voice. While continuing to pursue the thematic staples of his career—especially the search for (and articulation of) identity, whether personal, familial, or social—Chesnutt devises a variety of perspectives from which to approach a diversity of issues. This cluster of stories features some of the most provocative examples of his "raceless fiction," as well as an array of trickster figures who differ markedly from the type so well represented by Julius. Although each of these fictions is narrated by a single voice—unlike many of his earlier works, which place multiple voices in dialogue—Chesnutt employs a wide assortment of narrators, from ironic stylists to sympathetic commentators.

Though differing from many of his works in style and tone, Chesnutt's monologic or single-voiced narratives persist in exploring the parameters of identity. But while issues of identity-construction remain central to "The Passing of Grandison" and "A Miscarriage of Justice," those works lack the dark, often disturbing tone that pervades stories such as "The Sheriff's Children" and "Cicely's Dream." In fact, his monologic treatments of identity rely, for the most part, on irony and humor. "A Matter of Principle" and "Uncle Wellington's Wives," for example, comically undercut those who seek to improve their social situations through marriage; "Mr. Taylor's Funeral," "Stryker's Waterloo," "The Prophet Peter," and "The Exception" all lampoon those who attempt to disguise themselves for profit or diversion; and "How He Met Her" and "Walter Knox's Record" depict protagonists whose naiveté, about both love and work, is undone to comic effect. Thus, even when writing about what he considers important social matters, Chesnutt typically infuses these detached-narrator stories with an air of cultivated amusement.

The ironically titled "A Matter of Principle" satirically examines a case of intra race prejudice set in the northern city of "Groveland," modeled after Chesnutt's home of Cleveland. The crux of the story is Cicero Clayton's attempt to enhance his family's social position—like Mr. Ryder in "The Wife of His Youth," Mr. Clayton "declined to associate to any considerable extent with black people" (*CS* 150)—by having his daughter Alice marry a light-skinned, successful man. The story comically traces Mr. Clayton's efforts to ascertain whether a black congressman (and potential suitor) who will soon visit their town of Groveland is of light or dark complexion. He receives conflicting reports, and adjusts his strategies of engagement with Congressman Brown (!) accordingly. At first Clayton accepts the report of a friend who insists that Brown is light-skinned, prompting Alice's father to conclude that "'we must treat him white'" (157) by having a ball for him that will "'show the dark-eys of Groveland how to entertain a Congressman'" (157).

Featuring a highly ironic narrator, "A Matter of Principle" mirrors in many ways "The Wife of His Youth"; Mr. Clayton, however, lacks the self-awareness that finally allows Mr. Ryder to overcome his own hypocrisy. And while the initial treatment of these protagonists by their respective narrators is similar, Clayton, who suggestively has the same initials as Chesnutt,[6] is ultimately exposed as a ridiculous figure. Early in the story, for example, Clayton expresses his opinions on the race issue in a manner that strikingly recalls Ryder's speech on the same subject:

> "Of course we can't enforce our claims, or protect our-selves from being robbed of our birthright; but we can at least have principles, and try to live up to them the best we can. If we are not accepted as white, we can at any rate make it clear that we object to being called black. Our protest cannot fail in time to impress itself upon the better class of white people; for the Anglo-Saxon race loves justice, and will eventually do it, where it does not conflict with their own interests." (*CS* 150)

Like Ryder, Clayton indulges his high-toned language skills, but the result, when combined with the paucity of logic, is comic deflation. Chesnutt takes his satire of Clayton further than he does with Ryder by having the narrator offer commentary on Clayton's speech: "Whether or not the fact that Mr. Clayton meant no sarcasm, and was conscious of no inconsistency in this eulogy, tended to establish the racial identity he claimed may safely be left to the discerning reader" (*CS* 150). Chesnutt thus makes plain and unmistakable his satiric intentions toward Clayton. To put this narrative transaction in Wayne Booth's terms, the narrator is winking to the reader over the shoulder of his character.

A series of misassumptions, which Alice's lone dark-skinned suitor, Jack, subtly manipulates as a means of "writing" himself into her affections,[7] leads to the comic unraveling of Clayton's plot. For, when the complexion-obsessed father mistakenly identifies a very dark man at the train station as Brown, the narrative suddenly shifts into free indirect discourse to offer this assessment of the situation:

> He had invited to his house, had come down to meet, had made elaborate preparations to entertain on the following

evening, a light-colored man,—a white man by his theory, an
acceptable guest, a possible husband for his daughter, an
avowed suitor for her hand. If the Congressman had turned
out to be brown, even dark brown, with fairly good hair,
though he might not have desired him as a son-in-law, yet he
could have welcomed him as a guest. But even this softening of
the blow was denied him, for the man in the waiting-room was
palpably, aggressively black, with pronounced African features
and woolly hair, without apparently a single drop of *redeeming
white blood*. Could he, in the face of his well-known principles,
his lifelong rule of conduct, take this Negro into his home and
introduce him to his friends? Could he subject his wife and
daughter to the rude shock of such a disappointment? (*CS*
160, emphasis added)

The comically exaggerated language of this passage recalls
other works by Chesnutt, including the description of 'Liza Jane
in "The Wife of His Youth."[8]

From a narratological standpoint, Chesnutt's use of free
indirect discourse suggests a sophisticated manipulation of narrative techniques not often associated with his writing. Here,
the narrator's perspective merges linguistically with that of Clayton, resulting in a combination that paradoxically emphasizes
the narrative distance between the two figures. The effect is a
climactic irony that savages Clayton's pompous espousal of a
racial "theory" of redemption through admixture with white
blood. The story ends with the inevitable revelation that Congressman Brown is a light-skinned man—the man mistaken for
him was his traveling companion, Bishop Jones, "a splendid
type of the pure negro" (*CS* 165), according to the newspaper—whose trip to Groveland culminates in his betrothal to
Alice's chief rival.

The same sort of irony characterizes the treatment of the
protagonist in "Uncle Wellington's Wives." Deemed one of the
author's best by Howells,[9] this story, like "A Matter of Principle,"
offers a comic inversion of the quest for family identity
that so often appears in Chesnutt's fiction. While "The Wife of

His Youth," for example, examines the reunification of a couple married in slavery but separated by the Civil War, "Uncle Wellington's Wives" depicts the protagonist's farcical struggle to *exchange* his long-time black wife for a white one. Like Clayton, Wellington Braboy is a light-skinned black man whose attempts to enhance his social position—and to lighten his workload, he thinks—prompt him to leave his hard-working wife Milly in the South for the chance to marry a northern white woman. In fact, Wellington's conception of the North grows so laughably hyperbolic that he finally envisions it as a place of utopian social order that encourages miscegenation:

> The more uncle Wellington's mind dwelt upon the professor's speech, the more attractive seemed the picture of Northern life presented. . . . Giving full rein to his fancy, he saw in the North a land flowing with milk and honey,—a land peopled by noble men and beautiful women, among whom colored men and women moved with the ease and grace of acknowledged right. Then he placed himself in the foreground of the picture. What a fine figure he would have made in the world if he had been born at the free North! He imagined himself dressed like the professor, and passing the contribution-box in a white church; and most pleasant of his dreams, and the hardest to realize as possible, was that of the gracious white lady he might have called wife. (*CS* 206–7)

Once more, Chesnutt uses free indirect discourse to achieve a complex narrative situation and to deflate his character's pretensions: the linguistic mixing of voice amplifies our sense of Wellington's absurdity.

The notion that moving to the North will confer a new identity on Braboy proves too difficult a lure to resist, and the protagonist leaves his home in a parodic retelling of the slave's flight to the North: he clandestinely travels at night; he takes a literal train (as opposed to the Underground Railroad); and he conforms to the pattern of renaming himself that Kimberly W. Benston suggests is an integral part of slave narratives. "Social and economic freedom—a truly new self—was incomplete," writes Benston, "if not authenticated by self-designation" (153). In this story, the protagonist is consistently referred to as "'Wellin'ton,' 'Brer Wellin'ton,' or 'uncle Wellington'" (*CS* 219) while he lives in the South, but once he moves to the North he "authenticates" his new identity by having himself called "Mr. Braboy," a title he believes constitutes "one of the first fruits of Northern liberty" (219). When he finally returns to the South, figuratively with his tail between his legs, Braboy must retrace his escape route and be rebaptized, as the narrator pointedly suggests: "It would be painful to record in detail the return journey of uncle Wellington—Mr. Braboy no longer—to his native town; how many weary miles he walked; how many times he risked his life on railroad trucks and between freight cars; how he depended for sustenance on the grudging hand of back-door charity" (233). Braboy thus undergoes a sort of reverse metamorphosis in a story that borrows heavily from the slave narrative tradition.[10] The parodic thrust of this inverted slave narrative—again the emphasis on the journey by railroad, although this time heading South—is reserved solely for Wellington, whose "slight deviations from the path of rectitude" and "compulsory sojourn of thirty days in a city where he had no references" the narrator delights in pointing out (233). Here, Chesnutt uses the framework to mock the superficial ambitions of an unreflective man.

Braboy returns to his black wife and the South because the trappings of a new identity—an *unpleasant* white wife (rather than the "gracious white lady" he had envisioned) and the economics of responsibility—subvert his notion of the "free North":

> At times Wellington found himself wondering if his second marriage had been a wise one. Other circumstances combined to change his once rose-colored conception of life at the North. He had believed that all men were equal in this favored locality, but he discovered more degrees of inequality than he had

> ever perceived at the South. A colored man might be as good
> as a white man in theory, but neither of them was of any spe-
> cial consequence without money, or talent, or position. . . . On
> occasions when Mrs. Braboy [the second] would require of
> him some unusual physical exertion, or when too frequent
> applications to the bottle had loosened her tongue, uncle
> Wellington's mind would revert, with a remorseful twinge of
> conscience, to the *dolce far niente* of his Southern home. (228)

In fact, his reversions of mind prove so powerful that the voices
of his two wives merge as "the elegant brogue of Mrs. Braboy
would deliquesce into the soft dialect of North Carolina" (229).
Chesnutt emphasizes here, as he does elsewhere, the conflation
of voices to urge a character to action: in "The Wife of His
Youth," a similar scene has Mr. Ryder reverting to the "soft
dialect" of his youth as he acknowledges his long-lost wife. Here
the comic conflation of two women's voices motivates Braboy to
"escape" back to his southern home and his abandoned wife.

Both "A Matter of Principle" and "Uncle Wellington's
Wives" thus comically invert Chesnutt's paradigm of the search
for family formation. Clayton and Braboy corrupt the very
undertaking of such a quest because they do it for precisely
the wrong reasons: to improve social standing, to avoid work,
to lighten the black race. And Chesnutt's position on their
attempts to "pass" could not be more clear.[11] The pervasive
ironies that characterize both stories speak to the author's dis-
approval of this sort of intra-racial prejudice, and yet he has
been roundly attacked by those who claim *he* adhered to a
"racial theory" much like that which governs Mr. Clayton's philosophy.[12] Finally, though, his conclusions in this area would
seem to be evident: if, as one recent reader argues, "Chesnutt's
ultimate solution to the race problem is a wholesale racial
assimilation achieved by the genetic dilution of the black race"
(Ferguson 111), a strategy that would entail the infusion of
"curative white blood into a socially dysfunctional black race"
(114), why does he so ardently lampoon his characters who
advance, and indeed attempt to enact, this racial theory? In "A

Matter of Principle," Chesnutt exposes Clayton as a buffoon in this regard, and the thematic point of both "The Wife of His Youth" and "Uncle Wellington's Wives" seems to be precisely the opposite of "wholesale racial assimilation": both those stories suggest, in fact, that the only plausible "curative" for the two mulatto male protagonists (Ryder and Braboy) with dubious race theories is a return to their "genuine Negro" wives.[13]

Not all of Chesnutt's monologic examinations of identity-formation share this ironic, humorous tone, however. The most striking exception is "The Web of Circumstance," which melodramatically depicts the unraveling of the life and career of Ben Davis, a successful black businessman. His fall occurs through no fault of his own, and the plot relies heavily on circumstance, as the title implies. The protagonist's employee, Tom, frames his boss—by stealing Colonel Thornton's prized whip and hiding it in Davis's blacksmith shop—in an attempt to appropriate Davis's wife and business. Sentenced to prison for a disproportionate term (because of his poor legal defense, the prosecutor's ambitions, the judge's desire to make an example of him, and other "circumstances"), Davis is essentially robbed of his successful business, his wife, and his children. Upon his release from prison, Davis seeks revenge on Colonel Thornton, whom he mistakenly blames for his fall; the colonel is, in fact, the only character in the story who does *not* conspire against the blacksmith.[14] While waiting to kill Thornton, Davis comes across the colonel's daughter, and he briefly considers taking his revenge by killing her instead. But the idea "faded away and vanished into nothingness as soon as it came within the nimbus that surrounded the child's person" (*CS* 264). Indeed, her presence in large measure convinces him to abandon plans for vengeance. But when Thornton sees Davis "carrying in his hand a murderous bludgeon" and "running toward the child" in his attempt to flee, he mistakes Davis's intentions and shoots the blacksmith, who falls "dead at the child's feet" (264). Hence, two relatively blameless men are pitted against one another by the confluence of many circumstances, and their struggle results in Davis's death. Despite the ruin of his own life and the loss of his family, however, Davis refuses to exploit the opportunity of depriving Thornton of *his* family. Stripped of personal identity by a conniving fellow black and punished by whites who find entertainment and some degree of "vindication" in the blacksmith's fall, Davis sustains his reverence for the concept of family identity: it is no mere "circumstance" that he dies at the feet of a child.

Chesnutt depicts another intersection in the lives of an adult and a child in "The Bouquet," also published in *The Wife of His Youth.* Here, however, the gender and race of the two protagonists are partially inverted, with a white schoolteacher, Mary Myrover, befriending one of her black pupils, Sophy. The story considers the obstacles to such a friendship in the era of Reconstruction. Mary's mother and friends pointedly disapprove of her interaction with African Americans, and indeed Mary recognizes the restrictions to free intercourse between the races:

> Miss Myrover taught the colored children, but she could not be seen with them in public. If they occasionally met her on the street, they did not expect her to speak to them, unless she happened to be alone and no other white person was in sight. If any of the children felt slighted, she was not aware of it, for she intended no slight; she had not been brought up to speak to negroes on the street, and she could not act differently from other people. (*CS* 242)

The narrative detachment afforded by the monologic style is apparent here, as the narrator only subtly hints at the inadequacies of Mary's sensibilities. Certainly, Chesnutt does not treat her with the same unreserved admiration that characterizes his portrayals of Henrietta Noble and Martha Chandler, two of his other fictional white teachers who work with black children. Still, the narrator describes Mary as a mostly good-hearted, fairly progressive woman whose bonds with her students are emphasized in her ability to "speak" their language: "she was so familiar with their dialect that she might almost be said to speak it, barring certain characteristic grammatical inac-curacies" (*CS* 240). As in "The Wife of His Youth" and "Cicely's Dream," the bridging of race barriers thus occurs (or, in this case, nearly occurs) as a result of the merging of voices.

Finally, though, "The Bouquet" dramatizes the continuation of profound, possibly even permanent divisions between the races. Although Chesnutt once more uses voice to link his char-acters, the qualification apparent in the final clause of this pas-sage—Mary could not after all *quite* speak Sophy's language—foreshadows the teacher's ultimate separation from the one person who most loved her. Indeed, Mary had asked her favorite student—who "was far from the whitest of Miss Myrover's pupils; in fact, she was one of the darker ones" (*CS* 241)—to carry out her final wish: "'When I die, Sophy,' Miss Myrover said to the child one day, 'I want to be covered with roses. . . . I'm sure I shall rest better if my grave is banked with flowers, and roses are planted at my head and at my feet'" (241). But after Myrover's death, Sophy and all other African Americans are excluded from the funeral, which the girl is forced to watch from a concealed, but religiously significant, vantage point outside the church: "Time had dealt gently with the window, but just at the feet of the figure of Jesus a small tri-angular piece of glass had been broken out. To this aperture Sophy applied her eyes, and through it saw and heard what she could of the services within" (246). Chesnutt thus reverts to a familiar positioning of character in this passage, as Sophy, like the narrators of "Cartwright's Mistake" and "A Grass Widow," must play the role of voyeur. Similarly, Sophy cannot gain admittance to the whites-only cemetery where Mary finally rests. So once more, "Sophy stayed outside, and looked through the fence" at her beloved teacher's grave (247).

Chesnutt melodramatically depicts the physical and emo-tional separateness of the black child and her white friend, cast-ing Sophy in the role of well-meaning spectator who, like Wal-ton in "Cartwright's Mistake," can only catch glimpses of her friend's funeral and grave from a profoundly excluded position. And because Sophy cannot ultimately deliver on her promise to lay flowers at Mary's grave, she must, in a grimly ironic scene, enlist the aid of a dog (who *is* allowed on cemetery grounds) to carry the bouquet to the graveside: "When Prince had performed his mission he turned his eyes toward Sophy inquiringly, and when she gave him a nod of approval lay down and resumed his watch by the graveside. Sophy looked at him a moment with a feeling very much like envy, and then turned and moved slowly away" (*CS* 248). In many ways, the conclusion to this story is one of Chesnutt's bleakest assessments of the chances that the races can come together. The scene Chesnutt so effectively depicts at the gravesite literalizes the barriers that continued to divide the races throughout his life. The fence— through which Sophy watches as the dog lays her flowers on Mary's grave—constitutes one of the author's more striking objective correlatives. While the dog can move about freely, crossing back and forth between the black side of the fence and the white, Sophy can only look on in envy.

Chesnutt makes use of another powerful symbol in this set of monologic narratives, and indeed elsewhere. In several of these works, he emphasizes the degree to which his black characters' identities become interwoven with the houses they live in. Chesnutt's conflation of a character's identity with his house, echoing as it does Hawthorne's *The House of the Seven Gables* and anticipating Faulkner's "A Rose for Emily" and *Light in August,* is most apparent in *The House Behind the Cedars,* a work in which the partially obscured house parallels the similarly concealed identities of the mixed-blood family living within. The author uses this device often in *The Conjure Woman,* wherein he repeatedly describes, as Faulkner would in his Yoknapatawpha fiction, dilapidated mansions as symbols of southern socioeconomic decay. In the stories considered in this chapter, however, Chesnutt more positively makes use of this motif to suggest metaphorically the struggles of African Americans to build their lives at the turn of the century. The two stories in this cluster that most dramatically employ this symbol are "Uncle Peter's House" (1885) and "The Sway-Backed House" (1900). In the latter, an old man's death engenders intra-racial conflicts when he dies without leaving his asymmetrical house to his daughter's light-skinned fiancé as dowry.

In "Uncle Peter's House" the house becomes Peter's proxy, and its saga mirrors the difficulties blacks encountered during Reconstruction in trying to build viable lives for themselves. In addition to the refusal of white-owned banks to finance Peter's quest to build a house and of white landowners to sell him land, Peter faces even more direct obstacles: his earliest attempt at building the house, for example, ends when the Ku Klux Klan burns it down. But rather than abandon the effort, Peter starts again: "The ashes of the burnt house manured the crop of corn which he had planted in the clearing, and the work of accumulating lumber was begun anew" (*SF* 174). But in his next attempt to build, the now-old Peter is critically injured in a fall. Even on his deathbed, aware that he is headed toward "'A mansion in hebben'" (175), Peter charges his son with finishing the house. Significantly, the story ends with the narrator's description of how the house is progressing under the care of the son, Primus: "Several years have elapsed. Primus, true to his promise, has had the windows put in and the chimney built and is now lathing the interior" (176). The narrator's switch to the present tense and his depiction of Primus as the house's finisher speak to the idea that identity-formation, particularly for African Americans during Reconstruction, was an ongoing process that for the first time could involve continuity from one generation to the next.

Building a niche for oneself during the instability of the late nineteenth and early twentieth centuries was apparently no simple task for whites either, as stories such as "Walter Knox's Record" (written between 1899 and 1901), "The Kiss," and "A Miscarriage of Justice" (both written after September 1901) suggest. "The Kiss" is a well-handled melodrama depicting the final reconciliation of a long-estranged couple, and the other two stories offer penetrating appraisals of the uncertainties whites had to face as the country rebuilt itself.

"Walter Knox's Record" examines how naiveté leads to the near-corruption of a young man, Walter Knox, who enters city government because he believes that "'there is no greater career than to be a leader of men, and no higher cause than the promotion of good government'" (*SF* 375). Walter's idealism does not protect him against the political intrigue of his constituents, however, and he becomes entangled in the plotting of Mr. Street, a local businessman. His immediate superior then tries to enlist Knox in a counterplot to entrap Street, but the narrator explains Walter's refusal to play the role of a fellow conspirator:

> Walter had been carefully grounded, however, in correct principles, and possessed a very clear intelligence for so young a man. His second thoughts upon the Director's proposition were by no means so comfortable. Street had as yet committed no crime. Walter had been asked to do something without which no crime was possible—to perform one act in a series of acts which would constitute a crime, in order that a contemplated offense might become a real one. . . . He saw, too, that to approve the bills as suggested would place him in a false position, from which even the Director's word might not be able to release him. (*SF* 382)

By choosing therefore not to participate in the plot, Walter sacrifices his career in city government but preserves his integrity, a crucial component of this idealistic young man's identity. Knox chooses the ethical course, and that choice sets his career back but does not ruin the man. The story concludes with him hopeful that he might, armed with a newfound understanding of the world, one day have a chance to enter public life again. Such a conclusion reiterates Chesnutt's contention—evident in fictions such as "The Shadow of My Past" and "The Wife of His Youth"—that identity-construction is an ongoing process, and one that often requires extensive revision.

The other significant piece of "raceless" fiction Chesnutt

wrote using a single-voiced narrator is "A Miscarriage of Justice," which, like "The Kiss" and "Walter Knox's Record," remained unpublished until Render's collection. While "The Kiss" focuses on family re-formation and "Walter Knox's Record" on a man's attempts to craft a public self, "A Miscarriage of Justice" examines the reshuffling of the white social classes in the South. Like Faulkner nearly thirty years later, Chesnutt surprises the reader by infusing broad comedy into his treatment of a topic as potentially explosive as class conflict. This work follows a court case pitting a fading aristocrat, Colonel Westbrook, against the embodiment of the new southern businessman in Jim Carey, who had once worked for Westbrook. Carey's description of Westbrook establishes the dichotomy the two men represent:

> "Oh, he'll look just the same after he's lost," said Carey, "only he'll sit a little straighter and walk a little stiffer. I wouldn't have started the case if he had'nt been so darned stiff. He can't read the signs of the times—he still thinks of me as Jim the molder, or Carey the foreman. The world stopped moving for him just before I got started. He had already cooled in his mold while I was being poured into mine." (*SF* 358)

The legal dispute, having to do with patent rights to a plow, appears destined to go Carey's way, mostly because of a document—signed by the colonel—which "seemed, unless it could be successfully refuted, to be an acknowledgment of Carey's claim" (*SF* 360).

But circumstances conspire to thicken the plot. When, on the morning of the trial, Carey's horse throws him into a shallow creek, the colonel is the only witness to the event, and does not hesitate to rescue his foe. The crux of the story derives, however, from the colonel's reaction as he notices that the briefcase holding the crucial document is drifting away in the current. At this point the narration for the first time enters Westbrook's consciousness:

> As Colonel Westbrook deposited Carey's form upon the bank,
> he saw Carey's brown pocketbook floating slowly down the
> stream, and sinking slowly as it floated. The colonel was
> human. He had seen Carey, the evening before, place the only
> material evidence in the case in that brown pocketbook. . . .
> But if the papers yonder should never get to the jury, assurance
> would be rendered doubly sure. . . .
>
>   But the colonel's hesitation was only momentary. (*SF* 361)

As in "Walter Knox's Record," Chesnutt's thorough presentation of a complex ethical matter confers respect on his characters. Westbrook struggles with his decision, but like Knox makes
the moral if economically costly choice. After Carey learns of
Westbrook's action, he tries to have the case dropped, but the
colonel's pride intervenes. Ultimately, the story becomes comically complicated as both sides maneuver legally in attempts to
lose the case, and thus preserve "honor." Finally, Westbrook wins
the judgment—after Carey bribes the jury—and magnani-
mously refuses to collect his payment. The story concludes with
Carey's assessment of the case: "'The trial did one thing—the
colonel gave me his hand and "mistered" me. But the darned
old aristocrat had got the better of me all along the line. I gave
him fifty thousand dollars for my life, and he gave me ten thousand for nothing'" (*SF* 364).

   In depicting the reorganization of the southern social
classes, Chesnutt thus emphasizes the intersection between
economy and honor as this story comically enacts, in microcosm,
the "Reconstruction" of the South. As representative figures—
"They were the past and the future—Westbrook the old order,
Carey the new to which the old must give place" (*SF* 357)—the
two protagonists struggle to negotiate a new relationship. That
this comic story nevertheless predicates its concept of a "new
relationship" between the social classes on a misunderstanding
demonstrates Chesnutt's finely honed satirical sense.

   The same sort of comic tone pervades several of Chesnutt's
other detached-perspective works, some of which recall his por-

trayal of Julius in *The Conjure Woman*. In many of these works, the author depicts the attempts of protagonists—who might easily be classified as tricksters—to position themselves favorably in a shifting society. Like "Uncle Wellington's Wives," most of these stories feature likably dishonest characters who intentionally disguise themselves and who work very hard to avoid work. "Stryker's Waterloo," for example, traces the career of Napoleon Stryker, who "had tried almost every plan for capturing fortune except the only certain way—by means of a regular business and a settled life" (*SF* 365). The rest of the story chronicles his attempts to conceal his physical recovery from injuries sustained in a railway accident so that he can collect a large settlement from the railroad company. Similarly, in "The Prophet Peter" (1906) two white confidence men use Peter, a local "visionary" whose visions they manufacture, to convince the townspeople to sell all their property to the "apostles." Interestingly, Chesnutt infuses this story with religious imagery but has the day saved by a devout nonbeliever. And "The Exception" (written after September 1901) follows a troupe of actors— professional mask-wearers—as they relentlessly manipulate a reluctant stationmaster for railway tickets. Each of these stories offers a comic take on Chesnutt's theme of identity-formation.

One of the best of these monologic, third-person depictions of tricksters, published late in Chesnutt's career, appeared in W. E. B. Du Bois's *The Crisis* in 1915. "Mr. Taylor's Funeral" suggests that a man's identity (and reputation) can remain comically unstable even after his "death." The work treats the month-long disappearance and subsequent funeral(s) of Mr. Taylor, who becomes the subject of (mostly faulty) interpretation for a host of "readers." In essence, each member of the community reads Taylor in light of his or her own ideology and financial ambitions. One of the two ministers, for example, had envisioned Taylor as a romantic rival; he reads Taylor's "death," therefore, as an opportunity to marry an attractive and wealthy widow. The other minister instead views Taylor as the epitome of Christian probity. Like Chesnutt, then, Taylor becomes for his "readers" an amorphous subject, one capable of sustaining wildly divergent interpretations. Chesnutt therefore casts the "real" Taylor, the putative subject of the townspeople's interpretations, as largely irrelevant to those interpretations. For, as the omniscient narrator makes clear, those readings bear no resemblance to the truth about this particular "absent man" (*SF* 262).[15] Such a characterization might just as easily apply to an author who has been consigned to the periphery of a black tradition in fiction that he, in many ways, established.

Although comic in tone, the story nevertheless recapitulates and revises Chesnutt's interest in the creation of identity. In "Mr. Taylor's Funeral," the protagonist is physically positioned as a voyeur, watching "through the slats of a window" (*SF* 268), who is able to hear two distinctly different versions of himself as formulated by the two ministers. As in "Cicely's Dream," a central character is in effect defined by others, and has little input into his identity until the end of the story. And, more figuratively, one might say that Taylor is also positioned between this and the nether world. In that sense, he has perhaps the most profoundly divided identity of any Chesnutt character.

From a narratological standpoint, "Mr. Taylor's Funeral" typifies the way Chesnutt's detached narrators formulate identity. As a point on the continuum of his literary output, the story occupies a place very near both the chronological and tonal extreme. Published ten years after *The Colonel's Dream,* which is widely thought to have concluded Chesnutt's writing career, the story is a comic tribute to the inscrutability of identity. Chesnutt returns again and again to this theme in his works: he relentlessly dramatizes the profound complexity both blacks and whites face when trying to locate and articulate their relative positions in a confounding social landscape. His earlier works, however, bear more visibly the scars of his struggle with the theme. While the sheriff's son, Tom, of "The Sheriff's Children" and Tenie of "Po' Sandy" suffer horribly from their inability to craft meaningful identities for themselves and their families, "Mr. Taylor's Funeral" is a figurative shrug of the shoulders at man's powerlessness to define himself. "Mr. Taylor's Funeral" is not Chesnutt's finest work, but it does reiterate, with a comic difference, the thematic concerns that run throughout his career.

Ultimately, these monologic works treat many of the same themes that appear regularly in Chesnutt's writing; stories such as "Uncle Peter's House," "The Web of Circumstance," and "The Bouquet" attest to the suitability of this narrative format for advancing a literature of cause. Still, for the majority of Chesnutt's single-voiced, ironic narratives, one can detect a significant shift of perspective. The rhetoric of these eighteen works, with only a few exceptions, seems far less insistent and self-righteous than one finds in *The Marrow of Tradition,* the effect in many ways more disarming. Although differing in tone and perspective from his other works, this group of stories reconfirms Chesnutt's dazzling command of the literary conceit, as evidenced by the delicately calibrated plots of such works as "Uncle Wellington's Wives," "A Matter of Principle," and "Mr. Taylor's Funeral." In those stories and the others grouped with them, the narrators remain, as one imagines Chesnutt at forty-five, for the most part reserved and gently contemplative, commenting on the action cryptically in some works and not at all in others.

The narrative stance typical of these monologic stories seems, in many ways, the most comfortable for Chesnutt. In works such as "Mr. Taylor's Funeral" and "Uncle Wellington's Wives," he can remain an indistinct figure in the background. But in effacing his narrators, he paradoxically reveals a great deal about himself and his own conceptions of storytelling. While by the turn of the century Chesnutt's critical reputation derived from his remarkable renderings of multiple voices, it is in the single-voiced narration of "Mr. Taylor's Funeral" that he most cogently and accurately depicts the ultimate shape of his career as a writer: that of the "absent man" of the African-American literary tradition. It may be that in the reserved and detached voice characteristic of these eighteen stories Chesnutt found his own.

❧

"Mr. Taylor's Funeral" precisely lays out the terms of Chesnutt's twentieth-century reputation, but it is not his only story that invites readers to conflate the author with his protagonist. In "The Passing of Grandison," which will be the primary focus of this discussion, the titular character serves as a proxy in many ways for his creator. Both Chesnutt and Grandison encode messages that conceal as much as they reveal, and both resist the classifications that various readers—within and outside the text—attempt to impose. Although it reached print more than fifteen years after the publication of "Grandison," "Mr. Taylor's Funeral" seems nevertheless a preliminary work: it establishes the terms of Chesnutt's peculiarly inscribed authorial absence, while "The Passing of Grandison" presents a more polished tablet for that inscription.

Chesnutt constructs and articulates the parameters of identity for another essentially "absent man" in "The Passing of Grandison." As in "Mr. Taylor's Funeral," he thoroughly detaches the narrative apparatus from the perspective of the title character. Throughout the story, Grandison's thoughts remain unavailable to the reader and other characters, and we can form a composite idea of his identity only from what his fellow characters think and say of him. This complex narrative strategy plays an important role in our understanding of what Myles Raymond Hurd calls "one of [Chesnutt's] most technically sophisticated efforts in prose" (81). Indeed, the narrator ultimately relies on rendering only the *consequences* of Grandison's actions and then gathers the speculations of various focalizers in an effort to explain those consequences: like the befuddled Colonel Owens, who initially "owns" the protagonist, we can only infer from results what Grandison actually means.

Although he is one of several Chesnutt "masked" characters, Grandison differs materially from Julius, the trickster figure most commonly associated with Chesnutt's canon. In *The Conjure Woman,* the raconteur Julius seems to heighten his inscrutability despite, or perhaps because of, indulging his loquacious nature. But while the ambiguities of Julius's identity and motives are amplified by the wealth of information, mixed perhaps with a bit of disinformation, about himself that he seems quite willing to share, Grandison exists as a mute object of speculation for a host of characters and readers. The result is a protagonist who throughout remains opaque both to the reader and to the other characters, all of whom pride themselves on knowing just what this "simple" slave is up to.

The plot of the story seems laid out intentionally to misdirect the reader. The first few pages of "The Passing of Grandison," in fact, establish Dick Owens, the indolent son of a plantation owner, and not Grandison, as the protagonist of the work. Much of the early story directs our attention to young Owens's attempts to win the favor of Charity Lomax by running "one of his father's negro men off to Canada" as a test that will prove his worthiness as prospective husband (*CS* 187). His romantic quest proves more difficult than Owens had imagined, however, because running anyone off to Canada requires an inordinately relentless effort for which a plantation owner's lazy son seems profoundly ill-equipped. Chesnutt gives his readers an early clue to the difficulty of the task when Dick's attempts to requisition another slave, Tom, to accompany him North (and thereby become the beneficiary of his mission) are rejected by Colonel Owens, the patriarch of the plantation. Although the narrator tells us that Tom had always been "prudent enough . . . to dissemble his feelings" (190), the colonel's refusal to allow Tom to accompany his son to the North validates P. Jay Delmar's contention that Tom "had not dissembled his feelings quite well enough on previous occasions" (372). When Colonel Owens instead decides upon Grandison as a more trustworthy companion for his son, Chesnutt once more misdirects the reader's attention, here by seeming to affirm Colonel Owens's reading of Grandison.

Thus, Chesnutt lures readers into accepting a taxonomy of slaves developed by Colonel Owens, who "had pronounced views on the subject of negroes, having studied them, as he often said, for a great many years, and, as he asserted oftener, understanding them perfectly" (*CS* 191). Representing one group, Tom is, according to the colonel, "'too smart to trust among those low-down abolitionists. I strongly suspect him of having learned to read'" (191). Grandison can be trusted, on the other hand, because "'He's too fond of good eating to risk losing his regular meals; besides, he's sweet on your mother's maid, Betty, and I've promised to let 'em get married before long'" (192). Colonel Owens thereby devises a sliding scale for his slaves based on their relative abilities to "read." Ironically, he places Tom—who can *only* "read"—on the untrustworthy end of the spectrum while overlooking (or "misreading") the more potent threat to his ownership: Grandison can not only read, but in addition possesses a refined and subversive ability to *write* his own identity, albeit in code.

The implication that Grandison would not abandon Betty is a subtle and instructive bit of foreshadowing on Chesnutt's part, but the rest of the colonel's characterization establishes Grandison as lazy and stupid, an archetype of the "contented-slave" paradigm.[16] Grandison does nothing early in the story to dispel his image in the colonel's eyes. Told by the colonel, for example, that abolitionists may try to persuade him to escape, Grandison formulates a response that echoes the philosophy of his "master": "'Deed, suh, I would n' low none er dem cussed, low-down abolitioners ter come nigh me, suh. I'd—I'd—would I be 'lowed ter hit 'em, suh?'" (*CS* 193). This request convinces the colonel that Grandison is "'abolitionist-proof'" (194).

Hence, Chesnutt subtly satirizes the reading skills of the colonel and Dick, both of whom serve as proxies for the pre-dominantly white turn-of-the-century audience. When the younger Owens, alone with Grandison in the North, cannot execute his mission because his companion, maddeningly enough, continues to exemplify the contented slave by refusing to escape, readers might empathize with Dick and his mounting frustrations as liberator. Dick's efforts to fulfill his quest despite

Grandison's resistance are, in fact, comically herculean: he writes an anonymous letter to abolitionists inviting them to help Grandison escape; he leaves his charge alone in a Boston hotel for several days with a drawer full of money (which he first points out to his "slave"); he even takes Grandison over the border into Canada and abandons him there. But all to no effect. Dick becomes so frustrated, in fact, that

> he inwardly cursed the stupidity of a slave who could be free
> and would not, and registered a secret vow that if he were
> unable to get rid of Grandison without assassinating him, and
> were therefore compelled to take him back to Kentucky, he
> would see that Grandison got a taste of an article of slavery that
> would make him regret his wasted opportunities. (*CS* 197)

Dick's anger is, in fact, increased because he "could not express his feelings adequately. He did not even scold Grandison; how could he, indeed, find fault with one who so sensibly recognized his true place in the economy of civilization?" (*CS* 197).

This passage thus conflates the predicaments of the two protagonists: neither can "express his feelings adequately," at least in traditional terms. Dick Owens finds himself, if only briefly, in the uncomfortable position of masking his true intentions, the same position Grandison has learned to exploit. While the slave negotiates within and around the limitations of his status—he speaks disingenuously if at all—the master grows increasingly frustrated within *his* confines. And in fact the two men resolve their situations in markedly different fashions. Not recognizing the similarity of his situation and Grandison's, Dick at this point agrees with his father's view of the slave as "stupid." Grandison seems to reinforce that notion by resisting freedom so ardently that the younger Owens finally succeeds in liberating his "ebony encumbrance" (*CS* 199) only through force. Because Grandison consistently rebukes the attempts of Owens and various abolitionists to free him, Dick has him kidnapped and, ironically, imprisoned in the Canadian wilderness, a venue that usually represented a safe haven for runaway slaves. When

Grandison "escapes" from his northern captors, however, and makes his way back to Owens's plantation, the colonel tearfully welcomes him as the embodiment of the heroically loyal slave, "'all the time pining for the old plantation'" (202). Thus, Grandison still conforms in the reader's mind and in the minds of his masters to the paradigm of the contented slave.

His "heroic" efforts to return to the plantation comically revise the traditional slave narrative model. Like "Uncle Wellington's Wives," "The Passing of Grandison" inverts several elements of that genre of African-American literature: it features accounts of slave life in the Antebellum South, a harrowing journey, and an ultimately successful escape of the protagonist and his entire family.[17] The story, however, reworks these apparently typical slave narrative elements into an entirely different compound. The most dramatic divergence from the tradition is Chesnutt's reversal of the slave's journey to freedom in the North: since Grandison apparently prefers the Kentucky form of bondage to the Canadian version, he makes his way, despite overwhelming odds, back to the South. This inversion of the slave's escape culminates in what Richard O. Lewis calls "the irony of Grandison's using the North Star (symbol of escape away from the South and slavery) to guide his return to his slave master in Kentucky" (161).

But Grandison's final revision of the script deals a severe blow to Colonel Owens's faith in human nature: only three weeks later, Grandison, his wife, his parents, and his siblings all escape from the plantation together. Unlike Tom, Grandison was thus able to sustain his "dissembling" so successfully that his re-escape catches all of his "readers" by surprise. Delmar suggests that Chesnutt "plays Grandison's apparent characterization and the plot's apparent development against the reader's logical and more humane perception of the realities of slavery until he is ready to reveal the story's true meaning. Chesnutt, that is, so carefully manipulates irony and satire that the reader is not certain about whom or what is being satirized" (371). Although Delmar rightly identifies the skilled manipulations of irony and satire that so unsettle readers, "The Passing of Grandison" might best be read as a cautionary tale designed to ensnare those who would uncover too easily the "true meaning" of Chesnutt or his work.

"The Passing of Grandison" conforms to the thematic framework that governs much of Chesnutt's career. Implicitly a condemnation of slavery and the ill-conceived attitudes of those in power, the story also offers a sophisticated examination of identity formation. The narrative format seduces readers into characterizing Grandison as a stereotypical contented slave, whose lazy and stupid demeanor seems perfectly suited for a life of servitude. But finally, readers are forced to confront, albeit comically, the depths of not only Colonel Owens's misreading of the protagonist but their own as well. For Grandison has proven himself the master trickster here, duping the colonel, Dick, and the reader. Grandison is in many ways much more than merely a trickster, however: he also authors his own identity, and he encodes it so subtly that he remains inscrutable to all of his readers. Chesnutt too has established his own brand of authorial inscrutability, one predicated on *his* ability to disrupt, like Grandison, the reading positions of a complacent audience all too willing to accept black texts at face value.

Despite its layered satire and its reworking of several components of slave narratives, "The Passing of Grandison" ultimately fulfills its obligation to that genre. Although a trickster figure, Grandison takes the moral high ground, and his actions go far beyond proving that he is neither lazy nor stupid. His perilous return to the South and the elaborate planning necessary to execute the group escape that follows both result from Grandison's refusal to leave his family behind. In this way only, Colonel Owens's characterization of Grandison is accurate: he had assumed, remember, that his "abolitionist-proof" slave would be reluctant to leave because of both his love of good food and his betrothal to Betty. Grandison does indeed come back for Betty, and he picks up his other family members for good measure.

Chesnutt's design of the story comes finally together in a remarkably subtle arrangement that reiterates the author's career-long interest in the theme of family formation. The plot intersects where two men strive to build a family life: Grandison's efforts to marry Betty and engineer a free life for his family parallel Dick's far less dangerous attempts to impress Charity Lomax enough so that she will agree to marry him. The final success of both suitors suggests that masking often proves a valuable and positive device; both Grandison and Dick play roles counter to their natures, the one pretending fierce loyalty to the system that enslaved him, the other working hard to secure a life of indolence with Charity.

But ultimately, it is Chesnutt's accomplished and subtle characterization of the "absent man" that so distinguishes "The Passing of Grandison." In terms of defining oneself, no one would seem to be less empowered than a slave. And much of this fiction implicitly affirms the notion: in a story that bears his name, Grandison is the only major character who does not function as a focalizer. Even an unnamed waitress in a restaurant near the Canadian border acts as a reflector for a part of this story, but we see none of the action through Grandison's eyes. Indeed, although he does speak, in what turns out to be a consummate masking performance, to both Dick and Colonel Owens, we never gain any sort of direct access to what might be characterized as Grandison's real thoughts.

We do, however, witness the consequences of his actions, and those actions reveal that not only has Grandison emphatically defined himself, but he has defined everyone else as well. Although the colonel never suspects Grandison of being able—like Tom—to "read," the "abolitionist-proof" slave, ironically, has in large measure scripted the plot of his family's escape. Late in the story, the narrator hints at Grandison's detailed authorship of events when he tells us that "the underground railroad seemed to have had its tracks cleared and signals set for this particular train" (*CS* 203). "The Passing of Grandison" concludes by asserting once more the enigmatic nature of

Grandison, as Colonel Owens makes a last impotent attempt to recapture his onetime "property":

> One last glimpse he caught of his vanishing property, as he stood, accompanied by a United States marshal, on a wharf at a port on the south shore of Lake Erie. On the stern of a small steamboat which was receding rapidly from the wharf, with her nose pointing toward Canada, there stood a group of familiar dark faces, and the look they cast backward was not one of longing for the fleshpots of Egypt. *The colonel saw Grandison point him out to one of the crew of the vessel, who waved his hand derisively toward the colonel.* (*CS* 203–4, emphasis added)

Note how, even on the brink of freedom, Grandison still choreographs the action rather than acting himself: he does not deign to make a derisive gesture toward the colonel; rather, he inspires one of his band to make the gesture for him. An author himself, Grandison scripts his family's freedom while maintaining his own public silence. And like Chesnutt, this fictional "absent man" authored an identity for himself that remains, finally, inscrutable to his readers.

Indeed, Grandison's performance thus enacts precisely the authorial role to which Chesnutt aspired: the ex-slave draws on and exploits his readers' assumptions to compose his (literal) freedom, while Chesnutt sought to inscribe his own (artistic) liberty using the same means. Grandison becomes, then, an author modeled after his creator, and this 1899 story suggests the extent to which Chesnutt believed that he might, like his fictional proxy, *successfully* encode messages that both appealed to and subverted the expectations of his mostly white audience.

7/ Conclusion

The Blackballing of Charles W. Chesnutt

I f the "The Passing of Grandison" (1899) indicates the extent to which Chesnutt believed he could prosper as "an early 'spy in the enemy's country'" (Petesch 139), the publication five years later of "Baxter's Procrustes" (1904) attests to his recognition of a far more constrained authorial role for himself in the American literary tradition. Aware of his increasingly precarious relationship with predominantly white readers, Chesnutt drew on his experiences with the Rowfant Club to produce "Baxter's Procrustes," a multilayered satire of book collectors, hostile critics, and the *fin de siècle* reading audience who had responded unenthusiastically to most of his work.[1] Indeed, this story refracts Chesnutt's experiences with the club into provocative commentary on his attempts to inscribe himself as a black writer onto the "inviolate" pages of a white literary tradition. Even more tellingly, perhaps, its subsequent reissue by the same club sixty years later as a "rare" book ironically recapitulates the ongoing construction of Chesnutt's reputation.

In 1902 friends of Chesnutt proposed him for membership in the Rowfant Club, an association of bibliophiles who shared many of the preoccupations of the characters lampooned in "Baxter's Procrustes." The process by which the club considered new members called for at least two members to inscribe a candidate's name in their own handwriting; following a two-week deliberation period, the entire membership would secretly vote using black and white marbles. In Chesnutt's case, the balloting resulted in his rejection after two black marbles were cast among a host of white. Thus, Chesnutt found himself black-balled, primarily because the club was not yet ready for its first black member. Despite his disappointment, Chesnutt must have appreciated the irony inherent in the marble/d method of bal-loting: the club preserved its sanctuary of whiteness precisely through an irruption of blackness.

Two years after his blackballing by the Rowfant Club, Chesnutt satirized a similar group of book collectors in "Baxter's Procrustes," which became the seventh and final story he published in the *Atlantic Monthly*. When assessing the relative merit of books, the members of the fictional Bodleian Club favor expansive white margins over the clutter of black print. Hence, they value a predominance of whiteness on the page, with only "a beautiful, slender stream" of black text interrupting "a wide meadow of margin" (*CS* 274). Baxter, a cynical member of the club who serves in many ways as a proxy for Chesnutt, responds by "writing" a poem that enacts an extreme version of this philosophy: the result is a text of "all margin" (277). Because the club members have all had their copies sealed in order to enhance the book's worth, no one notices, until the end of the story when a visitor "cuts" his copy, that the text con-sists entirely of blank pages. Despite this Emperor's-new-clothes trickery, Baxter finds his attempt at subversion turned back on itself when the members of the Bodleian ultimately decide that a book composed exclusively of whiteness represents the acme of bookmaking: a sealed copy of Baxter's *Procrustes* thus sells for "the highest price ever brought by a single volume published by the club" (278).

Published late in Chesnutt's literary career—only *The Colonel's Dream* (1905) and a handful of short stories reached print after 1904—"Baxter's Procrustes" satirically encapsulates the attempts of "an unsuccessful author" (*CS* 269) to strike back at a reading establishment that consciously undervalues literary

merit: the narrator of the story, Jones, admits that, when considering manuscripts for publication, the club prizes "the qualities that make a book valuable in the eyes of collectors" (267),
which he articulates in the list below:

> Of these, age could not, of course, be imparted, but in the
> matter of fine and curious bindings, of hand-made linen
> papers, of uncut or deckle edges, of wide margins and limited
> editions, the club could control its own publications. *The matter
> of contents was, it must be confessed, a less important consideration.*
> (267, emphasis added)

Thus, Chesnutt offers what John B. Nicholson, Jr.—the editor of
the 1966 reissue of *Baxter's Procrustes* as a book—calls "a soft-
spoken ribbing of all whose hearts belong more to the physical
world of rare tomes than to their spiritual and intellectual contents" (*BP* 39).

At the center of this "ribbing" is the figure of Baxter himself, an author whose priorities from the outset differ from
those of his peers in the club. When Baxter tells the narrator
that he has thrown away the proof sheets for his poem, for
example, Jones is shocked by "[t]his indifference . . . to literary
values": indeed, he argues, "The proof sheets of 'Hamlet,' cor-
rected in Shakespeare's own hand, would be well-nigh price-
less" (*CS* 272). Chesnutt's marginalization of Baxter within the
literary milieu of the Bodleian Club takes on added significance
in light of how closely the description of Baxter corresponds
with Chesnutt's own appearance, demeanor, and experiences,
thereby making the character an apparent proxy for his creator:

> He was about thirty-five when he joined the club, and appar-
> ently some bitter experience—some disappointment in love or
> ambition—had left its mark upon his character. With light,
> curly hair, fair complexion and gray eyes, one would have
> expected Baxter to be genial of temper, with a tendency toward
> wordiness of speech. But though he had flashes of humor, his
> ordinary demeanor was characterized by a mild cynicism,
> which, with his gloomy, pessimistic philosophy, so foreign to

> the temperament that should accompany his physical type,
> could only be accounted for upon the hypothesis of some
> secret sorrow such as I have suggested. (268–69)

Although he was past forty-five when he published "Baxter's Procrustes," the rest of this passage rings true for the light-complected, gray-eyed, mildly cynical Chesnutt. And while William L. Andrews rightly cautions against affixing a too certain biographical reading to the work, he also suggests that the story "offers many tantalizing hints about its author's private frustrations, his self-concept, and his view of the literary life after his own full-time career had been cut short" (*Literary Career* 220).[2] Indeed, writes Andrews, "Baxter is Chesnutt's most elaborate self-dramatization, the most transparent and close-fitting of the many masks the author assumed in his fiction" (214).

Like Chesnutt and *his* audience, Baxter remains an inscrutable figure to the discriminating readers of the Bodleian Club: they profoundly and repeatedly misread him throughout the story. When a committee of three reviewers deliberates on the literary merits of the poem—despite none of them having read the text—they freely conflate author with poem, one of them declaring unequivocally that Baxter "'has written himself into the poem. By knowing Baxter we are able to appreciate the book, and after having read the book we feel that we are so much the more intimately acquainted with Baxter—the real Baxter'" (*CS* 273). The reviewers' unwillingness to unseal (and thus devalue) their own copies engenders this self-imposed critical myopia, but the scene also reveals their consistently inadequate reading skills, whether the text under consideration is Baxter or a bound collection of blank pages: indeed, the reviewers unintentionally indicate here how thoroughly they equate Baxter with blankness, a blankness onto which they blithely impose their own (inaccurate) "meaning." When the narrator steps out into the hall, for example, during this farcical literary discussion, he bumps into the eavesdropping Baxter, who is "smiling with an immensely pleased expression" (274). Jones promptly pronounces Baxter's merriment a ruse, concocted in a futile attempt to mask "his delight at our appreciation" (274–75).

But while the pretensions of the bookmen do serve to focus much of the satire of "Baxter's Procrustes," a modern audience might easily fall into the same reader traps that ensnare Jones and his fellow (mis)readers. For although Chesnutt embeds within the story a largely autobiographical description of Baxter—apparently locating himself in direct opposition to the bookmen—his relationship to the members of the club and their ideals remains enigmatic. He shared, for example, the passion he satirically attributes to them: Chesnutt too proved a considerable bibliophile, both before and after the publication of "Baxter's Procrustes." Houghton, Mifflin published his first collection of short stories in both a trade edition and a special limited large-paper edition. Helen M. Chesnutt attests to the degree to which her father prized the latter:

> The people of Cleveland were so interested [in the publication of *The Conjure Woman*] that some of the members of the Rowfant Club suggested to Houghton, Mifflin and Company that they issue a special limited Large-Paper Edition of the book. Subscription forms were sent out, and the subscriptions justified the issue of a Large-Paper Edition of one hundred and fifty numbered copies at the same time as the trade edition was issued. This Large-Paper Edition was printed on hand-made linen paper, and bound in linen-colored buckram. . . . Later on, when Chesnutt became a member of the Rowfant Club, he had his author's copy of the Large-Paper Edition rebound in blue morocco with hand-tooled designs at the Rowfant bindery; this volume remains a family treasure. (106)

Note how the language used to describe this large-paper edition of *The Conjure Woman*—the book, composed of "hand-made linen paper," is "rebound in blue morocco with hand-tooled designs"—closely parallels the language *Jones* invokes when outlining the standards which determine a book's "value" to collectors.

Chesnutt's subsequent reapplication (and admission) to the

Rowfant Club in 1910 after its initial rejection of him eight years earlier also indicates that he harbored no sustained antipathy for bibliophiles. He had been gently ironic about the 1902 snubbing—"It would be mighty nice to be a member of the club," he told his daughter, "but if they don't want me, I can get along without them" (H. Chesnutt 244)—and his attitude did not change appreciably after the club elected him. In a letter to Frederick Goff in 1910, he announces his intention to accept a place in the club, all the while maintaining a tone of ironic detachment:

> A month or two ago, Ginn asked me one day If I would care to join the Rowfant Club, observing that there would be no difficulty about it this time. I replied that if they could stand it, I could, but that I would like to have him feel pretty certain about the matter before he put my name up, as I would not care to go through the same experience. It went through all right, and I anticipate considerable pleasure from the company of gentlemen with whom I am "at last found worthy to associate." (H. Chesnutt 244–45)

And indeed Chesnutt did derive "considerable pleasure" from his association with the club, as his daughter verifies:

> Chesnutt enjoyed these Saturday nights at the Rowfant Club. There he met, in delightful fellowship, some of the finest and most scholarly men of Cleveland. . . .
>
> When his turn came to contribute to the Saturday night programs he was delighted, and spent a great deal of time in research and in writing. His first paper entitled "Who and Why was Samuel Johnson" was read in November, 1911. (H. Chesnutt 289)

Over several years, Chesnutt apparently enjoyed delivering several more papers, on such diverse figures as François Villon, Alexander Dumas, and George Meredith; in short, the club apparently suited him and he suited it. It seems entirely fitting that the Rowfant Club decided, nearly thirty-five years after Chesnutt's death, to republish one of his works.

In fact, its members—as represented by John Nicholson, the editor of the 1966 special edition of *Baxter's Procrustes*— embrace with good humor the satire Chesnutt directs their way. Nicholson devotes a significant portion of his biographical essay of Chesnutt to outlining a history of satirical treatments of bookmen, of which he places "Baxter's Procrustes" among the first rank:

> No group of men gathered together under so happy an order-ing of bookish pleasure could fail to enjoy exposure of the many-faceted idiosyncracies of their bibliolatrous fellows. Book-men have for centuries enjoyed literary exposures of their col-lective weaknesses. . . . Its expose of Rowfanters is sly but urbane, incisively pricking their precious conceits. (38–39)

Nicholson concludes his essay by invoking the "unique Row-fantian democracy" to claim that

> the man whose imagination brought this satirical story to life stands behind its printed pages, not as a man of any business or profession, not as a man of some particular race, not even as a man of any faith, but simply as a free creative mind sensing the foolishness of man prejudging man, and reacting with a kindly humorous wisdom to the nonsense in all men. (39)

Nicholson's reading of Chesnutt becomes crucial, then, to his editorial endeavor, and indeed he offers an astute and fair-minded assessment of his subject. Although Nicholson perhaps too confidently asserts where "the man whose imagination brought this satirical story to life stands" in relation to his sub-jects, Chesnutt likely would have appreciated Nicholson's read-ing. Nicholson's claim, in fact, that the central thrust of "Bax-ter's Procrustes" is aimed at "the foolishness of man prejudging man" attests to his perceptive grasp of Chesnutt's intentions in the story and indeed throughout his career.

Despite Nicholson's benevolence toward his fellow Rowfanter, however, much of his editorial work recapitulates both the modern construction of Chesnutt's literary reputation and the sort of interpretive practices originally satirized in the story. The Rowfant Club's reissue of "Baxter's Procrustes" as a limited edition volume *(Baxter's Procrustes)*—replete with the accouterments lampooned in the 1904 story—emphasizes only certain strands of the story's original multifaceted satire. Following the text of *Baxter's Procrustes,* for example, this note appears:

> . . . The paper [for this edition] was mould-made in Holland. The book has also been bound by The Prairie Press in Columbia Colonial Linen, stamped in genuine gold. Sides and endpapers are Dutch Charcoal, imported from Holland. The edition is limited to one hundred eighty copies.

Immediately following this note is the handwritten number indicating which of the one hundred and eighty copies the reader possesses. Hence, the subjects of Chesnutt's satire have appropriated his work in much the same way members of the Bodleian Club make use of Baxter's *Procrustes:* as a rare (and presumably profitable) book.

Nicholson's editorial revisions entail more, however, than arranging for pricey trappings. On page 31 of the 1966 edition of *Baxter's Procrustes,* the text of the story stops five lines from the bottom of the page, followed by this textual note:

> The next page is a facsimile of page 17 of the original edition of "Procrustes," as published by Mr. Baxter, excepting only the paper but including the wide margins and the rare typography—Publication Committee (*Baxter's Procrustes* 31)

The following page of the book is blank, and the story proper resumes on page thirty-three. None of the versions published during Chesnutt's lifetime includes either the blank page or the explanatory note. In the interest of contributing to the Baxter's gag, then, Nicholson and the "publication committee" have thus literalized Chesnutt's literary conceit, offering an odd inversion of Ralph Ellison's comment about black writers using their heritage to "change the joke and slip the yoke." Indeed, by here changing the joke, Nicholson inadvertently slips his subject back into a critical yoke that Chesnutt knew all too well in his own life.

For Nicholson has taken, albeit benevolently and with great good humor,[3] the same critical liberties as the ones that have resulted in Chesnutt's unfortunate reputation. His editorial revision of "Baxter's Procrustes" re-enacts the process by which Chesnutt has been marginalized by turn-of-the-century and modern readers. During his life, Chesnutt regularly encountered reviews by those who based their objections to his work on what Andrews calls "extra-literary" grounds, usually having something to do with race.[4] One anonymous reviewer of *The Marrow of Tradition,* for example, chastises Chesnutt for this "book of lies and slander" before admitting to not having read the work; a second reviewer "withholds" final judgment of *Marrow* until the author publishes a picture of himself so that his race can be determined. Even readers sympathetic to Chesnutt often misconstrue him, as happens when a reviewer who praises *The Wife of His Youth* lists "The Blue Vein Society"—a title Chesnutt never used—as one of the stronger pieces of the volume.[5] If turn-of-the-century reviewers mislabeled his works, though, they merely prepared the ground for more recent scholarship. One modern scholar who finds Chesnutt's works generally "defective" nevertheless lauds the achievement of a story called "Baxter's Procrust*ers*."[6] By adding the literal blank page, then, Nicholson inadvertently (and humorously, I might add) maintains a century-old tradition in which readers appropriate Chesnutt's work only to foreground "extra-literary" matters.

The way this tradition has evolved might well have appealed to the sense of irony of an author whose short fiction relied on subtlety and paradox to disorient readers. For, while the changes made to transform "Baxter's Procrustes" (1904) into *Baxter's Procrustes* (1966) literalize the critical impulse to appropriate his work, they also amplify the final bleak irony inherent in the original: although members of the Bodleian Club feel "badly sold" by Baxter's ruse (*CS* 277), they ultimately profit from the exchange, a result which must have irked Baxter no less than it depressed Chesnutt. In the coda to the story, the president of the Bodleian thus emphasizes the hopeless predicament of the marginalized writer, even one who attempts to strike back at the literary establishment. For the "rewards" of his plot accrue not to Baxter but to the Club, whose crass economic interests he had set out to expose and deflate: "'[Baxter's] *Procrustes*,'" the president says at the end of the story,

> "from the collector's point of view, is entirely logical, and might be considered as the acme of bookmaking. To the true collector, a book is a work of art, of which the contents are no more important than the words of an opera. Fine binding is a desideratum, and, for its cost, that of the *Procrustes* could not be improved upon. The paper is above criticism. The true collector loves wide margins, and the *Procrustes*, being all margin, merely touches the vanishing point of the perspective." (277)

Hence, those who value a "wide meadow of margin" (274) and the financial rather than literary elements of writing ultimately profit from a book with margins so wide as to preclude the trespass of text. And Chesnutt's story—which both satirizes bookmen and recapitulates his own marginalization as a black intellectual—ends with an acknowledgment that poor reading skills often prove profitable nevertheless, although rarely to the marginalized.

While "Baxter's Procrustes" has Baxter's satiric literalization of the bookmen's sense of value turned back on itself, the 1966 version heralds yet another ironic reversal, one even Chesnutt could not have forecast. The critical reputation of the story provides one last (although not "final") irony: "Baxter's Procrustes" is generally regarded as its author's finest work.[7] Thus, Chesnutt's attempt to inscribe himself—a black text— onto the white pages of the American literary tradition comes closest to achievement in a story that celebrates the obliteration of black text, an implicit acknowledgment of the value of "inviolateness" (*CS* 271).

If the story itself thus thematizes Chesnutt's "blackballing" in his own time, the Rowfant Club's 1966 reissue of "Baxter's Procrustes" as a wide-margin collector's edition ironically refigures a different version of that blackballing: the modern construction of Chesnutt's reputation. For in acting out—intentionally or not—much of the bibliophile behavior satirized in the story, as well as in adding a literal blank page to Chesnutt's text, the later editor anticipates the tenor of Chesnutt scholarship. Indeed, readers continue to undervalue a writer whose sophisticated narrative and metacritical strategies have paradoxically consigned him to his own procrustean bed.

Notes

1. See Joseph R. McElrath, Jr., and Robert C. Leitz, III, who, in their introduction to Chesnutt's letters, argue that Chesnutt was "not literally the first contributor to imaginative literature" by an African American (*"To Be an Author": Letters of Charles W. Chesnutt, 1889–1905* [hereafter abbreviated *Letters*] 8). They cite the attention Dunbar received, particularly Howells's review of *Lyrics of Lowly Life* in 1896. Indeed, Dunbar also published a novel in 1899, a full year before Chesnutt's first novel. I would nevertheless suggest that Dunbar's literary reputation was almost entirely (and not fairly) based on his poetry. Thus, I follow William L. Andrews in maintaining that Chesnutt is "the first important Afro-American writer of fiction" (*Literary Career* xi).

2. See McElrath and Leitz for commentary on Chesnutt's literary identity.

3. To exclude Chesnutt from any discussion of literary manipulations of double-consciousness is difficult. *The Conjure Woman* features the most frequently cited example of Chesnutt's handling of complex narrative interactions, but the same tendency is apparent, even foregrounded, in fictions such as "The Wife of His Youth," "A Grass Widow," and "Her Virginia Mammy." See also Sylvia Lyons Render's commentary on Chesnutt's "double vision" in *The Short Fiction of Charles W. Chesnutt* (hereafter abbreviated *SF*) 3.

4. Chesnutt no doubt would bristle at Jones's classification, particularly in that she explicitly compares his literary "sensibility" to that of William Wells Brown. In his journals, Chesnutt writes, "I have skimmed 'The Negro

in the [American] Rebellion,' by Dr. Brown, and it only strengthens me in my opinion, that the Negro is yet to become known who can write a good book" (*The Journals of Charles W. Chesnutt,* ed. Richard H. Brodhead [hereafter abbreviated *Journals*] 164).

5. See Howells, "Mr. Charles W. Chesnutt's Stories," for extended commentary on Chesnutt's work.

6. For a more comprehensive rendering of biographical data, see Helen Chesnutt's *Charles Waddell Chesnutt: Pioneer of the Color Line* (1952), Frances Richardson Keller's *An American Crusade: The Life of Charles Waddell Chesnutt* (1978), Sylvia Lyons Render's *Charles W. Chesnutt* (1980), and William L. Andrews's *The Literary Career of Charles W. Chesnutt* (1980). For Chesnutt's commentaries on his own life, see the recently published *Journals* (1993), which record Chesnutt's sporadic diary entries between 1874 and 1882, and *Letters* (1997).

7. See the *Letters,* especially missives to Houghton, Mifflin in 1891, to S. Alice Haldeman in 1896, and to Booker T. Washington in 1903, for Chesnutt's commentary on his own racial identity. See also the McElrath and Leitz note, in the *Letters,* citing an 1899 interview with Pauline C. Bouvé in which Chesnutt identified himself "as 'a descendant of three races,' the third being determined by 'Indian blood he inherits from an aboriginal ancestor'" (125). The *Journals* likewise chronicle Chesnutt's interest in his own racial identity; see particularly the 1881 entry in which he compares his position in the South to that of the Mahomet's Coffin (157–58).

8. Again, the *Journals* and the *Letters* record valuable evidence of Chesnutt's ambitions concerning a potential career as a writer. See especially the 1881 entry in the *Journals* in which he declares that "the dream of [his] life" is "to be an author!" (154). See also the 1890 letter to George Washington Cable for Chesnutt's assertion that "if it [the financial success of his business] continues . . . , I shall be able in a very few years to take the chances of devoting myself entirely to literary work, which I earnestly hope to do; meanwhile I look forward to a little leisure for writing during the summer" (*Letters* 64).

9. Although Chesnutt claimed in an 1899 letter to Walter Hines Page to "have retired from business since October 1, with the intention of devoting my time henceforth to literary pursuits of one kind or another" (*Letters* 133), it is not clear how long he remained "retired." See McElrath and Leitz's note (134) regarding the matter; they assert that "by August 1902 he [Chesnutt] was again fully involved in his old occupation" (*Letters* 134).

10. See, for example, the 1891 letter to George Washington Cable in

which Chesnutt writes, "My business for the past year has been very absorbing, and has netted me a handsome income. I stand at the parting of two ways: by strict attention to business, and its natural development, I see a speedy competence and possible wealth before me. On the other hand, I see probably a comfortable living and such compensations as the literary life has to offer. I think I have made my choice of the latter, though it will be a year yet before I can safely adopt it" (*Letters* 72). In another 1891 letter, this one to Walter Hines Page, Chesnutt laments that "[t]he only question with me is that the money returns from literature are so small and so uncertain, that I have not had the time to spare from an absorbing and profitable business to devote to it" (77). And in an 1893 letter to Albion Tourgée, he writes, "I am simply biding my time, and hope in the near future to devote the greater part of my time to literary production" (78). Despite the tone of optimism here, it would still be several years before Chesnutt could follow up on his dream to pursue exclusively the "literary life." McElrath and Leitz, in fact, title the section of the *Letters* recording Chesnutt's correspondence between 1891 and 1896 "A Dream Deferred, 1891–1896: The Businessman Prevails."

11. The final entry in the recently published *Letters* provides a sadly ironic commentary on Chesnutt's literary career. In a 1905 letter to Walter Hines Page, Chesnutt enthusiastically recalls his attendance at Mark Twain's seventieth birthday party at Delmonico's restaurant in New York. He calls the experience "very inspiring" (236), but although he had been briefly a shining light in American letters, his literary career was essentially over.

12. Sylvia Lyons Render collected those four fictions as well as virtually all of Chesnutt's previously unpublished and uncollected stories in *The Short Fiction of Charles W. Chesnutt* (1974, reprinted, with added bibliography,1981). Joseph R. McElrath has collected Chesnutt's speeches and essays for a forthcoming book .

13. Cable and Tourgée especially helped Chesnutt and served, in different ways, to inspire his literary ambitions. McElrath and Leitz, in fact, describe Cable as Chesnutt's "mentor" (20), and Tourgée also corresponded regularly, beginning in the late 1880s, with the budding author. See the entry in the *Journals* from 1880 for an account of how Tourgée's publication of *A Fool's Errand* (1879) particularly kindled Chesnutt's authorial ambitions, in large part because of the $20,000 Tourgée received for the novel:

> And if Judge Tourgee [*sic*], with his necessarily limited intercourse
> with colored people, and with his limited stay in the South, can write

such interesting descriptions, such vivid pictures of Southern life and character as to make himself rich and famous, why could not a colored man, who has lived among colored people all his life; who is familiar with their habits, their ruling passions, their prejudices; their whole moral and social condition; their public and private ambitions; their religious tendencies and habits;—why could not a colored man who knew all this, and who, besides, had possessed such opportunities for observation and conversation with the better class of white men in the south as to understand their modes of thinking; who was familiar with the political history of the country, and especially with all the phases of the slavery question;—why could not such a man, if he possessed the same ability, write a far better book about the South than Judge Tourgee or Mrs. Stowe has written? Answer who can! (125)

14. Chesnutt in his *Journals* emphasizes his experiences in the South during Reconstruction as a potentially rich source of information for his writing ambitions: "Fifteen years of life in the South, in one of the most eventful eras of its history; among a people whose life is rich in the elements of romance; under conditions calculated to stir one's soul to the very depths;—I think there is here a fund of experience, a supply of material, which a skillful pers[on] could work up with tremendous effect" (139).

15. Render similarly argues that in "Baxter's Procrustes" Chesnutt "demonstrated more impressively than ever before his mastery of the short-story form" (*Charles W. Chesnutt* 42).

16. Howells likewise emphasizes Chesnutt's reticence, a quality particularly well-suited for the production of realist fictions.

17. See especially Robert Hemenway's essay on the functions of folklore in *The Conjure Woman*.

18. References to *The Conjure Woman (CW)* are to the 1969 edition edited by Robert M. Farnsworth.

19. Some readers envision Chesnutt's ability to efface himself from his fiction as evidence of "masking" or "veiling." See particularly Donald A. Petesch, who suggests that "Chesnutt's narrative strategy should be viewed as the consummate masking, the 'sermon' made palatable" (138). Henry Louis Gates, Jr.'s, *Signifying Monkey* offers a lucid overview of this convention of African-American literature. See also Valerie Babb, P. Jay Delmar, and Lorne Fienberg ("Black Storytellers") for commentary on this issue.

20. Later, Dunbar famously commented on the tradition in "We Wear the Mask": "With torn and bleeding hearts we smile, / And mouth with myriad subtleties" (71).

21. Commentators continue to have difficulty asserting an authorial

identity for Chesnutt. See, for example, McElrath and Leitz: "Over a century later, though, the literary historian can still legitimately pose the question he [Chesnutt] did: what was Charles W. Chesnutt? How should we construct a frame of reference appropriate for him?" (4).

22. See Ralph Ellison's comments in "The Art of Fiction: An Interview," *Shadow and Act* (New York: Random House, 1953), p. 177.

23. In the Preface to *Uncle Tom's Cabin*, Harriet Beecher Stowe describes blacks as cipher in American culture, indeed as "a race hitherto ignored by the associations of polite and refined society" (v).

24. See Andrews, *To Tell a Free Story:* "Reaching 'the hearts of men' was the rhetorical aim of practically all black autobiography in the first century of its existence, whether produced by an ex-slave or not" (5).

25. Chesnutt remained more or less neutral in what Andrews calls "the schism in Afro-American leadership and politics [and] he avoided identifying himself with either side" (*Literary Career* 263). See Chesnutt's *Letters* for his correspondence with both Du Bois and Washington, especially the letter of 1903 to the latter (181–82).

26. In his introduction to *The African-American Novel in the Age of Reaction,* Andrews argues that "the cause of antislavery became an end in itself for the early African-American novel" (vii). See this introduction for a discussion of the development of the African-American novel.

27. See the *Journals* for Chesnutt's commentary on this matter: "I occupy here a position similar to that of the Mahomet's Coffin. I am neither fish[,] flesh, nor fowl—neither 'nigger', poor white, nor 'buckrah.' Too 'stuck-up' for the colored folks, and, of course, not recognized by the whites" (157).

28. See especially Elaine K. Ginsberg for commentary on the ways in which "both the process and the discourse of passing interrogate the ontology of identity categories and their construction" ("Introduction" 4).

29. Several writers—both black and white and including such figures as Griggs, Harper, Twain, and Howells—featured extended treatments of "passing" in the mid- to late-nineteenth century. See in particular Eric Sundquist's *To Wake the Nations* and the collection of essays titled *Passing and the Fictions of Identity,* edited by Elaine K. Ginsberg, for commentary on issues relating to the literary uses of passing.

30. See, for example, an anonymous review in the *Boston Journal* praising Chesnutt for treating his subject "courageously and with originality" (qtd. in Ellison and Metcalf 34). The reviewer for the *Boston Christian Register* likewise lauds the novel, suggesting that with it "Chesnutt has won for himself a secure place in the literary world." And an anonymous review for

the *Philadelphia Times* suggests that Chesnutt writes about this subject more convincingly than did Howells (qtd. in Ellison and Metcalf 33). Reviewers for the *Detroit Free Press* and the *Chicago Post* (33–34) likewise praise the novel.

31. See Render's introduction, especially p. 18, to *Short Fiction* for a discussion of Chesnutt's precise use of dialect.

32. In "A Black Grimm," a review of *The Short Fiction of Charles W. Chesnutt,* Jackson C. Boswell writes that Chesnutt's "specialty is the dramatic presentation of subtle characters against authentic backgrounds. Not unexpectedly he writes sympathetically about the conditions of colored in the Cape Fear River valley, and he makes his mark by his objective kindly treatment of poor whites" (31).

33. See Howells, "A Psychological Counter-Current in Recent Fiction." *North American Review* 173 (December 1901): 880.

34. See also Arlene A. Elder: "Chesnutt's progress toward assimilation and away from the common black experience can be traced easily in his business and social careers and, most tellingly, in his art" (127); see also SallyAnn H. Ferguson, who calls Chesnutt a "social accommodationist" (109).

35. Although I agree with McElrath and Leitz in suspecting that Chesnutt's reputation is "waxing," he nevertheless continues to receive less attention than he seems to deserve. According to a recent survey of the MLA bibliography, Chesnutt has been the subject of thirty-seven (37) articles, essays, books, and dissertations since 1988, not quite four a year; during the same period, Toni Morrison has prompted more than four hundred (more than forty a year), and Alice Walker and Zora Neale Hurston combine for nearly five hundred. And no book-length study devoted exclusively to Chesnutt appeared between 1980, when William L. Andrews published *The Literary Career of Charles W. Chesnutt,* and Ernestine Williams Pickens's *Charles W. Chesnutt and the Progressive Movement* in 1994. There appears to be a happy upswing in the amount of Chesnutt scholarship; McElrath has edited, for example, a collection of essays devoted exclusively to Chesnutt (*Critical Essays on Charles W. Chesnutt,* forthcoming from Twayne).

36. In his *Journals,* Chesnutt offers bitter commentary on his relationship with whites: "I hear colored men speak of their 'white friends'. I have no white friends. I could not degrade the sacred name of 'Friendship' by associating it with any man who feels himself too good to sit at table with me, or to sleep at the same hotel" (172). I do not quote this clearly emotional passage as a means of arguing that Chesnutt had a lifelong hostility toward whites, but it suggests, at the least, his ambivalent attitude on that subject. In such a context, it seems doubtful that he is being earnest here

in advocating that "genuine negroes' trust in their "best friends" for social help.

37. See Chesnutt's *Journals:* "If I do write, I shall write for a purpose, and this will inspire me to greater effort. The object of my writings would be not so much the elevation of the colored people as the elevation of the whites" (139).

38. The glossary of *The Dialogic Imagination* defines *polyglossia* this way: "The simultaneous presence of two or more national languages interacting within a single cultural system" (431). To apply this term to Chesnutt, one must make certain allowances, including the idea that American English and black vernacular both function as "national languages."

CHAPTER 2. THE WHITE AND THE BLACK . . . AND
THE LIMITS OF AUTHORSHIP

1. Many of Chesnutt's stories likewise take advantage of a kind of textual ambiguity, which results in what might be called "mulatto" texts. See Raymond Hedin for commentary on the pressures, for Chesnutt, of having to make "[t]he black story [which] had to look like a white story" (195). Also, see Samira Kawash, who argues that Johnson's *The Autobiography of an Ex-Colored Man* likewise constitutes an "unstable identity" (60): "the text itself passes back and forth between the poles of truth and fiction, autobiography and novel. . . . [The novel] is itself the subject of another passing narrative" (60). I want to suggest later in this chapter that "The Shadow of My Past" similarly calls into question the notion of stable racial and/or textual identities.

2. See also Chesnutt's essay "What Is a White Man?" There, the author taxonomizes how each southern state codified different classification systems for determining race identities for citizens. Chesnutt clearly enjoys satirizing the states' inability to reach consensus on distinguishing between whites and blacks.

3. See especially Eric J. Sundquist for commentary on "Chesnutt's career as a writer of racial fiction—a career in which he found himself caught, as he did in his professional life as an aspiring attorney, between two worlds and responsive to a multitude of problems marked by a color line that was drawn as starkly through the practice of literature as through American society at large" (271).

4. The exact date of composition is difficult to assert. I follow Render's dating in *Short Fiction* (427).

5. Although Chesnutt made no effort to conceal his racial identity, it

was not publicly well established until 1898. See his 1898 letter to Walter Hines Page (*Letters* 109–10), and also the note McElrath and Leitz provide (110), for further elaboration.

6. An *Atlanta Journal* reviewer of *The Marrow of Tradition* reserves judgment, for example, until Chesnutt publishes his picture so that readers can determine his race (qtd. in Ellison and Metcalf 50). Another contemporary reviewer dismisses one of Chesnutt's books without having read it: "Despite the fact that we have not seen the book, we have seen it reviewed and so know the truth of it" (qtd. in Ellison and Metcalf 53).

7. This shifting narrative persona also contributes to readers' uncertainty about Chesnutt's views and attitudes. Responding to "A Matter of Principle," for example, J. Saunders Redding asks, "But what is Chesnutt's conviction as an artist? Does he sympathize with the existence of a color caste within the race? . . . Of what is he trying to convince us?" (71). More recently, Jeannette S. White suggests that our unease as readers in the *Conjure* tales derives from our sense that Chesnutt, not Julius, is "the conjure man working his spell" on us (102).

8. In "The Shadow of My Past," Hal disguises his identity—checking in at a hotel under a pseudonym—in almost precisely the manner used by John Walden in *The House Behind the Cedars*. Both characters are thus established as "spies in the enemy's country," although Hal is, of course, a much more comic figure.

9. *The House Behind the Cedars* also relies on what Cooke would call "self-veiling." Much of that novel's plot depends on the ability of the mulatto protagonist to sustain her masquerade as a white woman, a mask she eventually discards. Indeed, the title of Chesnutt's second published novel metaphorically suggests her hidden state. Her entire family remains concealed for most of the novel behind the protective barrier of a row of cedars. While Cooke seems to foreground the social and financial considerations that encourage blacks to veil themselves, however, the practice might be viewed from a different perspective. In *The Conjure Woman, The Marrow of Tradition,* and *The House Behind the Cedars,* Chesnutt seems more concerned with the inability of his protagonists to position themselves within the hostile social matrix of Reconstruction. That is, these characters rarely benefit by "passing," or by blurring racial categories. If anything, these works convey the anguish of these characters as they try to establish a workable identity for themselves.

10. See especially such works as "The Passing of Grandison," "The Doll," and "Mars Jeems's Nightmare."

11. Note the melodramatic tone that characterizes the novel, which renders the struggles of "Rena [Walden] and her brother, upon whom God

had lavished his best gifts, and from whom society would have withheld all that made these gifts valuable" (128).

12. In those works, both protagonists adapt to social and personal circumstances. Both, in short, reinvent themselves: Grandison as a free man and Ryder as a husband and ex-slave.

13. In spite of its light tone, "The Shadow of My Past" seems to owe some debt to Edgar Allan Poe's literary gamesmanship, and especially to his use of dark doubles as distorted reflections of identity.

14. While works such as "Cicely's Dream," "The Sheriff's Children," and *The Marrow of Tradition* ground their treatments of the struggles of black Americans in historical fact—drawing on slavery, Reconstruction, and race riots, for example—"The Shadow of My Past" examines metaphorically the barriers to integration.

15. Despite the apparently stock comic situation of "The Shadow of My Past," the story nevertheless continues Chesnutt's dissection of what William L. Andrews calls "a great social paradox of his era—America's official praise of democracy and its unofficial practice of exclusivism and discrimination" (277).

16. In "Cicely's Dream," for example, the protagonist's attempts to build a life for herself with an amnesiac of indeterminate race ultimately fail. Because of the intrusion of a specifically white past—in the figure of her lover's betrothed—into the (black) present she has constructed, Cicely loses her fiancé and her dreams of a happy marriage. Similarly, "The Sheriff's Children" recounts the social turmoil foisted on Tom—the product of a biracial union—whose father sells him into slavery. Unable finally to position himself, despite some formal education, in the social matrix of Reconstruction, Tom dies a violent death at the hands of his white sister.

17. See Ginsberg for commentary on passing as a form of trespass, and Hedin for specific discussion of Chesnutt's struggles with questions of textual "identity."

18. While readers have credited Chesnutt with "broaden[ing] the cultural record by teaching Whites to read Negro 'texts'" (Molyneaux 164), "The Shadow of My Past" demonstrates how he also was able to blur such distinctions as "white" texts and "black" texts.

CHAPTER 3. "THROUGH MY LEAFY VEIL": CHESNUTT'S NARRATIVE WITNESSES

1. Except for the narrator of "Concerning Father," a story considered later in this chapter, all of Chesnutt's first-person narrators are men.

2. See especially Andrews's comments in *To Tell a Free Story*. See also

Gates's provocative description of the slave narrative as "a countergenre, a mediation between the novel of sentiment and the picaresque" (*Figures in Black* 81).

3. Issues of voice and narrative presence in this regard are often controversial. See, for example, Mary Helen Washington's discussion, in her foreword to Hurston's *Their Eyes Were Watching God,* of the debate concerning "voice" as a central issue of that book.

4. Genette objects to the term "first-person," and although his objections have considerable merit, I use the term here in an attempt to keep the focus on Chesnutt's work rather than on the terminology of narrative theory.

5. Even a casual glance at Chesnutt's correspondence is enough to convince one that he thought (and wrote) in terms of business and finance. See, for example, his response in 1891 to Houghton, Mifflin after that firm had "gracefully decline[d]" a volume of his stories: "You say you doubt if my own interests would be best regarded by a publication at this time. If you meant my pecuniary interests, that was a secondary consideration with me, as I could perhaps afford to assume all the expense of publication if necessary" (*Letters* 76).

6. Chesnutt worked to support a variety of socially unempowered groups at the turn of the century. See McElrath and Leitz, who comment in a note that "When Chesnutt expresses strong emotion in his letters, it is typically provoked by outrages perpetrated against the African-American community" (67). In addition to his many essays regarding the fundamental unfairness with which African Americans were treated, he also wrote an essay to promote voting rights for women.

7. See Render, *The Short Fiction of Charles W. Chesnutt,* who suggests that while Chesnutt did include some stereotypical descriptions of blacks, he "usually added another facet to some of the popular black stereotypes which he found more acceptable, thus investing them with new depth and dimension" (20). William L. Andrews comments on this oddity as well, suggesting that "Chesnutt wrote his earliest sketches about blacks from a superior and self-consciously 'literary' point of view, as if to underline the story teller's strict detachment from his subject" (*Literary Career* 18). Andrews also finds that "Chesnutt was not above exploiting standard 'darkey humor'" (19).

8. See Lorne Fienberg, "Charles W. Chesnutt and Uncle Julius: Black Storytellers at the Crossroads": "Both the narrative frame and the tales of Chesnutt's collection are permeated by the signs of the marketplace and by the concern for economic value" (165).

9. Perhaps Chesnutt's most thorough exploration of the intersection

of race and commerce is *The Colonel's Dream,* his last novel. It is also, to use Andrews's terms, "a harsher, more lurid, and more sensationalistic exposé of southern socioeconomic conditions than even *The Marrow of Tradition* had been" (*Literary Career* 222).

10. See Chesnutt's comments on what he calls the "subtler forms of moral evil" in the *Journals* (136–37).

11. Letters also play a crucial role in *The House Behind the Cedars,* especially in that they reveal family and race secrets. Chesnutt clearly drew on the epistolary and sentimental novel tradition for his use of letters to produce narrative tension, and he also seems fascinated with the consequences of written (rather than oral) discourse. See also "The March of Progress," which offers extended interpretations of handwriting samples as evidence of character.

12. One comic exception occurs in "A Matter of Principle," in which the Clayton family huddles together in an attempt to "read" Congressman Brown's race by examining his letter to Alice and his initials on her "dancing programme" (*CS* 155–56).

13. In "Aunt Mimy's Son," the narrator shares a narrative style and many personal characteristics with John in *The Conjure Woman.* Similarly, in "McDugald's Mule," the narrating voice appears to be that of Julius.

14. "Aunt Mimy's Son" and "Uncle Wellington's Wives" differ from most of Chesnutt's works in that they seem less than enthusiastic about African Americans leaving the South for the North. See, for example, *The Colonel's Dream* for Chesnutt's most despairing commentary on life in the South for blacks (or liberal whites, for that matter). See also his essay "A Multitude of Counselors."

15. *The Marrow of Tradition,* for example, sold fewer than four thousand copies in the first five years after its publication. See *Letters* for Chesnutt's concern over the poor showing of his novels especially, and also for McElrath and Leitz's notes on sales matters. By way of contrast to *Marrow,* they note that Thomas Dixon's *The Leopard's Spots* (1902) sold 105,000 copies in its first year (172).

16. See the *Journals* for Chesnutt's frequent attempts to distinguish between himself and other African Americans, particularly those who travel by "2nd class car" (112).

17. The same thing is a likely result of reading "The Goophered Grapevine" (as well as other *Conjure* tales); it is interesting to note that "Goophered Grapevine" and "A Grass Widow" were both published in 1887, suggesting perhaps that Chesnutt consciously worked to create similar effects with different narrative tactics.

18. Virtually all of Chesnutt's best works conform to this description.

Consider "The Wife of His Youth," "Her Virginia Mammy," and "Cicely's Dream," for example, each of which relies on characters' sharing (and reshaping) of narratives.

19. See Wayne Booth's classic *The Rhetoric of Fiction* for clear and helpful commentary on all matters narrative.

CHAPTER 4: NEGOTIATING BELIEF AND VOICING DIFFERENCE

1. See "Post-Bellum—Pre-Harlem." No page numbers given. And in an 1898 letter to Walter Hines Page, Chesnutt seems unconcerned with the organization of tales in *The Conjure Woman;* he stipulates that, while "The Goophered Grapevine" should appear first, "the order is not essential" (*Letters* 113).

2. See *The Conjure Woman and Other Conjure Tales* (1993), which collects the fourteen conjure tales for the first time.

3. See the 1889 letter to Albion W. Tourgée for Chesnutt's premature announcement of the demise of Uncle Julius: "I think I have about used up the old Negro who serves as mouthpiece, and I shall drop him in future stories, as well as much of the dialect" (*Letters* 44). For more discussion of the typical characteristics of the conjure tales, see Brodhead's introduction to *The Conjure Woman and Other Conjure Tales;* he contends that the tales "follow a single formula, which might be labeled the plot of cultural tourism" (2).

4. See Render's *Short Fiction* (427) for her dating of Chesnutt's previously unpublished short fiction.

5. The "other" conjure stories feature some interesting modifications of the original formula. "The Dumb Witness," "Lonesome Ben," "Tobe's Tribulations," and "The Marked Tree" all feature variations that will be discussed later in this chapter.

6. See the *Journals* (155–56) for what Brodhead calls "the germ" of "Tom's Warm Welcome."

7. In most other ways, these three short stories conform to, and of course anticipate, the narrative paradigm featured in the conjure works.

8. In particular, see Harris's *Uncle Remus: His Songs and His Sayings* (1881).

9. For concise histories of the literary and cultural milieu in which Chesnutt's conjure stories appeared, see Farnsworth's introduction to *The Conjure Woman,* Brodhead's introduction to *The Conjure Woman and Other Conjure Tales,* and Andrews's *Literary Career,* especially pp. 17–73.

10. The *Journals* and the *Letters* contain numerous references to Chesnutt's desire that his works provide economic gain for himself while promoting social change. See, for example, the 1901 letter to Houghton, Mif-

flin in which he claims that "I have not been writing primarily for money, but with an ethical purpose entirely apart from that; yet I have always hoped that I might perchance strike a popular vein, for, unless my books are read I shall not be able to accomplish even the ethical purpose which I have in view" (*Letters* 171).

11. See Rimmon-Kenan's discussion in *A Glance beyond Doubt* of how *Beloved* is "obsessed with narratives and narration" (104). Chesnutt's work, especially in *The Conjure Woman*, anticipates the issues of representation and what Rimmon-Kenan calls "access" that play such a crucial role in Morrison's novels.

12. Sundquist describes, for example, what he calls Chesnutt's "divided sensibilities" (453). See also McElrath and Leitz's introduction to Chesnutt's *Letters* for commentary on the dual impulses of Chesnutt's artistic identity.

13. Although Julius is often described as a shaper of anti-slavery narratives, Michael G. Cooke argues that Julius provides "a tainted medium of information" because he has become "dull, numb to the suffering of others, and all taken up with his own immediate material needs" (57). Such a conclusion, however, discounts the evocative power of several of these works, including "Dave's Neckliss." Cooke's assertion also fails to account for those conjure stories which do not result in the gratification of Julius's immediate needs. Even John is forced to conclude at the end of "Hot-Foot Hannibal," for example, that he cannot discover any ulterior motive on Julius's part.

14. Indeed, one of the strengths of the conjure tales is the interpretive flexibility they provide. Comprehensive interpretations that account for Chesnutt's motives in all fourteen tales are difficult, at best, to assert.

15. There have been many fine discussions of these works, including especially those by David Britt, Lorne Fienberg ("Black Storytellers"), Richard J. Patton, and Robert B. Stepto.

16. See McElrath and Leitz for their note explaining that it is not known who (presumably either Walter Hines Page or Chesnutt) originated the title for the collection (114). See also Brodhead's suggestion "that *The Conjure Woman* was partly the work of its author, but partly too of an institutional context that controlled the terms of this author's appearance" (17). The uncertainty regarding Chesnutt's involvement in the naming of the collection (and other aspects of its production) further clouds interpretive issues.

17. See Bone, *Down Home* (1975). See also Fienberg ("Black Storytellers") and Cooke for discussions of the importance of the transformations to these works.

18. Chesnutt claims in "Post-Bellum—Pre-Harlem" that only "The Goophered Grapevine" derived explicitly from folklore. See Andrews, *Literary Career,* for a discussion of Chesnutt's fear that he "would be misrepresented as a follower of Joel Chandler Harris" (45–46).

19. "Dave's Neckliss" is regarded as one of Chesnutt's best conjure tales, although it differs in material ways from others of its type. In an 1889 letter to Tourgée, Chesnutt writes, "I tried in this story to get out of the realm of superstition into the region of feeling and passion—with what degree of success the story itself can testify" (*Letters* 44). See also Brodhead's discussion, especially pp. 17–19, of "Dave's Neckliss."

20. See Pryse and Spillers for contextual information and provocative discussions of "conjure" as literary motif, especially in its relationship with women.

21. In works such as "The Sheriff's Children," "Her Virginia Mammy," "The Wife of His Youth," "The Web of Circumstance," and "The Doll," among others, Chesnutt trenchantly explores the processes by which families are formed, destroyed, or preserved.

22. "A Psychological Counter-Current in Recent Fiction," p. 882.

23. Despite having slavery as its subject—the story is, in fact, a comic inverse slave narrative—"The Passing of Grandison" is indeed one of Chesnutt's wittiest stories, and it likewise reveals the author's fine sense of comic situation. That said, however, I should also note that the story imparts serious messages as well. In chapter 6 I discuss "The Passing of Grandison" at some length.

24. "Post-Bellum—Pre-Harlem," *Colophon.* No page numbers given.

25. See Craig Werner for more discussion of this point: "Dividing 'himself' into two figures who, in the binary oppositions of the plantation tradition, are mutually exclusive and irresolvable, Chesnutt anticipates Saussure in deconstructing the linguistic convention, crucial to mimetic fiction, which asserts the identity of the signifier and signified" (352).

26. Once more, Chesnutt's sly wit is apparent. While John generally rejects the supernatural components of Julius's tales in favor of more empirical explanations, he does not recognize that the "philosophy" he reads aloud—suggesting that "transformations so many-sided" tend to "make a complete and deductive interpretation almost hopeless"—reiterates, in fancy language, one of Julius's favorite themes.

27. Regarding Chesnutt's flexibility on the order of stories in *The Conjure Woman,* see note 1 to this chapter.

28. See Stepto's suggestive reading of "The Dumb Witness," in which John usurps more of the narrating duties, as evidence of John's coming to a fuller understanding of Julius.

29. Raymond Hedin offers provocative commentary on those risks in his discussions of *The Conjure Woman, The Wife of His Youth and Other Stories of the Color Line,* and *The Marrow of Tradition.*

30. The slaveowners in Chesnutt's works are rarely depicted as "monsters" in the manner of masters described by Douglass or Jacobs. Instead, he tends to emphasize their greed, which typically diminishes their humanity. And in "The Passing of Grandison," Colonel Owens is portrayed as a fair-minded man who bristles at the notion of mistreating slaves. His "reading" skills are nonetheless satirized in the story as he consistently mistakes Grandison's plotting for devotion.

31. See especially Trudier Harris, "Chesnutt's Frank Fowler," for commentary on this point.

32. And, indeed, another literal "crossroads" is the site of the conclusion of the final story in *The Conjure Woman* ("Hot-Foot Hannibal"), wherein Annie makes her choice as to which road—in both literal and figurative senses—to take: she actively helps Julius, while John misses the signposts, reroute their course.

33. The conjure stories continue to evolve even after Chesnutt's death. See, for example, *Conjure Tales,* a children's book in which Ray Anthony Shepard retells Chesnutt's *Conjure Woman* tales, but without the dialect.

CHAPTER 5 — SPEAKING FOR (AND AGAINST) EACH OTHER: THE INSIDE NARRATIVES

1. For provocative discussions of "masking" or "veiling" as a prominent feature of black literature, see especially Gates's *Signifying Monkey* and Petesch's chapter on "'Masking' in Black Literature." For specific commentary on Chesnutt's use of the strategy see Michael G. Cooke, who finds Julius's masking to be a means of *"cancellation"* of self (54). Also, see Delmar on "The Sheriff's Children" and "The Passing of Grandison." Of the former story, Delmar suggests that both Sheriff Campbell and his son are brought down because they wear masks.

2. While almost all of Chesnutt's first-person narratives feature male protagonist-narrators (only "Concerning Father" departs from this norm), most of his "inside" narrators are women.

3. Chesnutt thus composes a narrative rubric which allows him to draw on his considerable skills to produce moving personal narratives, many of which are delivered in a form of dialect the author honed with his Julius stories.

4. All of the works discussed in this chapter foreground issues of family. Such a focus is not unique to this cluster of stories, and yet it is perhaps

most apparent here. Sundquist notes that "[n]o writer before Faulkner so completely made the family his means of delineating the racial crisis of American history as did Chesnutt" (394).

5. See Render (*Short Fiction* 427) for the approximate dates of Chesnutt's previously unpublished short stories.

6. See Sundquist for a fuller discussion of "White Weeds," a fascinating story about an elaborate revenge plot played out in near-Gothic (and highly racialized) terms.

7. Once more the precision of Chesnutt's plots is evident. Forsyth murdered a father who had come to defend his daughter. Forsyth is later allowed to live because another father decides that the best way for him to defend his daughter is to eschew revenge, as the conclusion of the story makes clear: "His own father had died in defense of his daughter; he must live to protect his own" (*SF* 412).

8. Chesnutt uses another judge, Judge Straight, in a similar capacity in *The House Behind the Cedars.* After establishing Straight as a fair-minded and thoughtful arbiter, Chesnutt has him conclude that race-based laws and conventions have little value. Straight is ultimately responsible for John Walden's becoming a lawyer and moving to South Carolina where he can practice law without revealing his race.

9. See the *Journals,* in which the young Chesnutt declares his "high and holy purpose for writing" to be a means of "elevating" white readers (139).

10. These "divided" narrative stories highlight Chesnutt's interest in and sensitivity to the perspectives of women. Not surprisingly, he also wrote an essay—"Women's Rights" in *The Crisis*—aligning himself with the women's movement.

11. As he does in *The House Behind the Cedars,* Chesnutt here appropriates the conventions of the "tragic mulatto" paradigm before overturning those very conventions. This sort of strategy has its risks, of course, including the possibility that Chesnutt's satiric intentions occasionally fall on deaf ears.

12. Although far different in artistic temperament, Chesnutt in this way anticipates the comic treatments of sensitive topics one finds in the works of Ralph Ellison and Ishmael Reed.

13. See also Redding on the question of miscegenation in Chesnutt's fiction: "Whether written in the spirit of comedy or tragedy, all the stories in *The Wife of His Youth* deal with the entanglements resulting from miscegenation" (72).

14. Fraiman suggests that "The Wife of His Youth" is the "narrative alter ego" (443) of "Her Virginia Mammy." In fact, one could convincingly

argue that "Cicely's Dream" also belongs in this group of interracial love stories.

15. See Elizabeth Abel's discussion of Morrison's "Recitatif," a story that "renders race a contested terrain variously mapped from diverse positions in the social landscape. By forcing us to construct racial categories from highly ambiguous social cues, 'Recitatif' elicits and exposes the unarticulated racial codes that operate at the boundaries of consciousness" (103). I want to suggest that much of Chesnutt's canon interrogates "racial categories" in similar ways.

16. See Stepto's commentary on how "The Dumb Witness," a conjure tale not included in *The Conjure Woman*, suggests that John does indeed come to listen to Julius. See also my chapter 4 for a discussion of how Chesnutt uses additional conjure tales, especially "The Marked Tree," to modify the relationship between John and Julius.

17. See Andrews, *Literary Career* (8–10 and 23, especially), for a discussion of Chesnutt's apparent desire to abandon dialect.

18. It is precisely the lack of this kind of narrative subtlety (combined with a stridency of tone not typical of the short fiction) that undermines Chesnutt's novels, especially *The Marrow of Tradition* and *The Colonel's Dream*.

19. Gayl Jones (131) argues that Chesnutt is emphasizing 'Liza Jane's "quaintness" in this story, a reading that seriously underestimates the rhetorical power of her narrative to effect Mr. Ryder's transformation.

20. Ryder's speech bears a striking resemblance to one made by Mr. Cicero Clayton in the ironically titled "A Matter of Principle." Note how differently Chesnutt has the fates of these two snobs play out.

21. This passage anticipates many of the same issues—particularly the legality of slave marriages and the promises of life in the North—Chesnutt handles comically in "Uncle Wellington's Wives."

22. In *The Conjure Woman* Julius's rhetorical powers seem superior to John's despite the latter's more formal diction. And in "The March of Progress," the apparently untutored Abe, speaking in heavy dialect, converts his seemingly more "articulate" colleagues, and the reader, to his way of thinking.

CHAPTER 6. SHORTENING HIS WEAPONS: THE MORE DETACHED VOICE OF REALISM

1. See McElrath and Leitz's introduction to Chesnutt's *Letters* (21–23) for discussion of his artistic duality.

2. Originally published by *Atlantic Monthly*, the story was reprinted in *Living Age* under the title "The Bunch of Yellow Roses" a year later. The latter version is substantially shorter.

3. See Render, *Short Fiction* (427), for a list of these approximate dates of composition.

4. See McElrath and Leitz for provocative commentary on George Washington Cable's influence on Chesnutt's writing career. The editors of the *Letters* gave Part I the title "Cable's Protégé," in fact.

5. The novels *(The House Behind the Cedars, The Marrow of Tradition, The Colonel's Dream)* in particular have been read primarily as documents of social commentary. See especially Sundquist and Andrews for discussion of Chesnutt's value as social critic.

6. Chesnutt does not hesitate to treat ironically those characters liable to be associated most closely with himself. Both Ryder and Clayton belong to "talented-tenth" clubs, as did Chesnutt himself, and yet he undercuts their brands of racial prejudice. Similarly, the ambitious young black schoolteacher of "The March of Progress," a figure sharing many biographical traits with the author, receives more than his share of jibes. And lawyers, especially the one in "Uncle Wellington's Wives," also tend to suffer satiric treatment at Chesnutt's hands.

7. "A Matter of Principle" concludes, in fact, by indicating that Jack and Alice will be married:

> Jack put his arm around [Alice's] waist, and, leaning over, kissed her.
>
> "'Never mind, dear,'" [Jack] said soothingly, 'you still have your "last chance" left, and I'll prove myself a better man than the Congressman.'" (*CS* 167)

The relationship between Jack and Alice here thus mirrors Frank Fowler's courtship of Rena in *The House Behind the Cedars,* but in "A Matter of Principle" that relationship seems destined to come to full fruition.

8. See also "The White and the Black" for an essayistic example of Chesnutt's highly ironic style, even about matters as delicate as race.

9. See "Mr. Charles W. Chesnutt's Stories": "It would be hard to say which is the finest in such admirably rendered effects as The Web of Circumstance, The Bouquet, and Uncle Wellington's Wives" (700).

10. Chesnutt worked the conventions of the slave narrative in several of his works, most notably in "The Passing of Grandison" and "The Wife of His Youth." This tendency anticipates the twentieth-century impulse to incorporate and revisit the slave narrative tradition. See, for example, Arna Bontemps's *Black Thunder,* Styron's *The Confessions of Nat Turner,* Reed's *Flight to Canada,* Morrison's *Beloved,* and Johnson's *Middle Passage.*

11. This is not to say that in other situations Chesnutt did not express some ambivalence about the notion of passing. His *Journals* mention the matter on several occasions. See, for example, an 1875 entry in which he bragged, "Twice to-day, or oftener I have been taken for 'white.' . . . I believe I'll leave here and pass anyhow, for I am as white as any of them" (78). But in much of his short fiction—including "Uncle Wellington's Wives," "The Wife of His Youth," and "A Matter of Principle"—he seems explicitly to condemn those who seek to "lighten" the race.

12. See Ferguson, Elder, Trudier, Harris, and Bruce.

13. Ferguson uses throughout her essay the term "genuine Negro" as if Chesnutt—who used the term ironically in "What Is a White Man?"—was "oddly callous" to the cause of dark-skinned blacks despite his "sensitivity" in other regards (118).

14. In yet another example of Chesnutt's apparent philosophy that good business makes for good social policy, Thornton, believing that Davis is guilty, privately tells the judge to "'[l]et him off easy. . . . He's the best blacksmith in the county'" (*CS* 256).

15. Chesnutt uses a similar convention—having peripheral characters in effect define protagonists—in other works as well, especially "Cicely's Dream." And in "The Shadow of My Past," the narrator pretends to be a stranger in his own home town so that he might investigate what the residents think of him. This strategy also recalls James's use of it in works such as *Daisy Miller* and *The Portrait of a Lady*.

16. See Taxel for a discussion of Grandison's ability to play the "Sambo" role.

17. In fact, Richard O. Lewis argues that in the composition of "The Passing of Grandison" Chesnutt borrowed heavily from a chapter having to do with a slave's escape in William Wells Brown's *My Southern Home; or The South and Its People*.

CHAPTER 7 — CONCLUSION: THE BLACKBALLING OF CHARLES W. CHESNUTT

1. None of Chesnutt's books sold particularly well, with *The Conjure Woman* being the most successful in terms of sales. See Andrews's *Literary Career* and Chesnutt's *Letters* for further information. See in *Letters*, for example, Chesnutt's comments on sales of *Marrow* (171) and McElrath and Leitz's notes on sales of *Conjure Woman* and *Marrow* (125, 172).

2. Andrews argues provocatively that, "chronologically and ideologically, Baxter stands between the heroes of Chesnutt's last two novels, Dr. Miller and Colonel French" (217). Such a reading also posits the extent to

which "Baxter's Procrustes" serves as a linchpin to an understanding of Chesnutt's career and subsequent reputation.

3. I do not intend here to malign Nicholson; indeed, his "addition" to "Baxter's Procrustes" is, I think, a piece of comedy Chesnutt would have appreciated. My point in using his commentary is merely to dramatize the extent to which Chesnutt's work allows great latitude of interpretation.

4. C. Alphonso Smith, for example, calls *The Marrow of Tradition* an "insidious" book in his *Baltimore Sun* review (1901), primarily because of its apparent endorsement of miscegenation. Even more wounding, no doubt, to the economic sensibilities of Chesnutt was the success of Thomas Dixon's *The Leopard's Spots* (1902). Like *Marrow* (1901), Dixon's book offers a fictional account of the Wilmington riot. But Dixon's characterization of Klansmen as heroes must have appealed more to popular sentiment: the book became a bestseller while *Marrow* sold fewer than five thousand copies by 1905.

5. See Ellison and Metcalf for summaries of these and other telling reviews.

6. Wintz repeatedly misnames one of Chesnutt's works, somehow transforming "Baxter's Procrustes" into "Baxter's Procrust*ers*" each time that work is mentioned.

7. In addition to Andrews, see Render, who writes that "Baxter's Procrustes" is "universally regarded as Chesnutt's best story" (*Short Fiction* 41).

Bibliography

Works by Charles W. Chesnutt

In the following list of primary works by Charles W. Chesnutt, *Short Fiction* refers to *The Short Fiction of Charles W. Chesnutt*, edited and introduced by Sylvia Lyons Render (Washington, D.C.: Howard University Press, 1981); *Collected Stories* refers to *Collected Stories of Charles W. Chesnutt*, edited and introduced by William L. Andrews (New York: Mentor, 1992); and *Conjure Woman* refers to *The Conjure Woman*, introduced by Robert M. Farnsworth (Ann Arbor: University of Michigan Press, 1969).

"Appreciation." *Short Fiction*, 64–65.
"Aunt Lucy's Search." *Short Fiction*, 209–13.
"Aunt Mimy's Son." *Short Fiction*, 202–8.
"The Averted Strike." *Short Fiction*, 383–90.
"A Bad Night." *Short Fiction*, 271–78.
"Baxter's Procrustes." *Collected Stories*, 266–78.
"The Bouquet." *Collected Stories*, 238–48.
"Busy Day in a Lawyer's Office." *Short Fiction*, 73–74.
"Cartwright's Mistake." *Short Fiction*, 315–20.
"A Cause Célèbre." *Short Fiction*, 68–69.
"Cicely's Dream." *Collected Stories*, 168–86.
Collected Stories of Charles W. Chesnutt. Ed. and Intro. by William L. Andrews. New York: Mentor, 1992.
The Colonel's Dream. New York: Doubleday Page, 1905.
"Concerning Father." *Short Fiction*, 89–96.
"The Conjurer's Revenge." *Conjure Woman*, 103–31.
The Conjure Woman. Intro. by Robert M. Farnsworth. Ann Arbor: University of Michigan Press, 1969.
The Conjure Woman and Other Conjure Tales. Ed. and Intro. by Richard H. Brodhead. Durham, N.C.: Duke University Press, 1993.

"Dave's Neckliss." *Short Fiction,* 132–41.

"A Deep Sleeper." *Short Fiction,* 115–22.

"The Disfranchisement of the Negro." In *The Negro Problem: A Series of Articles by Representative American Negroes of Today.* New York: James Pott, 1903.

"The Doctor's Wife." *Short Fiction,* 279–83.

"The Doll." *Short Fiction,* 405–12.

"The Dumb Witness." *Short Fiction,* 153–63.

"An Eloquent Appeal." *Short Fiction,* 66–67.

"The Exception." *Short Fiction,* 353–56.

"The Fall of Adam." *Short Fiction,* 177–82.

"A Fool's Paradise." *Short Fiction,* 321–29.

Frederick Douglass. Boston: Small Maynard, 1899.

"The Future American." 3-part series in the *Boston Evening Transcript* (1900). "The Future American: What the Race Is Likely to Become in the Process of Time." (18 August); "The Future American: A Stream of Dark Blood in the Veins of Southern Whites" (25 August); "The Future American: A Complete Race-Amalgamation Likely to Occur" (1 September).

"The Goophered Grapevine." *Atlantic Monthly* 60 (August 1887): 254–60.

"The Goophered Grapevine." *Conjure Woman,* 1–35.

"A Grass Widow." *Short Fiction,* 330–42.

"Gratitude." *Short Fiction,* 62–63.

"The Gray Wolf's Ha'nt." *Conjure Woman,* 162–94.

"Her Virginia Mammy." *Collected Stories,* 114–31.

"Hot-Foot Hannibal." *Conjure Woman,* 195–229.

The House Behind the Cedars. Boston: Houghton, Mifflin, 1901.

"How a Good Man Went Wrong." *Short Fiction,* 190–91.

"How Dasdy Came Through." *Short Fiction,* 249–52.

"How He Met Her." *Short Fiction,* 283–85.

"Jim's Romance." *Short Fiction,* 343–52.

The Journals of Charles W. Chesnutt. Ed. Richard H. Brodhead. Durham, N.C.: Duke University Press, 1993.

"The Kiss." *Short Fiction,* 306–14.

Letters. See *"To Be an Author": Letters of Charles W. Chesnutt, 1889–1905.*

"A Limb of Satan." *Short Fiction,* 195–201.

"Lonesome Ben." *Short Fiction,* 106–14.

Mandy Oxendine: A Novel. Ed. Charles Hackenberry. Foreword by William L. Andrews. Urbana: University of Illinois Press, 1997.

"The March of Progress." *Short Fiction,* 214–22.

"The Marked Tree." *Short Fiction,* 142–52.

The Marrow of Tradition. Boston: Houghton, Mifflin, 1901.

"Mars Jeems's Nightmare." *Conjure Woman,* 64–102.

"A Matter of Principle." *Collected Stories*, 149–67.

"McDugald's Mule." *Short Fiction*, 183–85.

"A Metropolitan Experience." *Short Fiction*, 286–91.

"A Midnight Adventure." *Short Fiction*, 85–88.

"A Miscarriage of Justice." *Short Fiction*, 357–64.

"Mr. Taylor's Funeral." *Short Fiction*, 261–70.

"A Multitude of Counselors." *New York Independent* 43 (2 April 1891): 4–5.

"The Negro in Art: How Shall He Be Portrayed?" *The Crisis* 33 (November 1926): 28–29.

"The Negro in Cleveland." *Clevelander* 5 (November 1930): 3–4, 24, 26–27.

"Obliterating the Color Line." *Cleveland World* (23 October 1901): 4.

"An Original Sentiment." *Short Fiction*, 78–79.

"The Origin of the Hatchet Story." *Short Fiction*, 83–84.

"The Partners." *Short Fiction*, 253–60.

"The Passing of Grandison." *Collected Stories*, 187–204.

"Peonage, Or the New Slavery." *Voice of the Negro*. 1 (September 1904): 394–97.

"A Plea for the American Negro." *Critic* 36 (February 1900): 160–63.

"Po' Sandy." *Conjure Woman*, 36–63.

"Post-Bellum—Pre-Harlem." *Colophon* 2, no. 5 (1931); reprinted in *The Crisis* 40 (June 1931): 193–94.

"The Prophet Peter." *Short Fiction*, 236–48.

"A Roman Antique." *Short Fiction*, 75–76.

"A Secret Ally." *Short Fiction*, 303–5.

"The Shadow of My Past." *Short Fiction*, 292–302.

"She Reminded Him." *Short Fiction*, 77.

"The Sheriff's Children." *Collected Stories*, 132–48.

The Short Fiction of Charles W. Chesnutt. Ed. and Intro. by Sylvia Lyons Render. Washington, D.C.: Howard University Press, 1981.

"Sis' Becky's Pickaninny." *Conjure Woman*, 132–61.

"A Soulless Corporation." *Short Fiction*, 70–72.

"Stryker's Waterloo." *Short Fiction*, 365–73.

"The Sway-Backed House." *Short Fiction*, 223–31.

"A Tight Boot." *Short Fiction*, 58–61.

"To Be an Author": Letters of Charles W. Chesnutt, 1889–1905. Ed. and Intro. by Joseph R. McElrath, Jr., and Robert C. Leitz, III. Princeton, N.J.: Princeton University Press, 1997.

"Tobe's Tribulations." *Short Fiction*, 97–105.

"Tom's Warm Welcome." *Short Fiction*, 186–89.

"Uncle Peter's House." *Short Fiction*, 168–76.

"Uncle Wellington's Wives." *Collected Stories*, 205–37.

"A Victim of Heredity." *Short Fiction*, 123–31.

"A Virginia Chicken." *Short Fiction*, 164–67.

"Walter Knox's Record." *Short Fiction*, 374–82.

"The Web of Circumstance." *Collected Stories*, 249–65.

"What Is a White Man?" *New York Independent* (30 May 1889): 5–6.

"The White and the Black." *Boston Evening Transcript* (20 March 1901): 13.

"White Weeds." *Short Fiction*, 391–404.

"The Wife of His Youth." *Collected Stories*, 102–13.

The Wife of His Youth and Other Stories of the Color Line. Boston: Houghton, Mifflin, 1899; Ann Arbor: University of Michigan Press, 1968.

"Wine and Water." *Short Fiction*, 232–35.

"Women's Rights." *The Crisis* 10 (August 1915): 182–83.

Secondary Sources

Abel, Elizabeth. "Black Writing, White Reading: Race and the Politics of Feminist Interpretation." In *Female Subjects in Black and White: Race, Psychoanalysis, Feminism,* ed. Elizabeth Abel et al., 102–31. Berkeley: University of California Press, 1997.

Abel, Elizabeth, Barbara Christian, and Helene Moglen, eds. *Female Subjects in Black and White: Race, Psychoanalysis, Feminism*. Berkeley: University of California Press, 1997.

Andrews, William L. Introduction to *Collected Stories of Charles W. Chesnutt*. New York: Mentor, 1992.

———. *The Literary Career of Charles W. Chesnutt*. Baton Rouge: Louisiana State University Press, 1980.

———. *To Tell a Free Story: The First Century of Afro-American Autobiography, 1769–1865*. Urbana: University of Illinois Press, 1986.

———, ed. *The African-American Novel in the Age of Reaction: Three Classics*. New York: Penguin, 1992.

Babb, Valerie. "Subversion and Repatriation in *The Conjure Woman*." *The Southern Quarterly* 25 (Winter 1987): 66–75.

Baker, Houston A., Jr., and Patricia Redmond. *Afro-American Literary Study in the 1990s*. Chicago: University of Chicago Press, 1989.

Bakhtin, M. M. *The Dialogic Imagination: Four Essays*. Ed. Michael Holquist. Trans. Caryl Emerson and Michael Holquist. Austin: University of Texas Press, 1981.

Benston, Kimberly W. "'I yam what I am'; the topos of (un)naming in Afro-American literature." In *Black Literature and Literary Theory*, ed. Henry Louis Gates, Jr., 151–72. New York: Methuen, 1984.

Bone, Robert. *Down Home: A History of Afro-American Short Fiction from Its Beginnings to the End of the Harlem Renaissance*. Ser. New Perspectives on Black America. Herbert Hill, General Editor. New York: G. P. Putnam's Sons, 1975.

Booth, Wayne C. *The Rhetoric of Fiction*. Chicago: University of Chicago Press, 1961.

Boswell, Jackson C. "A Black Grimm." Review of Sylvia Lyons Render, ed., *The Short Fiction of Charles W. Chesnutt*. *New Republic* 172 (1 March 1975): 31.

Britt, David. "Chesnutt's Conjure Tales: What You See Is What You Get." *CLA Journal* 15.3 (1972): 269–83.

Brodhead, Richard H. Introduction to *The Journals of Charles W. Chesnutt*, 1–28. Durham, N.C.: Duke University Press, 1993.

Bruce, Dickson D., Jr. *Black American Writing from the Nadir: The Evolution of a Literary Tradition, 1877–1915*. Baton Rouge: Louisiana State University Press, 1989.

Burnette, R. V. "Charles W. Chesnutt's *The Conjure Woman* Revisited." *CLA Journal* 30.4 (1987): 438–53.

Carafiol, Peter. "'Who I Was': Ethnic Identity and American Literary Ethnocentrism." In *Criticism and the Color Line: Desegregating American Literary Studies*, ed. Henry B. Wonham, 43–62. New Brunswick, N.J.: Rutgers University Press, 1996.

Chesnutt, Helen. *Charles Waddell Chesnutt: Pioneer of the Color Line*. Chapel Hill: University of North Carolina Press, 1952.

Cohn, Dorrit. *Transparent Minds: Narrative Modes for Presenting Consciousness in Fiction*. Princeton, N.J.: Princeton University Press, 1984.

Cooke, Michael G. *Afro-American Literature in the Twentieth Century: The Achievement of Intimacy*. New Haven, Conn.: Yale University Press, 1984.

Cunningham, Joan. "The Uncollected Short Stories of Charles Waddell Chesnutt." *Negro American Literature Forum* 9.2 (Summer 1975): 57–58.

Davis, Charles T., and Henry Louis Gates, Jr., eds. *The Slave's Narrative*. Oxford: Oxford University Press, 1985.

Delmar, P. Jay. "The Mask as Theme and Structure: Charles W. Chesnutt's 'The Sheriff's Children' and 'The Passing of Grandison.'" *American Literature* 51 (November 1979): 364–75.

Douglass, Frederick. *Narrative of the Life of Frederick Douglass, an American Slave*. Boston: Anti-Slavery Office, 1845.

Du Bois, W. E. B. *The Souls of Black Folk*. In *Three Negro Classics*, ed. John Hope Franklin, 207–389. New York: Avon, 1965.

Dunbar, Paul Laurence. *The Complete Poems of Paul Laurence Dunbar*. New York: Dodd, Mead, 1922.

Edwards, Jay. "Structural analysis of the Afro-American trickster tale." In *Black Literature and Literary Theory*, ed. Henry Louis Gates, Jr., 81–103. New York: Methuen, 1984.

Elder, Arlene A. "'The Future American Race': Charles W. Chesnutt's Utopian Illusion." *MELUS* 15.3 (Fall 1988): 121–29.

Ellison, Curtis W. and E. W. Metcalf, Jr. *Charles W. Chesnutt: A Reference Guide*. Boston: G. K. Hall, 1977.

Ellison, Ralph. "The Art of Fiction: An Interview." In *Shadow and Act*, 169–83. New York: Random House, 1953.

Farnsworth, Robert M. Introduction to *The Conjure Woman*. Ann Arbor: University of Michigan Press, 1969.

Ferguson, SallyAnn H. "Chesnutt's Genuine Blacks and Future Americans." *MELUS* 15.3 (Fall 1988): 109–19.

Fienberg, Lorne. "Charles W. Chesnutt and Uncle Julius: Black Storytellers at the Crossroads." *Studies in American Fiction* 15 (1987): 161–73.

———. "Charles W. Chesnutt's *The Wife of His Youth:* The Unveiling of the Black Storyteller." *ATQ* 4 (1990): 219–37.

Fraiman, Susan. "Mother-Daughter Romance in Charles W. Chesnutt's 'Her Virginia Mammy.'" *Studies in Short Fiction* 22.4 (Fall 1985): 443–48.

Gates, Henry Louis, Jr., ed. *Black Literature and Literary Theory*. New York: Methuen, 1984.

———. "Criticism in the Jungle." In *Black Literature and Literary Theory*, 1–24. New York: Methuen, 1984.

———. *Figures in Black: Words, Signs, and the "Racial" Self*. New York: Oxford University Press, 1987.

———. "The Master's Pieces: On Canon Formation and the Afro-American Tradition." In *The Bounds of Race: Perspectives on Hegemony and Resistance*, ed. Dominick LaCapra, 17–38. Ithaca, N.Y.: Cornell University Press, 1991.

———. *"Race," Writing, and Difference*. Chicago: University of Chicago Press, 1986.

———. *The Signifying Monkey: A Theory of African-American Literary Criticism*. New York: Oxford University Press, 1988.

Gatewood, Willard B. *The Black Elite, 1880–1920*. Bloomington: Indiana University Press, 1990.

Genette, Gérard. *Narrative Discourse: An Essay in Method*. Trans. Jane E. Lewin. Ithaca, N.Y.: Cornell University Press, 1980.

Gibson, Donald B. *The Politics of Literary Expression: A Study of Major Black Writers*. Ser. *Contributions in Afro-American and African Studies* 63. Westport, Conn.: Greenwood Press, 1981.

Ginsberg, Elaine K. "Introduction: The Politics of Passing." In *Passing and the Fictions of Identity*, 1–18. Durham, N.C.: Duke University Press, 1996.

———, ed. *Passing and the Fictions of Identity*. Durham, N.C.: Duke University Press, 1996.

Harris, Trudier. "Chesnutt's Frank Fowler: A Failure of Purpose." *CLA Journal* 22 (1979): 215–28.

Hedin, Raymond. "Probable Readers, Possible Stories: The Limits of Nineteenth-Century Black Narrative." In *Readers in History: Nineteenth-*

Century American Literature and the Contexts of Response, ed. James L. Machor, 180–205. Baltimore: Johns Hopkins University Press, 1993.

Hemenway, Robert. "The Functions of Folklore in Charles Chesnutt's *The Conjure Woman." Journal of the Folk Institute* 13 (1976): 283–309.

Howells, W. D. "Mr. Charles W. Chesnutt's Stories." *Atlantic Monthly* 85 (May 1900): 699–701.

———. "A Psychological Counter-Current in Recent Fiction." *North American Review* 173 (December 1901): 872–88.

Hughes, Langston, ed. *The Best Short Stories by Negro Writers: An Anthology from 1899 to the Present.* Boston: Little, Brown, 1967.

Hurd, Myles Raymond. "Step by Step: Codification and Construction in Chesnutt's 'The Passing of Grandison.'" *Obsidian II* 4.3 (Winter 1989): 78–90.

James, Henry. *The Art of the Novel.* New York: Scribners, 1934.

Johnson, Barbara. "The Quicksands of the Self: Nella Larsen and Heinz Kohut." In *Female Subjects in Black and White: Race, Psychoanalysis, Feminism,* ed. Elizabeth Abel et al., 252–65. Berkeley: University of California Press, 1997.

Jones, Gayl. *Liberating Voices: Oral Tradition in African American Literature.* New York: Penguin, 1991.

Kawash, Samira. "*The Autobiography of an Ex-Coloured Man:* (Passing for) Black Passing for White." In *Passing and the Fictions of Identity,* ed. Elaine K. Ginsberg, 59–74. Durham, N.C.: Duke University Press, 1996.

Keller, Frances Richardson. *An American Crusade: The Life of Charles Waddell Chesnutt.* Provo: Brigham Young University Press, 1978.

LaCapra, Dominick, ed. *The Bounds of Race: Perspectives on Hegemony and Resistance.* Ithaca, N.Y.: Cornell University Press, 1991.

Lewis, Richard O. "Romanticism in the Fiction of Charles W. Chesnutt: The Influence of Dickens, Scott, Tourgee, and Douglas." *CLA Journal* 26 (December 1982): 145–71.

McElrath, Joseph R., Jr., and Robert C. Leitz, III, eds. Introduction to "*To Be an Author": Letters of Charles W. Chesnutt, 1889–1905,* 3–23. Princeton, N.J.: Princeton University Press, 1997.

Meese, Elizabeth, and Alice Parker, eds. *The Difference Within: Feminism and Critical Theory.* Amsterdam and Philadelphia: John Benjamins, 1989.

Molyneaux, Sandra. "Expanding the Collective Memory: Charles W. Chesnutt's *The Conjure Woman* Tales." In *Memory, Narrative, and Identity: New Essays in Ethnic American Literatures,* ed. Amritjit Singh, Joseph T. Skerrett, Jr., and Robert E. Hogan. Boston: Northeastern University Press, 1994.

Nicholson, John B., Jr. "Biographical Essay about the Author." *Baxter's Procrustes.* Cleveland: Rowfant Club, 1966.

Patton, Richard J. "Studyin' 'bout Ole Julius: A Note on Charles W. Chesnutt's Uncle Julius McAdoo." *American Literary Realism 1870–1910* 24 (1992): 72–79.

Petesch, Donald A. *A Spy in the Enemy's Country: The Emergence of Modern Black Literature.* Iowa City: University of Iowa Press, 1989.

Pickens, Ernestine Williams. *Charles W. Chesnutt and the Progressive Movement.* New York: Pace University Press, 1994.

Pryse, Marjorie, and Hortense J. Spillers, eds. *Conjuring: Black Women, Fiction, and Literary Tradition.* Bloomington: Indiana University Press, 1985.

Redding, J. Saunders. *To Make a Poet Black.* Ithaca, N.Y.: Cornell University Press, 1988.

Render, Sylvia Lyons. *Charles W. Chesnutt.* Twayne's United States Authors Series 373. Boston: Twayne, 1980.

———. Introduction to *The Short Fiction of Charles W. Chesnutt,* 3–56. Washington, D.C.: Howard University Press, 1981.

Rimmon-Kenan, Shlomith. *A Glance beyond Doubt: Narration, Representation, Subjectivity.* Columbus: Ohio State University Press, 1996.

Shepard, Ray Anthony. *Conjure Tales by Charles W. Chesnutt Retold by Ray Anthony Shepard.* New York: Dell, 1978.

Smith, C. Alphonso. "An Insidious Book." *Baltimore Sun,* 5 December 1901.

Spillers, Hortense J. "Notes on an alternative model—neither/nor." In *The Difference Within: Feminism and Critical Theory,* ed. Elizabeth Meese and Alice Parker, 165–87. Amsterdam and Philadelphia: John Benjamins, 1989.

Stepto, Robert B. *From Behind the Veil: A Study of Afro-American Narrative.* Urbana: University of Illinois Press, 1979.

———. "'The Simple but Intensely Human Inner Life of Slavery': Storytelling and the Revision of History in Charles W. Chesnutt's 'Uncle Julius Stories.'" In *History and Tradition in Afro-American Culture,* ed. Gunter H. Lenz, 29–54. Frankfurt: Campus Verlag, 1984.

Stowe, Harriet Beecher. *Uncle Tom's Cabin.* 1852. Afterword by John William Ward. New York: NAL Penguin, 1966.

Sundquist, Eric J. *To Wake the Nations: Race in the Making of American Literature.* Cambridge, Mass.: Belknap Press, Harvard University Press, 1993.

Taxel, Joel. "Charles Waddell Chesnutt's Sambo: Myth and Reality." *Negro American Literature Forum* 9 (1975): 105–8.

Terry, Eugene. "The Shadow of Slavery in Charles Chesnutt's *The Conjure Woman.*" *Ethnic Groups* 4 (1982): 103–25.

Walcott, Ronald. "Chesnutt's 'The Sheriff's Children' as Parable." *Negro American Literature Forum* 7.3 (Fall 1973): 83–85.

Washington, Mary Helen. Foreword. *Their Eyes Were Watching God.* By Zora Neale Hurston. New York: Harper and Row, 1990.

Werner, Craig. "The Framing of Charles W. Chesnutt: Practical Deconstruction in the Afro-American Tradition." In *Southern Literature and Literary Theory*, ed. Jefferson Humphries, 339–65. Athens, Ga.: University of Georgia Press, 1990.

White, Jeannette S. "Baring Slavery's Darkest Secrets: Charles Chesnutt's *Conjure Tales* as Masks of Truth." *Southern Literary Journal* 27 (Fall 1994): 85–103.

Wideman, John Edgar. "Charles Chesnutt and the WPA Narratives: The Oral and Literate Roots of Afro-American Literature." In *The Slave's Narrative*, ed. Charles T. Davis and Henry Louis Gates, Jr., 59–78. Oxford: Oxford University Press, 1985.

Wiegman, Robyn. *American Anatomies: Theorizing Race and Gender.* Durham, N.C.: Duke University Press, 1995.

Wintz, Cary D. "Race and Realism in the Fiction of Charles W. Chesnutt." *Ohio History* 81.2 (Spring 1972): 122–30.

Yarborough, Richard. "The First-Person in Afro-American Fiction." In *Afro-American Literary Study in the 1990s*, ed. Houston A. Baker, Jr., and Patricia Redmond, 105–21. Chicago: University of Chicago Press, 1989.

Index

Abel, Elizabeth, 193
Absalom, Absalom! (Faulkner), 112
African-American fiction tradition,
   Chesnutt's contributions to, 1–2,
   7–8, 10–11, 23, 49
*African-American Novel in the Age of
   Reaction: Three Classics, The*
   (Andrews), 181
*Afro-American Literature in the Twentieth
   Century* (Cooke), 41–42
Alger, Horatio, 12
*American Anatomies: Theorizing Race
   and Gender* (Wiegman), 27
*American Crusade: The Life of Charles
   Waddell Chesnutt, An* (Keller), 178
Andrews, William L., 3, 5, 14, 20, 51,
   55, 56, 64, 65, 67, 79, 98, 99, 118,
   126, 169, 177–78, 181–82,
   185–86, 188, 190, 193–96
Antebellum South, 8, 19, 25–26,
   101, 162
"Appreciation," 50, 56, 62
Atlanta Journal, 184
Atlantic Monthly, xi, 47, 78, 105, 126,
   167
"Aunt Lucy's Search," 83, 108–9, 115
"Aunt Mimy's Son," 19, 50, 53, 56,
   59–60, 62–68, 70, 187
*Autobiography of an Ex-Colored Man,
   The* (Johnson), 10, 14–15, 183
"Averted Strike, The," 138

Babb, Valerie, 81–82, 180
"Bad Night, A," 19, 34–36, 42, 83
Baker, Houston A., Jr., 17

Bakhtin, M. M., 25
Baldwin, James, 76
Baltimore Sun, 196
"Baxter's Procrustes," xii, 5, 7, 19,
   24, 37, 50, 52, 54–55, 59, 61,
   166–76, 180, 196
Baxter's Procrustes, 168, 172–76
Beloved (Morrison), 85, 189, 194
"Benito Cereno" (Melville), 110
Benston, Kimberly W., 110, 144–45
Bibb, Henry, 9
Billy Budd, Sailor (Melville), 60–61
Black Literature and Literary Theory
   (Gates), 23
Black Thunder (Bontemps), 194
Blithedale Romance, The (Hawthorne),
   63, 66
Bodleian Club, 167–76
Bone, Robert, 83–84
Bontemps, Arna, 194
Booth, Wayne, 37, 142, 188
Boston Christian Register, 181
Boston Evening Transcript, xi, 27
Boston Journal, 181
Boswell, Jackson C., 182
"Bouquet, The" (*see also* "The Bunch
   of Yellow Roses"), 47–48, 138, 140,
   148–50, 157, 194
Bouvé, Pauline C., 178
Bradford, William, 10
Britt, David, 81–82, 86, 189
Brodhead, Richard H., 41, 178,
   188–89, 190
Brown, Charles Brockden, 10
Brown, William Wells, 1, 9, 11, 195

Bruce, Dickson D., Jr., 21, 57, 82, 195
"Bunch of Yellow Roses, The" (shortened version of "The Bouquet"), 194
Burnette, R. V., 82, 105–6

Cable, George Washington, 4, 8, 178–79, 194
Carafiol, Peter, 12
Carraway, Nick, 49
"Cartwright's Mistake," 19, 50, 52, 55–64, 67–68, 69, 75, 83, 149
Century, 8
Charles Waddell Chesnutt: Pioneer of the Color Line (H. Chesnutt), 178
Charles W. Chesnutt (Render), 178, 180
Charles W. Chesnutt and the Progressive Movement (Pickens), 182
Chesnutt, Charles Waddell
African Americans as outsiders in works of, 47–48
ancestry, de-emphasis of, 118–19
as advocate of women's rights, 3, 186, 192
business concerns, sensibilities, and practices, 2–3, 52, 55, 75–76, 80, 195, 178–79, 182, 186, 188–89, 196
characters and narrators as proxies for author, 41, 52, 64–66, 76, 82, 142, 155–65, 166–76, 194
characters and narrators as proxies for readers, 50, 90
class prejudice of, 66, 187
"colorless" or "raceless" narrators/fiction, 53–55, 57, 61–62, 140, 153–54
comic tone in works of, 34–36, 38–46, 88–89, 91–93, 98, 117–18, 137–47, 154–65, 166–76, 184, 190, 192–93
conception of authorship, 43, 46, 69–71, 79–80
controversial race attitudes in works of, 52–53, 186
"dark double" figures in works of, 44–45, 185
dialect in works of, 17, 24, 77, 83, 98, 129–35, 182
divided/fragmented authorial

presence of, 31–34, 80–106, 138, 183, 189–90
duality as motif in works of, 38–46, 107, 122, 155–56
economics, importance of in fiction, 54–55, 85–87, 99–106, 191
family, as theme in works of, 4–5, 85, 110–36, 146, 164, 190–92
fragmentation as theme in works of, 37–38
gender, as focus in works of, 53, 108, 115–136, 191–92
irony in works of, 22, 117–18, 125–27, 137–47, 174–76, 194
letters as fictional devices in works of (textual voyeurism), 64–65, 70–71, 75, 187
misdirection as plot device, 159
mixed blood figures (mulattoes) in works of, 13–16, 20–22, 28–33, 63–64, 105–6, 112, 116–21, 124, 184
"mulatto texts" (textual passing) of, 15, 30–31, 37–46, 183, 185
mutability of identity as motif, 31–32, 34–46, 74–76
narrative formats of. *See* narration, modes of
narrators as "detectives" ("shadows"), 39, 43–44, 62
narrators as self-conscious storytellers, 71–76
narrators silenced or effaced at end of stories, 60–61, 68–69, 75–76
nature of interpretation as theme, 47–48, 50, 57–61, 65–66, 74–75
purpose in writing, self-described, 23–24, 183
racial classification/definition, commentary on, 27–33, 57, 183
racial identity of, 11, 20, 28–33, 55–56, 178, 183–84
railroad scenes, importance of, 27–33, 37
realistic sensibilities of, 3–4, 58, 125, 127, 138–39
Reconstruction as motif in works of, 4–5, 99–106, 115–36
reputation as dialect writer, 126, 193
romantic sensibilities of, 3

search for/construction of identity as motif in works of, 38–46, 125, 130–35

"self-made man" as theme, 38, 40–41

social commentary in works of, 20, 51, 66, 138, 140, 157, 188–89, 194

spatial placement of narrators within fictions, 62–64

trickster figures in works of, 51, 77–106, 158–65, 166–76

voice, importance of, 12–13, 17–19, 82–83, 87, 122, 124–25, 129–35, 146, 148–49, 193

voyeurs, narrators and characters as, 63–67, 69–71, 75, 149, 156

white reading audience, relationship with, 5–8, 12, 19–20, 25, 30–33, 36–37, 45–46, 50–51, 61, 90, 104–06, 114, 121, 138, 165, 166, 169–76, 184

Chesnutt, Helen, 170, 178

Chicago Post, 182

Chopin, Kate, 4

"Cicely's Dream," 41, 45, 53, 108–11, 115, 117, 120–25, 135–36, 138, 141, 185, 188, 193, 195

Civil War, 2, 4–5, 8–10, 62, 79, 101, 107, 144

Cleveland News and Herald, xi

Cleveland Social Circle, 126

Clotel, or The President's Daughter (Brown), 11

Cohn, Dorrit, 58, 74

Collected Stories of Charles W. Chesnutt (Andrews, "Introduction"), 3, 20, 98–99

Colonel's Dream, The, xi, 4, 13, 62, 68, 96, 126–27, 140, 156, 167, 186–87, 194

colonial literature, 10–11

Colophon, 88, 190

"colorless" fiction in African-American literary tradition, 53–54

Color Purple, The (Walker), 119

"Concerning Father," 3, 50, 53, 70, 185, 191

Confessions of Nat Turner, The (Styron), 194

"Conjurer's Revenge, The," 78, 83, 85, 93–94, 104

conjure stories (not collected in *The Conjure Woman*), 51, 64, 77–79, 83, 95–98, 188–89, 191

Conjure Tales by Charles W. Chesnutt, 191

Conjure Woman, The, xi, 2–3, 5–7, 16–18, 26, 30–31, 36–37, 41–42, 49, 54, 61–62, 64, 66, 68, 77–106, 125–26, 132–34, 150, 155, 159, 177–78, 180, 184, 187–88, 191, 193

Annie's role in, 77, 91–95, 98–99, 102–6, 191

Aunt Peggy (primary conjure woman), 80, 83–84, 87, 89, 99, 102

belief as central issue, 78, 81, 88–91, 95–98, 102–5

as cultural dialogue, 78–99

dialect in, 17, 24, 77, 83, 98, 182

economics, importance of, 54, 85–87, 99–106, 191

evolution/revision of series, 77–78, 81, 86–87, 94–98, 103–6, 191

folklore roots, 6, 84–85, 87, 180, 190

humor in, 88–89, 91–93, 98, 190

Julius's race designation, importance of, 105–6

as novel, 77

order of, 94, 188, 190

reaction to, and commentary on, 30–31, 41–42, 81–86, 184, 189

sales of, 195

title, origin of, 80, 189

typical slaveowners in, 100, 191

use of transformations in, 83–84, 87, 105–6

use of magic/goopher in, 80–81, 83–106

Conjure Woman, The (special limited large-paper edition), 170

Conjure Woman and Other Conjure Tales, The, 188

Conjure Woman, The (Introduction), 188

consonant self-narration, 58, 74

Cooke, Michael G., 41–42, 184, 189, 191

Cooper, James Fenimore, 10

Coverdale, Miles (*Blithedale Romance*),

Coverdale, Miles, *(cont.)*
64, 66
Crisis, The (magazine), xi, 78, 89,
110, 155, 192

Daisy Miller (James), 195
"Dave's Neckliss," 78, 84, 190
"Deep Sleeper, A," 78
Delmar, P. Jay, 159, 162–63, 180, 191
Detroit Free Press, 182
Dialogic Imagination, The (Bakhtin),
25, 183
"Disfranchisement of the Negro,
The," 126
dissonant self-narration, 74
Dixon, Thomas, 19, 187, 196
"Doll, The," 3, 109–15, 124, 135–36,
184, 190
double-consciousness as fictional
device, 1, 46, 177
double-voicedness, 17–18
Douglass, Frederick, 6–9, 11, 23,
33–34, 126, 180, 191
Du Bois, W. E. B., xi, 10, 46, 89, 155,
181
Dumas, Alexander, 171
"Dumb Witness, The," 78, 83, 95,
188, 190, 193
Dunbar, Paul Laurence, 1, 10–11,
180

economics, importance of in African-
American literary tradition, 55
Elder, Arlene A., 182, 195
Ellison, Curtis W., 196
Ellison, Ralph, 8, 15–17, 30, 41, 46,
49, 76, 173–74, 181
"Eloquent Appeal, An," 19, 50, 59,
62
Emancipation, 9–10
Emerson, Ralph Waldo, 33
epistolary novel tradition, 187
Equiano, Olaudah, 8
"Exception, The," 42, 138, 141, 155

"Fall of Adam, The," 108–9
Family Fiction, 78
Farnsworth, Robert, 79, 81–82, 92,
180, 188
Faulkner, William, 25–26, 112, 150,
153, 192
Ferguson, SallyAnn H., 21–22,
146–47, 182, 195

Fienberg, Lorne, 18–19, 55, 81–82,
86, 133, 180, 186, 189
Figures in Black (Gates), 185–86
Fisher, Rudolph, 1
Flight to Canada (Reed), 194
folktale tradition, 6, 84–85, 87, 180,
190
Fool's Errand, A (Tourgée), 179–80
"Fool's Paradise, A," 19, 50, 52,
55–56, 59–60, 62, 64, 67, 74–75
Fraiman, Susan, 116, 120, 192
frame tales, 77–106
Franklin, Benjamin, 10
Frederick Douglass, xi, 3, 37
free indirect discourse, 13, 143–44
Freeman, Mary Wilkins, 2, 4, 26
"Future American, The" (series of
articles), 52–53, 57, 126

Gates, Henry Louis, Jr., 17–18, 23,
31, 180, 185–86, 191
Genette, Gérard, 49, 73–74, 186
Gibson, Donald B., 82
Gil Blas (Le Sage), 49
Gilder, Richard Watson, 8
Ginsberg, Elaine K., 30, 45–46, 181,
185
Glance beyond Doubt, A (Rimmon-
Kenan), 189
"Goophered Grapevine, The," 6, 78,
80, 84–85, 98–106, 187–88, 190
"Grass Widow, A," 19, 50, 52, 56, 64,
68–76, 83, 149, 177, 187
"Gratitude," 34
"Gray Wolf's Ha'nt, The," 78, 85, 93
Great Expectations (Dickens), 74
Great Gatsby, The (Fitzgerald), 49
Griggs, Sutton, 10–11, 13–14, 19,
119, 181
Groveland, 141, 143

Haldeman, S. Alice, 178
Harlem Renaissance, 1–2, 76, 87
Harper, Frances E. W., 10–11, 13–14,
181
Harris, Joel Chandler, 4, 79, 84, 98,
188, 190
Harris, Trudier, 55, 195
Harte, Bret, 4
Hawthorne, Nathaniel, 3, 63–64, 66,
105, 150
Hedin, Raymond, 14, 30–31, 183,
185, 191

Hemenway, Robert, 180
Hemingway, Ernest, 1
Heroic Slave, The (Douglass), 11
"Her Virginia Mammy," 5, 25, 53, 66,
  108–11, 115–21, 123–24, 131,
  135–36, 177, 188, 190, 192
Himes, Chester, 49
Hindered Hand, The (Griggs), 13–14
"Hot-Foot Hannibal," 78, 84–85,
  88–91, 94, 96, 191
Houghton, Mifflin & Co., 94, 170,
  178, 186
House Behind the Cedars, The, xi, 4,
  13–16, 36–37, 42, 62–64, 184–85,
  126, 150, 187, 192, 194
Household Realm, 78
House of the Seven Gables, The
  (Hawthorne), 150
"How Dasdy Came Through," 83
Howells, William Dean, 2–3, 19–21,
  24, 26, 33–34, 83, 88, 177–78, 94,
  125, 137, 143–44, 180–82, 190,
  194
"How He Met Her," 42, 138, 141
Huck Finn, 49
Huckleberry Finn (Twain), 15, 49
Hurd, Myles Raymond, 138, 158
Hurston, Zora Neale, 1, 76, 114,
  182, 186

Imperium in Imperio (Griggs), 119
Invisible Man (Ellison), 15, 17, 46
Iola Leroy (Harper), 13–14
Irving, Washington, 10

Jacobs, Harriet, 6, 9, 23, 41, 180,
  191
James, Henry, 2–3, 26, 48, 137–38,
  195
Jewett, Sarah Orne, 4, 26
Jim Crow Laws, 27–33
"Jim's Romance," 139
Johnson, Barbara, 29–30
Johnson, Charles, 85, 194
Johnson, James Weldon, 10, 14–15,
  41, 183
Johnson, Samuel, 171
Jones, Gayl, 1–2, 177–78, 193
Journals of Charles W. Chesnutt, The,
  51, 177–83, 187–89, 192

Kawash, Samira, 183
Keller, Frances Richardson, 178

"Kiss, The," 138, 151–53
Ku Klux Klan, 151

LaCapra, Dominick, 24–25
Lardner, Ring, 1
Leitz, Robert C., III, 8, 13, 177–82,
  184, 186–87, 189, 193–95
Leopard's Spots, The (Dixon), 187, 196
Lewis, Richard O., 162, 195
*Liberating Voices: Oral Tradition in
  African American Literature* (Jones),
  1–2, 177–78
Light in August (Faulkner), 150
"Limb of Satan, A," 83, 108–09, 115
*Literary Career of Charles W. Chesnutt,
  The* (Andrews), 5, 177–78, 182,
  188, 190, 193, 195
Living Age, 194
local color tradition, 4, 79, 84
"Lonesome Ben," 42, 78, 86, 92,
  95–96, 188
Lyrics of Lowly Life (Dunbar), 177

"March of Progress, The," 82, 109,
  115, 117, 120, 132, 135, 187,
  193–94
"Marked Tree, The," 3, 78, 83, 87,
  90, 96–98, 106, 188, 193
Marrow of Tradition, The, xi, 4, 7–8,
  12–13, 27–30, 36–37, 54, 62, 88,
  94, 113, 126–27, 137, 140, 157,
  174, 184–85, 187, 191, 194–96
"Mars Jeems's Nightmare," 78,
  90–91, 184, 190
masking (as motif in African-Ameri-
  can literature), 6–7, 41–42, 107–8,
  159–65, 180, 184, 191
Matheus, John, 1
"Matter of Principle, A," 7, 19, 82,
  125–26, 138–44, 146–47, 157,
  184, 187, 193–95
Maupassant, Guy de, 26
"McDugald's Mule," 78, 187
McElrath, Joseph R., Jr., 8, 13,
  177–82, 184, 186–87, 189, 193–95
Melville, Herman, 60–61, 110
Meredith, George, 171
Metcalf, E. W., Jr., 196
"Metropolitan Experience, A," 34, 83
Middle Passage, 194
"Midnight Adventure, A," 19, 34
"Miscarriage of Justice, A," 138–39,
  141, 151, 153–54

miscegenation, 109, 118–21, 140, 144–46, 192, 196
"Mr. Charles W. Chesnutt's Stories" (Howells), 2, 19–20, 26, 178, 194
"Mr. Taylor's Funeral," 3, 7, 19, 138–41, 155–58
modernism, 87
Molyneaux, Sandra, 185
Morrison, Toni, 85, 119, 182, 189, 193–94
multiculturalism, 24
"Multitude of Counselors, A," 187
My Southern Home; or The South and Its People (Brown), 195

narration, modes of
   in Chesnutt's fiction
      detached third-person (single- or monologic-voiced), xii, 108, 137–65
      divided or imbalanced (combination of first- and third-person narrators in same fiction), xii, 107–36, 192; as means of giving voice to traditionally unempowered, 108, 112–13
      dual-narrators, both first-person (*Conjure* tales), xii, 77–106, 125
      first-person protagonist-narrators (involved first-person), xii, 27–46
      first-person "witness" narrators, xii, 47–76
   detached third-person in African-American literary tradition, 49
   first-person in African-American literary tradition, 33–34, 48–49
Narrative Discourse: An Essay in Method, 49
narrative levels (Genette's classification)
   diegetic, 73–74
   extradiegetic, 73–74
   metadiegetic, 73–74
Narrative of the Life of Frederick Douglass (Douglass), 6–7
Native Son (Wright), 17
The Negro in the American Rebellion (Brown), 177–78
"Negro in Cleveland, The," 3
"New Negro," 64
New South, 79
Nicholson, John B., Jr., 168, 172–74, 196

Northrup, Solomon, 9
Nugent, Bruce, 1

"Obliterating the Color Line," 52–53, 126
"Origin of the Hatchet Story, The," 50
Our Nig (Wilson), 11
Overland Monthly, 78

Page, Thomas Nelson, 4, 19, 79, 98
Page, Walter Hines, 178–79, 184, 188–89
"Partners, The," 19, 138
"passing," 12–16, 30–31, 37, 42, 45–46, 59–60, 63–64, 117, 122, 146, 181, 184–85, 192
"passing" (textual). *See* Chesnutt, "mulatto texts" of
Passing and the Fictions of Identity, 30, 181
"Passing of Grandison, The," 7, 44, 59, 88, 125, 138–41, 158–65, 166, 184–85, 190–91, 195
"Patesville," 6, 80, 104
Patton, Richard J., 189
"Peonage, Or the New Slavery," 52–53
Petesch, Donald A., 9, 23, 46, 166, 180, 191
Philadelphia Times, 181–82
Pickens, Ernestine Williams, 182, plantation tradition in literature, 79
"Plea for the American Negro, A," 57
Plessy v. Ferguson, 10
Poe, Edgar Allan, 7, 48, 185
polyglossia, 25, 183
Portrait of a Lady, The (James), 195
"Po' Sandy," 78, 83–85, 92–93, 156–57
"Post-Bellum—Pre-Harlem," 77, 188, 190
"Prophet Peter, The," 3, 138, 141, 155
Pryse, Marjorie, 190
"Psychological Counter-Current in Recent Fiction, A" (Howells), 137, 182, 190
Puck, 137

"Quietus," 17–18

race
  as basis of identity in fiction, 57,
    115–21
  as source of prejudice and discrim-
    ination, 7, 27–33, 129, 140
  intra-racial prejudice in Chesnutt's
    works, 126–29, 141–42, 146
"Race," Writing, and Difference (Gates),
  31
Reconstruction, 2, 4–5, 10, 24, 27,
  61–62, 87, 107, 109, 115, 122,
  148, 151, 184–85
Reed, Ishmael, 192, 194
Redding, J. Saunders, 7, 184, 192
Render, Sylvia Lyons, 11, 138
  178–80, 182–83, 186, 188, 192,
  194, 196
Rhetoric of Fiction, The (Booth), 188
Rimmon-Kenan, Shlomith, 80
"Roman Antique, A," 19
"Rose for Emily, A" (Faulkner), 150
Rowfant Club, 166–76
Russell, Charlie, 17–18

Salinger, J. D., 1
Self-Culture Magazine, 78
sentimental novel tradition, 187
Shadow and Act (Ellison), 181
"Shadow of My Past, The," 7, 19, 34,
  36–46, 62, 152, 183–84, 195
Shepard, Ray Anthony, 191
"Sheriff's Children, The," 42, 45,
  107–09, 115, 120, 138, 141,
  156–57, 185, 190–91
Short Fiction of Charles W. Chesnutt, The
  (Render), 11, 179, 183, 186, 188,
  194
"Sights from a Steeple," 63
Signifying Monkey, The (Gates), 17,
  180, 191
"Sis' Becky's Pickaninny," 78, 84–85,
  91, 96, 104
slave marriages, 132, 144, 193
slave narrative tradition, xii, 6, 8–11,
  23, 48–49, 104–5, 144–45,
  162–64, 185–86, 194
slavery, 4, 8–10, 18, 77–106, 111,
  116–17, 135, 158–65, 180, 185
Smith, C. Alphonso, 196
Song of Solomon (Morrison), 85, 119
Southern Workman, 78, 89
Spillers, Hortense J., 29–30, 190

Spy in the Enemy's Country, A
  (Petesch), 180
Stepto, Robert B., 189–90, 193
St. Jean De Crèvecoeur, 10
Stowe, Harriet Beecher, 9, 180
"Stryker's Waterloo," 138, 141, 155
Stuart, Ruth McEnery, 4
Styron, William, 194
Sundquist, Eric J., 8, 13–14, 16, 105,
  181, 183, 189, 192, 194
"Sway-Backed House, The," 138, 151

Taxel, Joel, 195
Tennyson, Alfred Lord, 130
Terry, Eugene, 20, 81–82, 85–86
Their Eyes Were Watching God
  (Hurston), 114, 186
Thoreau, Henry David, 33
Tid-Bits, 137
*"To Be an Author": The Letters of Charles
  W. Chesnutt, 1889–1905*, 177–79,
  181, 184, 187–89, 193, 195
"Tobe's Tribulations," 78, 89, 95–96,
  188
To Make a Poet Black (Cullen), 7
"Tom's Warm Welcome," 78
Toomer, Jean, 1
To Tell a Free Story (Andrews), 181,
  185
Tourgée, Albion, 4, 179–80, 188, 190
To Wake the Nations (Sundquist), 8,
  181
tragic mulatto tradition, 13–16, 117,
  192
*Transparent Minds: Narrative Modes for
  Presenting Consciousness in Fiction*
  (Cohn), 58
Turgenev, Ivan, 2, 26
Twain, Mark (Samuel Clemens), 1, 4,
  179, 181
Two Tales, 78

"Uncle Peter's House," xi, 138, 151,
  157
Uncle Remus: His Songs and His Sayings
  (Harris), 89, 188
Uncle Tom's Cabin (Stowe), 9
"Uncle Wellington's Wives," 41,
  138–41, 143–47, 155, 157, 162,
  187, 193–95
Underground Railroad, 144, 165
United States Constitution, 9, 22

"Victim of Heredity, A," 78, 84–85
Villon, François, 171
"Virginia Chicken, A," 78

Walker, Alice, 119, 182
Walrond, Eric, 1
"Walter Knox's Record," 19, 138,
    141, 151–54
Washington, Booker T., 10, 12, 178,
    181
Washington, Mary Helen, 186
"Web of Circumstance, The," 66,
    138, 140, 147–48, 157, 190, 194
Werner, Craig, 190
"We Wear the Mask" (Dunbar), 180
"What Is a White Man?" 21–22, 57,
    183, 195
Wheatley, Phillis, 8
White, Jeannette S., 184

"White and the Black, The," 27–33,
    194
"White Weeds," 108–09, 115, 192

Wiegman, Robyn, 27, 29
"Wife of His Youth, The," 19, 24, 44,
    53, 66, 82, 108–11, 115, 117,
    124–36, 141–44, 146–47, 152,
    177, 185, 188, 190, 192, 194–95
*Wife of His Youth and Other Stories of the
    Color Line, The,* xi, 3, 5, 18, 26, 37,
    57, 83, 115, 126, 138, 148, 174,
    191–92
    "Blue Vein Society," 126–29,
    131–33
    intra-racial prejudice, focus on,
    126–29, 141–43, 146
Willis, Susan, 17
Wilson, Harriet, 11
Winthrop, John, 10
Wintz, Cary D., 196
women's rights, 3, 192
"Women's Rights," 3, 186, 192
Wright, Richard, 12, 17, 76

Yarborough, Richard, 48–49, 53–54
Yoknapatawpha, 150

WITHDRAWN